Physical Medicine and Rehabilitation

Spasticity

Guest Editor:

Richard T. Katz, MD

SSM Rehabilitation Institute
St. Mary's Health Center
St. Louis, Missouri

Volume 8/Number 3   October 1994
HANLEY & BELFUS, INC.   Philadelphia

Publisher: **HANLEY & BELFUS, INC.**
210 South 13th Street
Philadelphia, PA 19107
(215) 546-7293
(215) 790-9330 (Fax)

PHYSICAL MEDICINE AND REHABILITATION: State of the Art Reviews is included in *BioSciences Information Service, Current Contents, ISI/BIOMED,* and *Cumulative Index to Nursing & Allied Health Literature.*

PHYSICAL MEDICINE AND REHABILITATION: State of the Art Reviews   ISSN 0888-7357
Volume 8, Number 3   ISBN 1-56053-143-6

PHYSICAL MEDICINE AND REHABILITATION: State of the Art Reviews is published triannually (three times per year) by Hanley & Belfus, Inc., 210 South 13th Street, Philadelphia, Pennsylvania 19107.

POSTMASTER: Send address changes to PHYSICAL MEDICINE AND REHABILITATION: State of the Art Reviews, Hanley & Belfus, Inc., 210 South 13th Street, Philadelphia, PA 19107.

The 1994 subscription price is $69.00 per year U.S., $80.00 outside U.S. (add $30.00 for air mail). Single copies $34.00 U.S., $37.00 outside U.S. (add $10.00 for single copy air mail).

Physical Medicine and Rehabilitation: State of the Art Reviews
Vol. 8, No. 3, October 1994

SPASTICITY
Richard T. Katz, MD, Editor

CONTENTS

The mechanisms of spasticity have proved difficult to quantify. Here, the authors review various mechanisms that have been proposed in the literature. Also discussed is the upper motor neuron syndrome, an abnormal motor function that is secondary to lesions of cortical, subcortical, or spinal cord structures.

Because mechanical measurements of spasticity are not routinely available, clinicians must rely on their own observations of the severity of spasticity. In addition to describing scales that can help clinicians to make such assessments, the authors discuss quantification techniques that they hope will eventually spread from laboratory use to the clinic.

A variety of electrophysiologic studies have been performed to examine changes in spinal cord function and segmental reflexes in spastic patients. However, the test results often correlate poorly and have little clinical usefulness. This chapter provides an overview of a number of electrophysiologic studies and their results.

The pharmacologic management of spastic hypertonia is an integral component of the care of many neurologically impaired patients. This chapter reviews baclofen, diazepam, and dentrolene, the three drugs most commonly used for the treatment of spastic hypertonia. It also discusses experimental medications and medications that have not been approved for use in the United States.

Depending on the individual case, nerve blocks may or may not be appropriate for the treatment of spasticity. In this comprehensive review, Dr. Glenn outlines the use of nerve blocks with phenol, alcohol, and local anesthetics, including their side effects, complications, and clinical applications.

Historically, studies of whether electrical stimulation helps to reduce spasticity have lacked consistent protocols and, therefore, have led to inconclusive and diverse results. Here, the authors use a mechanical approach in their own attempt to measure the effect of electrical stimulation.

Most patients who suffer a spastic stroke or other brain injury achieve limited ambulation. In this chapter, the authors describe the basics of ambulation, gait analysis, and the use of orthotics as they apply to these patients. Surgical and pharmacologic interventions also are discussed.

Some patients with upper extremity spasticity may be appropriate candidates for ameliorative surgery. Surgery must be followed by a carefully planned rehabilitation program. In addition to describing surgery for the shoulder, elbow, wrist, and hand, the author discusses the evaluation of spasticities and includes scales by which hand placement and voluntary motor capacity can be graded.

This chapter details the preoperative evaluation for lower extremity surgery and the surgical approach to various clinical problems, including limb scissoring, crouched gait, stiff-knee gait, equinovarus foot, and valgus foot. Various types of contractures that occur in the hip, knee, and foot also are addressed.

The author reports that the intrathecal administration of baclofen, which was developed to avoid side effects associated with the oral route, is "a highly effective alternative" in the treatment of various types of spasticity. Issues he broaches include how to select patients to receive a baclofen pump, perioperative concerns such as dose determination and insertion of the pump, postoperative care, and complications.

Selective dorsal rhizotomy, the neurosurgical ablation of selected dorsal rootlets, is increasingly used to treat spasticity in carefully chosen patients. In this detailed review, the authors describe patient selection, the role of intraoperative monitoring, side effects, and the procedure's effects on spasticity, range of motion, gait, and various other functions.

CONTRIBUTORS

Craig Jeffrey Anmuth, DO
Clinical Assistant Professor, Department of Physical Medicine and Rehabilitation, Temple University School of Medicine, Philadelphia; Division of Physical Medicine and Rehabilitation, Abington Memorial Hospital, Abington, Pennsylvania

Richard D. Bucholz, MD, FACS
Associate Professor, Division of Neurological Surgery, Department of Surgery, St. Louis University School of Medicine, St. Louis, Missouri

Denise I. Campagnolo, MD
Kessler Institute for Rehabilitation, University of Medicine and Dentistry of New Jersey–New Jersey Medical School, Newark, New Jersey

Julius P. A. Dewald, PT, PhD
Senior Clinical Research Associate/Clinical Assistant Professor, Sensory Motor Performance Program, Programs in Physical Therapy, Rehabilitation Institute of Chicago, Northwestern University Medical School, Chicago, Illinois

Alberto Esquenazi, MD
Director, Gait and Motion Analysis Laboratory, MossRehab Hospital; Associate Professor, Department of Physical Medicine and Rehabilitation, Temple University School of Medicine, Philadelphia, Pennsylvania

Joseph D. Given, PhD
Research Associate, Sensory Motor Performance Program, Rehabilitation Institute of Chicago, Chicago, Illinois

Mel B. Glenn, MD
Professor and Chairman, Department of Rehabilitation Medicine, Boston University School of Medicine; Chief, Department of Rehabilitation Medicine, Boston University Medical Center Hospital; Director, Department of Rehabilitation Medicine, Boston City Hospital and Boston Specialty and Rehabilitation Hospital, Boston, Massachusetts

Ross M. Hays, MD
Department of Rehabilitation Medicine and Department of Pediatrics, University of Washington, Seattle, Washington

Barbara A. Hirai, BS
Coordinator, Gait and Motion Analysis Laboratory, MossRehab Hospital, Philadelphia, Pennsylvania

Richard T. Katz, MD
Medical Director and Vice President of Medical Affairs, SSM Rehabilitation Institute, St. Mary's Health Center; Associate Professor of Clinical Internal Medicine, St. Louis University Medical School, St. Louis, Missouri

Mary Ann E. Keenan, MD
Chairman, Department of Orthopaedic Surgery, Albert Einstein Medical Center; Professor of Orthopaedic Surgery and Professor of Physical Medicine and Rehabilitation, Temple University School of Medicine, Philadelphia, Pennsylvania

Craig M. McDonald, MD
Assistant Professor, Department of Physical Medicine and Rehabilitation and Department of Pediatrics, University of California, Davis, School of Medicine; Director, Neuromuscular Disease Clinics; Director, Pediatric Rehabilitation Clinics, University of California, Davis, Medical Center, Sacramento, California

Michael S. Pinzur, MD
Professor, Department of Orthopaedic Surgery, Loyola University Stritch School of Medicine, Maywood, Illinois

William Z. Rymer, MD, PhD
Director of Research and John G. Searle Professor, Rehabilitation Institute of Chicago; Professor, Departments of Physiology, Physical Medicine and Rehabilitation, and Biomedical Engineering, Northwestern University Medical School, Chicago, Illinois

PUBLISHED ISSUES 1987-1991
(available from the publisher)

PUBLISHED ISSUES 1992–1994

FUTURE ISSUES

Subscriptions and single issues available from the publisher—Hanley & Belfus, Inc.,
Medical Publishers, 210 South 13th Street, Philadelphia, PA 19107. Telephone (215) 546-7293;
(800) 962-1892. Fax (215) 790-9330.

PREFACE

The purpose of this issue is to provide an overview of the mechanisms, measurement, and management of spastic hypertonia. Chapters have been dedicated to a broad understanding of the mechanisms of spastic hypertonia and alterations in motor control that occur after central nervous system injury. Spastic hypertonia has been quantified using clinical scales, measurement of limb torque with simultaneous electromyographic pick-up, other mechanical measures, and by a host of electrophysiologic studies. These topics are covered in two separate chapters. The wide variety of treatment options—pharmacology, intrathecal pump, electrical stimulation, orthopedic and neurologic surgery—compose a large portion of this text and will surely benefit the physician involved in the process of maximizing function in an individual spastic patient.

This issue does not cover every aspect of spastic hypertonia in detail but intends to serve the clinician as a broad overview with an emphasis on the "state of the art." In this spirit, it is worthwhile to offer some introductory comments concerning the treatment of spastic hypertonia.

GENERAL CONSIDERATIONS

Spastic hypertonia, better known as "spasticity," is easier to recognize than characterize and perhaps more difficult to treat successfully. It may result from a variety of central nervous system disorders and has both diagnostic and therapeutic significance. Diagnostically, spasticity is a hallmark of an upper motor neuron disorder, and therapeutically, it represents one of the most important impairments for individuals who care for patients with central nervous system disease. As stated in the chapter on pharmacologic management, before treatment is initiated, the physician needs to address several important questions:

- Is there a functional impairment due to the spastic hypertonia?
- Is there a disturbance of gait?
- Do flexor spasms force the patient from his chair or interfere with transfers?
- Does the pain that can be associated with "spasms" disturb the patient's sleep?
- Does the lower extremity extensor tone support the patient during ambulation?

A stereotyped therapeutic approach has been proposed,[19] but, as in many aspects of rehabilitation, treatment is best individualized to a particular patient.

Basic Patient Management to Reduce Spasticity

Good nursing care can reduce nociceptive and exteroreceptive stimuli that may be exacerbating the patient's hypertonia. The avoidance of noxious stimuli is therefore an important initial management step. This includes prompt treatment of urinary tract complications (infections, stones), prevention of pressure sores and contractures, releasing of tightly wrapped leg bags and clothes, proper bowel and bladder management to prevent fecal impaction and bladder distension, and prophylaxis for deep venous thrombosis. Heterotopic bone has been suggested as an exacerbant, but the prevention of this complication is difficult.

Proper bed positioning early after spinal cord injury has been suggested as an important step in the long-term reduction of spastic hypertonia.[10] However, this assertion has never been systematically evaluated. A daily stretching program is an integral component of any management program for spastic hypertonia. A common bedside observation is that the resistance perceived as the physician continuously ranges a limb progressively diminishes as the motion is repeated.

Regular ranging of a patient's limbs helps prevent contractures and can reduce the severity of spastic tone for several hours. The reasons for the "carry-over" of ranging for several hours are not completely clear, but they could be related to mechanical changes in the musculotendinous unit or to plastic changes that occur within the central nervous system. These plastic events may correlate with short- and long-term modulation of synaptic efficacy associated with neurotransmitter changes on a cellular level. Habituation of reflex activity has been studied in *Aplysia californica,* a marine snail that has a simple nervous system. The snail has a reflex for withdrawing its respiratory organ and siphon, which is similar to the leg-flexion withdrawal reflex in humans. Repetitive activation results in a decrease in synaptic transmission, partly due to an inactivation of calcium channels in the presynaptic terminal. The decrease in calcium influx diminishes the release of neurotransmitter, probably due to the calcium-dependent exocytosis of neurotransmitter vesicles.[5,6]

SHORT-TERM STRATEGIES

Certain interventions may be valuable as temporizing strategies when a specific goal has been set. Several schools of therapeutic exercise have suggested that reflex-inhibiting postures may temporarily decrease spastic hypertonia so that underlying movements may be unmasked.[2,4,15] Using these strategies, therapists are able to help patients with hemiplegic and cerebral palsy to produce voluntary movements.

Topical cold has been reported to decrease tendon reflex excitability, reduce clonus, increase range of motion of the joint, and improve power in the antagonistic muscle group. These effects can be used to facilitate improved motor function for short periods of time.[11,14-16,18,20-22] Tone may be decreased shortly after the application of ice, probably due to decreased sensitivity in cutaneous receptors and slowing of nerve conduction. Central factors such as changes in central nervous system excitability may take longer to occur. Thus, a therapist might apply a cold pack for 20 or more minutes to obtain maximum effect.[7] Topical anesthesia may have similar effects.[23,25]

Due to hypertonic contracture, casting and splinting techniques can improve the range of motion in a joint, and positioning the limb in a tonic stretch has been observed to decrease reflex tone.[3,8,9,12,13,17,26,27] In one study, long-term but not short-term casting resulted in a significant decrease in both dynamic and static reflex sensitivity. Elongation of the series elastic component of the musculotendinous unit and an increase in the number of sarcomeres within muscle fibers may each have contributed to the decrease in tone.[24] Biofeedback techniques have also been observed to modulate spastic hyertonia but have not demonstrated much widespread usefulness.[1,28,29]

READING THIS ISSUE

It is hoped that the reader of this issue will benefit from a variety of authors' insights into the mechanisms and management of spastic hypertonia. The breadth of basic science and clinical experience provided here present the "state of the art" for the clinician interested in providing the best clinical care for a common problem in patients undergoing rehabilitation. While the text may be examined in any order, it is suggested that the reader review the first two chapters carefully to establish a solid understanding of the basic mechanisms of spasticity, thus establishing a framework for understanding strategies in clinical management.

Richard T. Katz, MD
Guest Editor

REFERENCES

1. Basmajian JV: Biofeedback in rehabilitation: A review of principles and practices. Arch Phys Med Rehabil 62:469–475, 1981.
2. Bobath B: Adult Hemiplegia: Evaluation and Treatment. London, Heinemann Medical Books, 1970.
3. Booth BJ, Doyle M, Montgomery J: Serial casting for the management of spasticity in the head-injured adult. Phys Ther 63:1960–1966, 1983.
4. Brunnstrom S: Movement Therapy in Hemiplegia. New York, Harper & Row, 1970.
5. Castellucci VF, Carew TJ, Kandel ER: Cellular analysis of long-term habituation of the gill withdrawal reflex of *Aplysia californica.* Science 202:1306–1308, 1978.
6. Castellucci VF, Kandel ER: A quantal analysis of the synaptic depression underlying habituation of the gill-withdrawal reflex in *Aplysia.* Proc Natl Acad Sci USA 71:5004–5008, 1974.
7. Chan CWY: Some techniques for the relief of spasticity and their physiological basis. Physiotherapy Canada 38:85–89, 1986.
8. Cherry DB, Weigand GM: Plaster drop-out casts as a dynamic means to reduce muscle contracture. Phys Ther 61:1601–1603, 1981.
9. Collins K, Oswald P, Burger G, Nolden G: Customized adjustable orthoses: Their use in spasticity. Arch Phys Med Rehabil 66:397–398, 1985.
10. Guttman L: Spinal Cord Injury—Comprehensive Management and Research. Oxford, England, Blackwell Scientific Publications, 1976.

11. Hartviksen K: Ice therapy in spasticity. Acta Neurologica Scandinavica 38(suppl 3):79–84, 1962.
12. Kaplan N: Effect of splinting on reflex inhibition and sensorimotor stimulation in treatment of spasticity. Arch Phys Med Rehabil 43:565–569, 1962.
13. King T: Plaster splinting to reduce elbow flexor spasticity. Am J Occup Ther 36:671–673, 1982.
14. Knutsson E: On effects of local cooling upon motor functions in spastic paresis. Prog Phys Ther 1:124–131, 1970.
15. Levine MG, Kabat H, Knott M, Voss DE: Relaxation of spasticity by physiological technics. Arch Phys Med Rehabil 35:214–223, 1954.
16. Lightfoot E, Verrier M, Ashby P: Neurophysiological effects of prolonged cooling of the calf in patients with complete spinal transection. Phys Ther 55:251–258, 1975.
17. McPherson JJ, Becker AH, Franszczak N: Dynamic splint to reduce the passive component of hypertonicity. Arch Phys Med Rehabil 66:249–252, 1985.
18. Mecomber SA, Herman RM: Effects of local hypothermia on reflex and voluntary activity. Phys Ther 51:271–282, 1971.
19. Merritt J: Management of spasticity in spinal cord injury. Mayo Clin Proc 56:614–622, 1981.
20. Miglietta O: Action of cold on spasticity. Am J Phys Med 52:198–205, 1973.
21. Miglietta O: Electromyographic characteristics of clonus and influence of cold. Arch Phys Med Rehabil 45:508–512, 1964.
22. Miglietta O: Evaluation of cold in spasticity. Am J Phys Med 41:148–151, 1962.
23. Mills WJ, Pozos RS: Decrease in clonus amplitude by topical anesthesia. Electroencephalogr Clin Neurophysiol 61:509–518, 1985.
24. Otis JC, Root L, Kroll MA: Measurement of plantar flexor spasticity during treatment with tone-reducing casts. J Pediatr Orthop 5:682–686, 1985.
25. Sabbahi MA, De Luca CJ, Powers WR: Topical anesthesia: A possible treatment for spasticity. Arch Phys Med Rehabil 62:310–314, 1981.
26. Snook J: Spasticity reduction splint. Am J Occup Ther 33:648–651, 1979.
27. Te Groen JA, Dommisse FG: Plaster casts in the conservative treatment of cerebral palsy. S Afr Med J 502–505, July 18, 1964.
28. Wolf SL, Binder-MacLeod SA: Electromyographic biofeedback applications to the hemiplegic patient: Changes in upper extremity neuromuscular and functional status. Phys Ther 63:1393–1403, 1983.
29. Wolf SL, Binder-MacLeod SA: Electromyographic biofeedback applications to the hemiplegic patient: Changes in lower extremity neuromuscular and functional status. Phys Ther 63:1404–1413, 1983.

WILLIAM Z. RYMER, MD, PhD
RICHARD T. KATZ, MD

MECHANISMS OF SPASTIC HYPERTONIA

From the Departments of
   Physiology, Physical Medicine
   and Rehabilitation, and
   Biomedical Engineering
Northwestern University Medical
   School and
Sensory-Motor Performance
   Program
Rehabilitation Institute of Chicago
Chicago, Illinois (WZR)
      and
St. Louis University Medical
   School and
SSM Rehabilitation Institute
St. Louis, Missouri (RTK)

Reprint requests to:
William Z. Rymer, MD, PhD
Rehabilitation Institute of Chicago
Room 1406
345 East Superior Street
Chicago, IL 60617

Spasticity is a hallmark of an upper motoneuron disorder, and it represents one of the most important impairments for clinicians who care for patients with central nervous system disease. A widely accepted definition of spasticity, provided by Lance in 1970, is that of

> a motor disorder characterized by a velocity-dependent increase in tonic stretch reflexes (muscle tone) with exaggerated tendon jerks, resulting from hyperexcitability of the stretch reflex, as one component of the upper motor neuron syndrome.[42]

Muscle tone is often characterized as "the sensation of resistance felt as one manipulates a joint through a range of motion, with the subject attempting to relax."[43] Although this definition is adequate for the bedside clinical examination, a more rigorous analysis indicates that muscle tone is made up of viscoelastic characteristics of muscular and connective tissues and reflex muscle contraction (tonic stretch reflexes). The heightened resistance on bedside examination represents changes in the musculotendinous unit (e.g., contracture), and/or changes within the segmental reflex arc (hyperactive stretch reflexes). This and succeeding chapters will provide the reader with a critical review of past literature concerning spastic hypertonia and will discuss in what ways spasticity can be quantified.

MECHANICAL CHANGES INTRINSIC TO MUSCLE

The intrinsic mechanical stiffness of a muscle is simply one of several contributors to muscle tone. The mechanical stiffness of a muscle may be estimated, at least in part, by studying the tension elicited when a joint is extended over a given angle at a designated angular velocity. The slope of the curve relating muscle force to length (or, in this case, angle of joint displacement) is influenced by both the intrinsic stiffness of muscle as well as by stretch reflex action. This response simulates the behavior of a simple spring, which generates a restoring force that is proportional to its change in length. The restoring force typically develops only after a certain amount of stretch is imposed. This initial length change is like the "slack length" of a spring, which will generate resistance only when the slack is taken up. The slack length is governed by the threshold of the stretch reflex, although some spring-like properties of skeletal muscle persist even when the tissue is stripped of its reflex controls.[52]

Given that muscle normally exhibits spring-like behavior, the possibility exists that an increase in the intrinsic mechanical stiffness of the muscle is responsible for spastic hypertonia. Furthermore, it is possible that this stiffness could be mediated by permanent structural changes in muscle connective tissues, or be variable in character, residing in the contractile apparatus of muscle itself. In either case, the changes in muscle stiffness would appear as an increase in the resistance to limb extension without a commensurate increase in muscle excitation as measured by the electromyogram.

In relation to this latter possibility, several investigators have recently advanced the idea that changes in the intrinsic muscle mechanical properties (rather than stretch reflex enhancement) are largely responsible for spastic hypertonia.[5,24-26,35] These claims are based on electromyographic and force analyses of leg muscles in hemiplegic adults and during ambulation in children with cerebral palsy; abnormally high tension developed in the spastic triceps surae during passive stretch without a parallel increase in electromyographic activity. On the basis of these EMG findings, coupled with observations of temperature effects on muscle response, the authors argued for a change in the intrinsic mechanical response of muscle to stretch, akin to the "stretch activation" that is described in slow amphibian or myotonic mammalian muscle.[1] Stretch activation refers to a stretch-induced excitation of muscle that occurs without a change in the efferent neural command.

Although this idea is both novel and provocative, in our view the experimental findings that were presented may be equally well explained by some form of degenerative or atrophic change in muscle structure, e.g., severe muscle atrophy with collagenous and elastic tissue replacement. There are no present grounds to propose an anomalous change in the physiological muscle response to stretch. Moreover, this "intrinsic" muscle hypothesis does not easily account for many established findings—such as enhanced phasic muscle stretch reflexes and increased tendon jerks—which indicate that motoneuron excitability is also markedly increased.

NEURAL MECHANISMS FOR MUSCULAR HYPERTONIA

The most basic neural circuit contributing to spastic hypertonia is the segmental reflex arc, which consists of muscle spindle receptors, their central connections with spinal cord neurons, and the motoneuronal output to muscle. Within this arc, the α-motor neuron may be likened to a final conduit, or final common pathway for motoneuronal outflow. This outflow is the summation of a host of different synaptic and modulatory influences, including

1. excitatory postsynaptic potentials from group Ia and II muscle spindle afferents,
2. inhibitory postsynaptic potentials from interneuronal connections from antagonistic muscles and from golgi tendon organs, and
3. presynaptic inhibition initiated by descending fiber output.[70]

Presynaptic inhibition is exerted by axons that end on primary afferent nerve terminals and that reduce the ability of sensory afferents to depolarize the post-synaptic membrane. Exteroceptive (e.g., cutaneous) and interoceptive (e.g., visceral) afferent information also can provide important input into the segmental milieu. It is upon these basic pathways that spinal and supraspinal influences modulate reflex behavior.

With the above segmental configuration in mind, two distinctly different ways exist in which the nervous system could produce an enhanced reflex response to muscle stretch. The first is by selectively increasing motoneuronal excitability, which is reflected as an increased motoneuronal response to a particular level of stretch-evoked synaptic input. The second is by increasing the amount of excitatory synaptic input elicited by muscle extension. Various mechanisms may be responsible for such changes (Table 1).[19,54] While it is quite possible that both enhanced stretch-evoked motoneuronal excitability and increased synaptic input may coexist, it is convenient to treat them independently for the present.

Increased Motoneuronal Excitability

α-motoneuron hyperexcitability is said to exist if motoneuronal recruitment and/or increased discharge are elicited with smaller than normal levels of excitatory input.[72] Clinically, an increase in motoneuronal excitability would mean that either a smaller stretch amplitude or a slower than usual stretch velocity would excite motoneurons. Similarly, synaptic input elicited by synchronous electrical excitation of Ia afferent fibers (H reflex) or mechanical excitation (muscle stretch reflex) would result in an augmented evoked response in the tested muscle. The evidence for enhanced motoneuronal excitability in spasticity is very

TABLE 1. Possible Neural Mechanisms for Spastic Hypertonia

I. Increased motoneuronal excitability

  A. Excitatory synaptic input is enhanced
    1. Segmental afferents
    2. Regional excitatory interneurons
    3. Descending pathways, i.e., lateral vestibulospinal tract

  B. Inhibitory synaptic input is reduced
    1. Renshaw cell recurrent inhibition
    2. Ia inhibitory interneurons
    3. Ib afferent fibers

  C. Change in the intrinsic electrical properties of the neuron
    1. Changes in passive membrane electrical properties
    2. Changes in voltage sensitive membrane conductance

II. Enhanced stretch-evoked synaptic excitation of motoneurons

  A. Gamma efferent hyperactivity

  B. Excitatory interneurons more sensitive to muscle afferent
    1. Collateral sprouting
    2. Denervation hypersensitivity
    3. Decrease in presynaptic inhibition

---

strong,[2,46] although the sources of such an increase are not yet clearly established. Several possibilities are worth considering.

For example, a state of increased excitability would arise quite simply if motoneurons are continuously more depolarized than normal so that they are set close to their threshold for recruitment. Little added synaptic input would then be required to achieve activation. This increased depolarization could arise either because tonic excitatory input is enhanced (e.g., from segmental afferents, regional excitatory interneurons, or descending pathways such as the lateral vestibulospinal tracts) or because there is a tonic reduction of inhibitory synaptic input from regional inhibitory interneurons (such as Renshaw cell recurrent inhibitions, Ia inhibitory interneurons, or Ib afferent neurons).[54] There is substantial evidence for this type of disturbance in spasticity, and it will be dealt with more fully below.

A different way that motoneurons may show increased excitability is via a change in the intrinsic electrical properties of the neurons. This could include changes in passive membrane electrical properties (such as increased input resistance and/or reduced capacitance) or changes in the normal ionic conductance mechanisms. Both types of disturbance could have the net effect that a given synaptic current (elicited in response to stretch-induced afferent excitation) would evoke a larger than normal voltage change and a resulting increase in motoneuronal activity without commensurate change in stretch reflex threshold.

No good evidence exists to support a change in the intrinsic membrane properties in chronic spastic animals.[32] However, most studies have been performed in anesthetized animals rather than in decerebrate-unanesthetized preparations, and other changes in neuronal intrinsic behavior are still quite feasible. Such changes would be expressed as alterations in voltage-sensitive membrane conductances mediated by changes in concentrations of neural modulators carried by various descending brainstem pathways. Substances such as serotonin (an indoleamine) or substance P (a peptide) may "gate" neuronal responses to transmitter-induced voltage changes, dramatically changing the way neurons respond to a given change in voltage.

For example, in the presence of serotonin, spinal motoneurons respond to a square wave depolarizing pulse with a rather prolonged depolarization that far outlasts the stimulus and that may return to the baseline only after the application of a hyperpolarizing pulse.[34] Changes in the intrinsic properties of the neuron would be expressed as an enhanced responsiveness of motoneurons during muscle stretch, which might appear as an abnormal and progressive increase in reflex force during muscle extension.

Increased Stretch-evoked Synaptic Excitation of Motoneurons

The second way in which an increased motoneuronal response to stretch could arise is by means of an augmented stretch-evoked excitatory synaptic input. That is, muscle afferent discharge in spastic muscle gives rise to increased excitatory synaptic current flowing into motoneurons, either directly from muscle afferent terminals or via interposed interneurons. This increased synaptic current could arise in two ways:

1. muscle spindle afferents show enhanced response to stretch because of increased dynamic fusimotor bias,[22,23,58]
2. interposed excitatory interneurons are more responsive to muscle afferent input.

Previously, it was widely believed that spastic hypertonia was due to hyperactivity of the γ-efferent fibers (called gamma spasticity in older nomenclature), causing an increased sensitivity of the muscle spindle receptor to length change. This hypothesis was based on the observation that spasticity diminished when nerves were infiltrated with dilute local anesthetic, with concentration appropriate to block fusimotor input. Although stretch reflexes can indeed be diminished by such γ-efferent blockade, this does not prove that spasticity is due to hyperactivity within afferent limbs of the reflex arc.[72] Since voluntary alpha mononeuronal activation is normally accompanied by significant γ activation,[66] blockade of gamma fibers would induce loss of tone in normal as well as abnormal muscle. To determine whether the level of gamma activity is abnormal in spastic muscle would require the effects of gamma blockade to be compared in normal and spastic muscle at equivalent levels of motor output, a prohibitively difficult experimental protocol to implement.

An alternative approach to evaluating the role of fusimotor input in spasticity is to use microneurographic recordings of spindle afferent discharge to evaluate the level of γ activation. Such studies, in which an insulated tungsten microelectrode is used to impale a single human nerve axon,[31] also have failed to confirm γ fusimotor hyperactivity.[15,30,31] Moreover, studies of spindle responses in monkeys after cortical ablation also have failed to reveal an excess of fusimotor activity after the development of spastic hypertonia.[29] Studies by Gilman et al. were performed in anesthetized animals rather than decerebrate-unanesthetized preparations. In summary, no present evidence supports the concept of enhanced dynamic fusimotor bias.

The second possible mechanism is an increase in segmental excitatory input to the motoneuron. Three mechanisms have been proposed that may cause motoneurons or interposed excitatory interneurons to become more responsive to muscle afferent input: collateral afferent sprouting, denervation hypersensitivity, and changes in presynaptic inhibition.

In the course of postinjury recovery, muscle afferents could undergo sprouting of their terminal branches to accommodate synaptic sites vacated by destruction of supraspinal tracts.[49] Collateral sprouting has been observed in spinal cord and autonomic nervous systems as well as several specific regions of the brain.[7] In principle, sprouting could also help explain the significant delay before spastic hypertonia appears after a spinal cord injury.[17,19,68] Regrettably, recent investigation offers little support for the view that collateral sprouting is an important process in spinal cord reorganization following partial deafferentation.[57] Models of sprouting in the mammalian central nervous system typically require much more radical removal of afferent input to a spinal neuron than is likely to arise in most supraspinal lesions.

Secondly, synapses that lose their presynaptic terminals may become more sensitive to ambient transmitter effects in the postsynaptic region. Studies using chemical destruction of descending spinal cord tracts mediated by serotonin and norepinephrine lend support to the idea of denervation sensitivity as a contributing factor to spastic hypertonia.[50,51] Exaggerated extensor hindlimb reflexes are observed after administration of serotonergic agonists in animals whose serotonergic systems were chemically destroyed, and similarly exaggerated flexor reflexes were noted in animals with noradrenergic destruction. Histochemical studies of serotonergic and noradrenergic receptor density demonstrated a nearly complete degeneration of these receptors approximately 2 weeks after axonotomy, followed by a regeneration of terminal density to 50–66% of original levels after 3 to 6 months. The regeneration of these terminals suggests that surviving fibers may have produced new sprouts by the mechanisms of collateral sprouting and reinnervated the empty synaptic sites.

Finally, enhanced synaptic excitation could also arise if the level of baseline "presynaptic inhibition" were reduced, since this would result in a greater than normal release of transmitter for each incoming afferent impulse.[70] Evidence for this assertion has been largely based on the failure of the tonic vibration reflex (TVR) to suppress the H reflex in the spastic patient.[12,36] In this paradigm a tonic vibratory stimulus is applied to a limb, usually the lower extremity. Tonic vibratory stimuli have been shown to preferentially and repetitively drive Ia afferent fibers. They exert their inhibitory characteristics by way of an interneuron that is both excited by Ia afferent input and then acts on terminal Ia fiber arborisations.[14] This interneuron is strongly modulated by descending pyramidal and extrapyramidal (vestibulospinal, reticulospinal, rubrospinal) tracts,[3,12,18] and therefore the TVR can help to elucidate the role of these descending fibers on the segmental reflex arc.

When an electrical stimulus is applied to the tibial nerve in normal subjects, the predominantly monosynaptic H reflex is noted approximately 30 ms later in the triceps surae. This H reflex is partially suppressed in normal subjects when the TVR is applied to the limb. The failure of the TVR to effectively inhibit the H reflex has been a strong argument implicating presynaptic inhibition as a mechanism contributing to spastic hypertonia. Presynaptic inhibition may act by limiting the magnitude of calcium current moving into primary afferent terminals, which in turn limits neurotransmitter release.[72]

Additional evidence for altered presynaptic mechanisms comes from a recent study by Thompson[64] in which the H reflex studies in the spastic hindlimbs of a chronic spinal hemisectioned rat were found to have reduced dependence on H reflex stimulus frequency. The authors argue that frequency-dependent H reflex reduction is related to increased presynaptic inhibition and that failure to show such reduction is an indication of a diminished presynaptic inhibition in motoneurons innervating spastic muscles. Whether the effects are indeed attributable to presynaptic inhibition, or to other presynaptic phenomena, the finding does point to systematic differences in spinal-lesioned animals that may be important in mediating hindlimb spasticity.

This list of possible sources of augmented reflexes is certainly incomplete, but it is already apparent that many factors may be involved. The problem of distinguishing these possibilities may appear, at first, to be insurmountable in an intact human; however, several likely differences in the patterns of mechanical and electromyographic response to muscle extension exist that should help to distinguish the broad categories of disturbance.

THRESHOLD VERSUS GAIN DISTURBANCES

In principle, two distinct parameters may be altered in the pathologic stretch reflex in spasticity, and these have important implications for the neurophysiologic disturbances outlined above (Fig. 1). First, the "slack length" or threshold of the stretch reflex could be reduced. In this scenario, a smaller and/or slower motion is sufficient to reach the reflex threshold, which is manifested clinically as a catch point after which the resistance to manual stretch abruptly increases. Once the stretch reflex is activated, the torque or force of the muscle increases in proportion

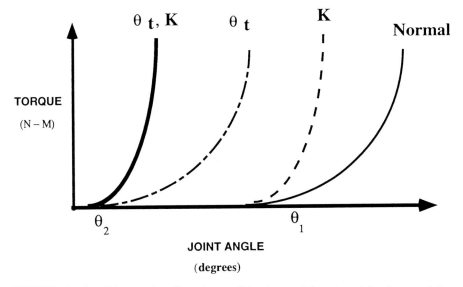

FIGURE 1. Possible stretch reflex abnormalities in spasticity. As a joint is extended, torque elicited by muscle stretch begins to increase after a certain threshold angle (θ) is reached. The amount of torque per unit angle, or muscle stiffness, is the slope of the curve. (θ_1) denotes a "normal" threshold angle; (θ_2) a reduced threshold for motoneuron recruitment. Curve (θ_t, K) represents a state in which both reduced threshold and increased stiffness exist. Curve θ_t and K represent the cases where only reduced threshold or increased stiffness exist alone, respectively. Curve N represents the normal state of reflex threshold and stiffness.

to the increasing joint angle. Both the slope of the force-length relationship and the increase in force with a standard velocity of stretch are similar to those recorded in normal muscle.

The most likely physiologic substrate for this pattern of response is simply that motoneurons are more depolarized as a result of a net increase in tonic excitatory synaptic input from descending pathways or regional interneurons so that motoneuron recruitment takes place more readily. There is no additional requirement for enhanced synaptic input during stretch.

The second possible disturbance of the stretch reflex is an increase in reflex gain, characterized by an abnormal increase in reflex force with increasing extension without substantial change in the reflex threshold angle. Expressed in quantitative terms, the angular stiffness, which is a measure of stretch reflex gain, is increased above normal.

Experimental Differentiation

Increased reflex gain would arise if the excitatory response to ongoing stretch were augmented because of increased dynamic γ bias (increasing spindle afferent discharge rates), afferent terminal sprouting (increasing the number of active terminals), postsynaptic receptor hypersensitivity (increasing the impact of released transmitter), reductions in presynaptic inhibition (increasing the amount of transmitter released for each incoming action potential), or changes in intrinsic motoneuronal properties (increasing the voltage change induced by release of a given amount of transmitter).

It is conceivable then that changes in reflex gain and threshold can be used to distinguish between normal and spastic-hypertonic reflexes. If the reflex threshold is reduced, motoneurons are probably in a state of sustained depolarization. If reflex stiffness is enhanced, either stretch-evoked afferent input or the postsynaptic effects of that input are enhanced. If both threshold and reflex stiffness are changed, then both forms of disturbance probably coexist.

Recent investigations at our laboratory at the Rehabilitation Institute of Chicago suggest that reflex gain is not enhanced in hypertonic muscles of hemiplegic subjects.[45,55,56] Rather, our analysis suggested that reflex threshold disturbances are the principal abnormalities in spastic hypertonia. These concepts will be addressed more rigorously below.

SUPRASPINAL MECHANISMS

Descending tracts contribute to spastic muscle hypertonia either via direct or monosynaptic excitatory projections to lower motoneurons (e.g., from the corticospinal or lateral vestibulospinal tracts) or indirectly by inhibition or facilitation of interneurons within spinal reflex pathways.[20] Operationally, the synaptic effects of descending pathways may be categorized, at least in principle, as mediating changes in the excitability of spinal motoneurons and/or as mediating changes in the responses of segmental reflex pathways. We will address each of these possibilities.

Changes in Motoneuron Excitability

It has been proposed that changes in motoneuronal excitability may be contingent primarily on changes in the "baseline" levels of depolarization of the motoneuron rather than on changes in intrinsic motoneuron membrane properties. The increased baseline depolarization depends, in turn, on the net tonic excitatory synaptic input that is converging on the neuron, from either descending pathways or from segmental interneuronal input.

For example, the lateral vestibulospinal pathway is apparently very important for the development of the increased excitability in axial and extensor α motoneurons that characterizes spastic hypertonia,[43] at least in supraspinal forms of spasticity. While this effect is due partly to monosynaptic input, more powerful excitatory contributions from the vestibulospinal system are almost certainly provided by local excitatory interneurons. Similarly, it is also likely that the excitation or inhibition of motoneurons mediated by descending reticulospinal fibers originating in medullary and pontine centers is mediated largely by segmental interneurons.

Changes in Segmental Reflex Function

While the activity of many descending pathways is likely to be impaired in either supraspinal or spinal injury, loss of the inhibitory effects of descending pathways (especially reticulospinal) on regional interneurons receiving input from cutaneous and muscle segmental afferents is also believed to be very important, especially in spinal forms of spasticity. This loss of inhibition may arise as a result of direct pathway interruption (as in spinal or brainstem injury) or as a result of the loss of supraspinal facilitation of brainstem reticulospinal neurons, whose discharge may be reduced or even silenced. These reductions in descending input release a number of powerful segmental reflexes, which are normally completely suppressed.[9-11,41]

For example, the Babinski reflex—a characteristic accompaniment of spastic hypertonia—represents a transition from the normal plantar reflex to a more diffusely organized flexion withdrawal reflex. The normal plantar reflex appears to promote postural stability by increasing the grip of the digits on the terrain and thus resembles the feline plantar cushion reflex. The Babinski reflex is a more diffusely organized flexion withdrawal reflex in which toes, ankles, and even more proximal joints are progressively flexed.

The clasp-knife reflex is a second, although less common, manifestation of this phenomenon of interneuronal release in spasticity. This reflex is characterized by an abrupt reduction of EMG activity and force once a spastic muscle is stretched through a particular length (or joint angle). The term "clasp-knife" is applied because the initial high resistance of spastic hypertonia is interrupted by the onset of inhibition, making the resistance of the hypertonic limb decline abruptly, rather like the behavior of an old-fashioned clasp-knife. Although initially attributed to tendon organ action[28] and then to secondary spindle afferent input,[18] recent evidence suggests that the clasp-knife is a reflection of the activity of group III and IV mechanoreceptors, whose central effects become pronounced because of the reduced descending inhibition of segmental interneurons.[59]

There are numerous other illustrations of alterations in reflex responsiveness that arise in supraspinal or spinal types of spasticity. Many of them are characterized by the pairing of increased flexor reflexes with the inhibition of antagonist extensors, presumably via the Ia reciprocal inhibitory interneuron. This is well illustrated by the clasp-knife reflex, in which inhibition of antigravity muscles, such as the triceps and quadriceps, is accompanied by an excitation of the opposing flexors.

To summarize, spasticity can be characterized by a combination of two major disturbances, both mediated by alterations in the balance of descending pathway activity. The first induces an increase in excitability of motoneurons innervating antigravity muscles (which are physiological extensors in the legs, and flexors in the arms), and the second changes the patterns of reflex responsiveness of many segmental reflexes, often promoting flexor muscle activity and reduced extensor activity.

Pathways Responsible for Modification in Descending Control in Spasticity

Cortex, basal ganglia, and cerebellum all provide important modulation of brainstem structures in normal motor control. Selective destruction of corticospinal tracts does not result in spastic hypertonia, but hypotonia and loss of fine hand movements.[65] Interruption of extrapyramidal fibers is evidently needed before spastic hypertonia develops. Lesions of particular premotor cortical sites, specifically areas 4 and 6 of Brodman, result in hypotonia followed by hypertonic hemiparesis.[29] With bilateral premotor damage spasticity is more severe.[19]

We do not yet understand which pathways are instrumental in mediating the increase in motoneuron excitability. However, it seems likely that the alterations in segmental interneuronal responsiveness follow loss of activity in the so-called dorsal reticulospinal system.[33] This pathway appears to require substantial facilitation from corticobulbar projections so that extensive white matter lesions, which diminish the excitatory inflow to the brainstem, have the effect of reducing the descending inhibition of segmental interneurons.[12]

Another, similar possibility is that descending moaminergic systems, such as the locus ceruleus pathways, are involved in regulating the excitability of segmental circuits. These pathways may be damaged directly in spinal cord injury or lose cortical excitatory drive, causing them to reduce their inhibitory control of segmental interneurons. This reduced inhibition may release segmental interneurons, such as those subserving cutaneous or muscle-based inhibitory pathways, or it may release excitatory interneurons, such as those receiving input from secondary spindle afferents.

UPPER MOTOR NEURON SYNDROME

A wide variety of motor dysfunctions that occur in patients with "spasticity" are not simply a result of the hypertonic changes that have been discussed above. The upper motor neuron (UMN) syndrome is a more general term used to describe patients with abnormal motor function secondary to lesions of cortical, subcortical, or spinal cord structures. Careful study of patients with UMN syndrome reveals that the patient's motor difficulties can be divided into a series of abnormal behaviors (positive symptoms) and performance deficits (negative symptoms) (Table 2).[44,61,71]

Positive symptoms are easily recognized in disorders of the spinal cord, as in the patient suffering from transverse myelitis or spinal cord injury. These symptoms include spasticity, the exaggerated flexion reflexes addressed earlier, and the related Babinski response. The release of reflexes from descending inhibitory control causes flexor or adductor spasms. Flexor spasms may become so severe as to require a paraplegic to be restrained to remain in a wheelchair. Hip adductor spasms cause "scissoring" of the lower extremities, limiting a patient's ability to ambulate effectively. Clonus, a cyclical hyperactivity of antagonistic muscles in response to stretch, may become so severe as to prohibit potentially functional muscle groups from performing effectively for the patient.

A final positive symptomatic component of the upper motor neuron syndrome that is frequently overlooked is the loss of precise autonomic control. A loss of upper motor neuron modulation on spinal autonomic mechanisms can result in a disorganization of autonomic function below the level of a spinal cord injury. In patients with spinal cord lesions above approximately the sixth thoracic level, seemingly innocuous sensory input can result in a potential hypertensive crisis. This hypertensive response is one component of autonomic dysreflexia, a gross nonselective "mass response." Disorganization of sympathetic activity below the level of spinal cord injury may be responsible for autonomic dysreflexia,[67] but mechanisms other than exaggerated sympathetic outflow also may contribute.[62]

Negative symptoms or performance deficits are more frequently observed in hemiparetic patients, such as those suffering from cerebrovascular accidents or

TABLE 2.   Upper Motor Neuron Syndrome

Abnormal behaviors (positive symptoms)
Reflex release phenomena
Hyperactive proprioceptive reflexes
Increased resistance to stretch
Relaxed cutaneous reflexes
Loss of precise autonomic control
Performance deficits (negative symptoms)
Decreased dexterity
Paresis/weakness
Fatigability

traumatic brain injury, but also may be found in patients with multiple sclerosis or spinal cord injury. Motoric actions are often weak, easily fatigued, and lacking in dexterity.[44,61,71] Several physiologic factors may contribute to these performance deficits.

The loss of orderly recruitment and rate modulation of motoneurons within a given motoneuron pool leads to inefficient muscle activation, inducing early loss of force, augmented subject effort, and the clinical perception of weakness.[27,69,71] High threshold motor units with rapid rates of adaptation are evidently recruited early, and these "fast twitch" units are poorly suited to maintain sustained muscle contractions.[53] Changes in mean motor unit discharge rates in paretic muscles may be the cause of abnormal EMG-force relationships, where surface electromyographic activity is augmented per unit force generated.[63] Twitch-contraction time of fast motor units also have been shown to change in hand muscles of hemiplegic limbs.[47]

Intramuscular and surface EMG recordings from spastic patients demonstrate disturbances of spatial selection of muscles in hemiparetic limbs. Recordings from normal limbs during isometric torque generation at the elbow reveal an orderly spatial distribution of muscle action. Each muscle is activated over a broad angular range in a symmetrical pattern, with EMG scaling with increasing force, and with the peak EMG value located at the angle of calculated maximum mechanical advantage. In contrast, spastic paretic limbs exhibit severe disturbances in the pattern of muscle activation so that the angular range and spatial orientation are radically disturbed. For example, normal elbow flexor muscles are activated maximally in the direction of flexion. However, in hemiparetic patients these muscles show a substantial shift in the angle of peak EMG and are maximally activated 90° or even 135° away from the normal angle.[8]

The final major type of distrubance appears as an alteration in the time-course of EMG activation in agonist and antagonist muscles. For example, in normal limbs, rapid flexion of a joint is associated with a so-called triphasic pattern of EMG activation, in which the agonist muscle is activated in two sequential bursts and the antagonist is activated in the intervening interval. In the UMN syndrome, the orderly timing is lost so that only a portion of the triphasic pattern is expressed. In the extreme case, a poorly-timed and ineffective simultaneous cocontraction of agonist and antagonist occurs.[46] Impaired agonist control and antagonist relaxation has been shown in various movement schema.[4,6,48,60]

Kinesiologic analysis of hemiplegic ambulation offers valuable insight into abnormal motor behaviors in patients with spastic hypertonia. Spastic reflexes tested in a passive limb are not identical with those in movements performed by the patients themselves. In some patients a low threshold for stretch reflex activation can be found at bedside examination in muscles that are not activated by the stretch imposed by ambulation.[37] These studies have demonstrated that there is a wide interindividual variation in gait patterns among affected patients. However, all patients demonstrated varying degrees of a lowered stretch reflex threshold, inadequate muscular activation, and stereotyped coactivation of muscles in primitive locomotor patterns.[37-40]

In summary, relief of the hypertonic "spastic" components of the upper motor neuron syndrome does not necessarily infer enhanced performance. Cocontraction of agonist and antagonist, dyssynergic patterns of contraction, flexor spasms, paresis, and loss of dexterity are probably more disabling than hypertonia for patients suffering from this motor disorder.[7,16,21,40-42,72]

REFERENCES

1. Abbott RH: The effects of fiber length and calcium ion concentration on the dynamic response of glycerol extracted insect fibrillar muscle. J Physiol 231:195–208, 1973.
2. Angel RW, Hoffmann WW: The H reflex in normal spastic and rigid subjects. Arch Neurol 8:591–596, 1963.
3. Ashby P, Verrier M: Neurological changes following spinal cord lesions in man. Can J Neurol Sci 2:91–100, 1975.
4. Benecke R, Conrad B, Meinck HM, Hohne J: Electromyographic analysis of bicycling on an ergometer for evaluation of spasticity of lower limbs in man. In Desmedt JE (ed): Motor Control: Mechanisms in Health and Disease. New York, Raven, 1983, pp 1035–1046.
5. Berger W, Quintern J, Dietz V: Pathophysiology of gait in children with cerebral palsy. Electroencephalogr Clin Neurophysiol 53:538–548, 1982.
6. Bernadelli A, Accornero N, Hallett M, et al: EMG burst duration during fast arm movements in patients with the upper motor neuron syndrome. In Delwaide PJ, Young RR (eds): Clinical Neurophysiology in Spasticity: Contribution to Assessment and Pathophysiology. Amsterdam, Elsevier, 1985, pp 77–82.
7. Bishop B: Spasticity: Its physiology and management. Phys Ther 57:371–401, 1977.
8. Bourbonnais D, VanDen Novin S, Carey K, Rymer WZ: Abnormal spatial patterns of elbow muscle activation in hemiparetic subjects. Brain 112:85–102, 1989.
9. Burke D, Gillies JD, Lance J: The quadriceps stretch reflex in human spasticity. J Neurol Neurosurg Psychiatry 33:216–223, 1970.
10. Burke D, Andrews CJ, Gillies JD: Reflex response to sinusoidal stretch in spastic man. Brain 94:455–470, 1971.
11. Burke D, Gillies JD: Hamstrings stretch reflex in human spasticity. J Neurol Neurosurg Psychiatry 34:231–235, 1971.
12. Burke D, Ashby P: Are spinal "presynaptic" inhibitory mechanisms suppressed in spasticity? J Neurol Sci 15:321–326, 1972.
13. Burke D, Lance JW: Studies of the reflex effects of primary and secondary spindle endings in spasticity. In Desmedt JE (ed): New Developments in Electromyography and Clinical Neurophysiology, Vol 3. Basel, Karger, 1973, pp 475–495.
14. Burke D, Hagbarth KE, Lofstedt L, Wallin BG: The responses of human muscle spindle endings to vibration of non-contracting muscles. J Physiol 261:673–693, 1976.
15. Burke D: A reassessment of the muscle spindle contribution to muscle tone in normal and spastic man. In Feldman RG, Young RR, Koella WP (eds): Spasticity: Disordered Motor Control. Chicago, Year Book, 1980, pp 261–278.
16. Burry HC: Objective measurements of spasticity. Dev Med Child Neurol 14:508–510, 1972.
17. Chambers WW, Liu CN, McCouch GP: Anatomical and physiological correlates of plasticity in the central nervous system. Brain Behav Evol 8:5–26, 1973.
18. Chan CWY: Some techniques for the relief of spasticity and their physiological basis. Physiother Can 38:85–89, 1986.
19. Chapman CE, Wiesendanger M: The physiological and anatomical basis of spasticity: A review. Physiother Can 34:125–136, 1982.
20. Clemente CD: Neurophysiologic mechanisms and neuroanatomic substrates related to spasticity. Neurology 28:40–45, 1978.
21. Davidoff RA: Antispasticity drugs: Mechanisms of action. Ann Neurol 17:107–116, 1985.
22. Dietrichson P: Phasic ankle reflexes in spasticity and Parkinsonian rigidity. The possible role of the fusimotor system. Acta Neurol Scand 47:22–51, 1971.
23. Dietrichson P: Tonic ankle reflexes in Parkinsonian rigidity and spasticity. The possible role of the fusimotor system. Acta Neurol Scand 47:163–182, 1971.
24. Dietz V, Quintern J, Berger W: Electrophysiological studies of gait in spasticity and rigidity: Evidence that altered mechanical properties of muscle contribute to hypertonia. Brain 104:431–449, 1981.
25. Dietz V, Berger W: Normal and impaired regulation of muscle stiffness in gait: A new hypothesis about muscle hypertonia. Exp Neurol 79:680–687, 1983.
26. Dietz V, Berger W: Interlimb coordination of posture in patients with spastic paresis: Impaired function of spinal reflexes. Brain 107:965–978, 1984.
27. Dietz V, Ketelsen UP, Berger W, Quintern J: Motor unit involvement in spastic paresis: Relationship between leg muscle activation and histochemistry. J Neurol Sci 75:89–103, 1986.
28. Fulton JF, Pi-Suner J: A note concerning the probable function of various afferent end organs in skeletal muscle. Am J Physiol 83:554–562, 1927–1928.

29. Gilman S, Lieberman JS, Marco LA: Spinal mechanisms underlying the effects of unilateral ablation of areas 4 and 6 in monkeys. Brain 97:49–64, 1974.
30. Hagbarth KE, Wallin G, Lofstedt L: Muscle spindle responses to stretch in normal and spastic subjects. Scand J of Rehabil Med 5:156–159, 1973.
31. Hagbarth KE: Exteroceptive, proprioceptive and sympathetic activity recorded with microelectrodes from human peripheral nerves. Mayo Clin Proc 54:353–364, 1979.
32. Hochman S, McCrea DA: The effect of chronic spinal transection on homonymous Ia EPSP rise times in triceps surae motoneurons in the cat. Abstr Soc Neurosci 186:12, 1987.
33. Hongo T, Lundberg A, Jankowska E: The rubrospinal tract: II. Facilitation of interneuronal transmission in reflex paths to motoneurons. Exp Brain Res 7:365–391, 1969.
34. Hounsgard J, Hultborn H, Jesperson B, Kiehr O: Intrinsic membrane properties causing a bistable behavior of alpha-motoneurons. Exp Brain Res 55:391–394, 1984.
35. Hufschmidt A, Mauritz KH: Chronic transformation of muscle in spasticity: A peripheral contribution to increased tone. J Neurol Neurosurg Psychiatry 48:676–685, 1985.
36. Iles JF, Roberts RC: Presynaptic inhibition of monosynaptic reflexes in the lower limbs of subjects with upper motoneuron disease. J Neurol Neurosurg Psychiatry 49:937–944, 1986.
37. Knutsson E, Richards C: Different types of disturbed motor control in gait of hemiparetic patients. Brain 102:405–430, 1979.
38. Knutsson E: Restraint of spastic muscles in different types of movement. In Feldman RG, Young RR, Koella WP (eds): Spasticity: Disordered Motor Control. Chicago, Year Book, 1980, pp 123–132.
39. Knutsson E, Martensson A: Dynamic motor capacity in spastic paresis and its relation to prime mover dysfunction, spastic reflexes and antagonist co-activation. Scand J Rehabil Med 12:93–106, 1980.
40. Knutsson E: Analysis of gait and isokinetic movements for evaluation of antispastic drugs or physical therapies. In Desmedt JE (ed): Motor Control: Mechanisms in Health and Disease. New York, Raven, 1983, pp 1013–1034.
41. Lance JW: Pathophysiology of spasticity and clinical experience with baclofen. In Feldman RG, Young RR, Koella WP (eds): Spasticity: Disordered Motor Control. Chicago, Year Book, 1980, pp 185–204.
42. Lance JW: Symposium synopsis. In Feldman RG, Young RR, Koella WP (eds): Spasticity: Disordered Motor Control. Chicago, Year Book, 1980, pp 487–489.
43. Lance JW, McLeod JG: Physiological Approach to Clinical Neurology. Boston, Butterworths, 1981.
44. Landau WM: Spasticity: What is it? What is it not? In Feldman RG, Young RR, Koella WP (eds): Spasticity: Disordered Motor Control. Chicago, Year Book, 1980, pp 17–24.
45. Lee WA, Boughton A, Rymer WZ: Absence of stretch reflex gain enhancement in voluntarily activated spastic muscle. Exp Neurol 98:317–335, 1987.
46. Matthews WB: Ratio of maximum H reflex to maximum M response as a measure of spasticity. J Neurol Neurosurg Psychiatry 29:201–204, 1966.
47. Mayer RF, Young JL: Effects of hemiplegia with spasticity on single motor units. In Feldman RG, Young RR, Koella WP (eds): Spasticity: Disordered Motor Control. Chicago, Year Book, 1980, pp 133–146.
48. McClellan DL, Hassan N, Hodgson JA: Tracking tasks in the assessment of spasticity. In Delwaide PJ, Young RR (eds): Clinical Neurophysiology in Spasticity: Contributing to Assessment and Pathophysiology. Amsterdam, Elsevier, 1985, pp 131–139.
49. McCouch GP, Austin GM, Liu CN, Liu CY: Sprouting as a cause of spasticity. J Neurophysiol 21:205–216, 1958.
50. Nygren LG, Fuxe K, Gosta J, Olson L: Functional regeneration of 5-hydroxytryptamine nerve terminals in the rat spinal cord following 5,6-dihydroxytryptamine induced degeneration. Brain Res 78:377–394, 1974.
51. Nygren LG, Olson L: On spinal noradrenaline receptor supersensitivity: Correlation between nerve terminal densities and flexor reflexes various time after intracisternal 6-hydroxydopamine. Brain Res 116:455–470, 1976.
52. Partridge LD, Benton LA: Muscle, the motor. In Brooks V (ed): Handbook of Physiology, Vol 2. Bethesda, MD, American Physiological Society, 1981, pp 43–106.
53. Petajan JH: Disordered motor unit control in spasticity. In Feldman RG, Young RR, Koella WP (eds): Spasticity: Disordered Motor Control. Chicago, Year Book, 1980, pp 233–248.
54. Pierrot-Desilligny E, Mazieres L: Spinal mechanisms underlying spasticity. In Delwaide PJ, Young RR (eds): Clinical Neurophysiology in Spasticity: Contribution to Assessment and Pathophysiology. Amsterdam, Elsevier, 1985, pp 63–76.

55. Powers RK, Campbell DL, Rymer WZ: Stretch reflex dynamics in spastic elbow flexor muscles. Ann Neurol 25:32–42, 1989.
56. Powers RK, Marder-Meyer J, Rymer WZ: Quantitative relations between hypertonia and stretch reflex threshold in spastic hemiparesis. Ann Neurol 23:115–124, 1988.
57. Rodin BE, Sampogna SL, Kruger: An examination of intraspinal sprouting in dorsal root axons with the tracer horseradish peroxidase. J Comp Neurol 215:187–198, 1983.
58. Rushworth G: Spasticity and rigidity: An experimental study and review. J Neurol Neurosurg Psychiatry 23:99–118, 1960.
59. Rymer WZ, Houk JC, Crago PE: Mechanisms of the clasp-knife reflex studied in an animal model. Exp Brain Res 37:93–113, 1979.
60. Sahrmann SA, Norton BJ: The relationship of voluntary movement to spasticity in the upper motor neuron syndrome. Ann Neurol 2:460–465, 1977.
61. Shahani BT, Young RR: The flexor reflex in spasticity. In Feldman RG, Young RR, Koella WP (eds): Spasticity: Disordered Motor Control. Chicago, Year Book, 1980, pp 287–296.
62. Stjernberg L, Blumberg H, Wallin BG: Sympathetic activity in man after spinal cord injury: Outflow to muscle below the lesion. Brain 109:695–715, 1986.
63. Tang A, Rymer WZ: Abnormal force-EMG relations in paretic limbs of hemiparetic human subjects. J Neurol Neurosurg Psychiatry 44:690–698, 1981.
64. Thompson FJ, Reier PJ, Lucas CC, Parmer R: Altered patterns of reflex excitability subsequent to contusion injury of the rat spinal cord. J Neurophysiol 68:1473–1486, 1992.
65. Tower SS: Pyramidal lesion in the monkey. Brain 63:36–90, 1940.
66. Vallbo AB: Human muscle spindle discharge during isometric voluntary contractions. Amplitude relations between spindle frequency and torque. Acta Physiol Scand 90:319–336, 1974.
67. Wallin BG, Stjernberg A: Sympathetic activity in man after spinal cord injury. Brain 107:183–198, 1984.
68. Wiesendanger M: Is there an animal model of spasticity? In Delwaide PJ, Young RR (eds): Clinical Neurophysiology in Spasticity: Contribution to Assessment and Pathophysiology. Amsterdam, Elsevier, 1985.
69. Young RR, Shahani BT: A clinical neurophysiological analysis of single motor unit discharge patterns in spasticity. In Feldman RG, Young RR, Koella WP (eds): Spasticity: Disordered Motor Control. Chicago, Year Book, 1980, pp 219–232.
70. Young RR, Delwaide PJ: Drug therapy: Spasticity. N Engl J Med 304:28–33,96–99, 1981.
71. Young RR, Wierzbicka MD: Behavior of single motor units in normal subjects and in patients with spastic paresis. In Delwaide PJ, Young RR (eds): Clinical Neurophysiology in Spasticity: Contribution to Assessment and Pathophysiology. Amsterdam, Elsevier, 1985, pp 27–40.
72. Young RR, Shahani BT: Spasticity in spinal cord injured patients. In Bloch RF, Basbaum M (eds): Management of Spinal Cord Injuries. Baltimore, Williams & Wilkins, 1986, pp 241–283.

WILLIAM Z. RYMER, MD, PhD
RICHARD T. KATZ, MD

MECHANICAL QUANTIFICATION OF SPASTIC HYPERTONIA

From the Departments of
  Physiology, Physical Medicine
  and Rehabilitation, and
  Biomedical Engineering
Northwestern University Medical
  School and
Sensory-Motor Performance
  Program
Rehabilitation Institute of Chicago
Chicago, Illinois (WZR)
  and
St. Louis University Medical
  School and
SSM Rehabilitation Institute
St. Louis, Missouri (RTK)

Reprint requests to:
William Z. Rymer, MD, PhD
Rehabilitation Institute of Chicago
Room 1406
345 East Superior Street
Chicago, IL 60617

The quantification of spasticity has been a difficult and challenging problem that has been based primarily on highly observer-dependent measurements. The lack of effective measurement techniques has been quite restrictive, since quantification is necessary to assess severity of the spastic state, to define its key characteristics for research analyses, and to evaluate various modes of treatment. For example, measurement of day-to-day torque variations for a particular joint within a given patient is likely to be extremely valuable in quantifying the effects of a therapeutic intervention such as a drug or surgical procedure.

Previous quantitative efforts have concentrated on such approaches as the tabulation of functional activities, electromyographic and biomechanic analysis of limb resistance to mechanical displacement, rectified surface electromyographic responses to perturbation or voluntary movement, gait analysis, and a host of electrophysiologic reflex studies.[15,31,38] Nonetheless, for a variety of reasons, including varying definitions, different observer standards, and interinstitutional differences in practice, no uniformly useful clinical measurements have emerged. The quantification of spasticity has been further hampered by a host of complicated issues. Changes in performance due to training effects, emotional status, and various systemic factors may all hamper a detailed analysis.[15]

SCALES

Gross clinical scales[2,40] assessing muscle tone on a scale of 0 (normal) to 4 (severe) offer ease of measurement but may lack temporal and interexaminer reproducibility. Moreover, these scales suffer from a "clustering" effect in which most of the patients are grouped within the middle grades.

The patient is examined in a comfortable position, usually supine, and muscle stretch reflexes and passive muscle tone are assessed bilaterally and separately for the upper and lower extremities. A modification of these scales has been created that adds an additional intermediate grade, and it has been shown to have high interrater reliability when testing elbow flexors (Table 1).[8] Although clinical scales such as those proposed by Pedersen[40] and Ashworth[2] offer only qualitative information, they have been widely used in the study of spasticity and are the present yardstick against which newer, more exact methods must be compared.

The Fugl-Meyer Scale is an accurate and objective method of assessing function (but not necessarily spastic hypertonia) in hemiplegic patients,[20] based on the natural progression of functional return observed by previous investigators.[10,47] Twitchell and Brunnstrom noted the recurrence of muscle stretch reflexes before volitional motor action, followed by synergistic movement patterns, return of voluntary selective motor function, and, finally, a decrease in hyperreflexic stretch reflexes. Motor evaluation with the Fugl-Meyer Scale in the upper extremity assesses movement within and independent of synergistic patterns, including coordination and speed of movement. The intricate movements of the hand and wrist are assessed separately, as is the patient's ability to maintain body posture. Light touch, position sense, joint movement, and pain-free movement add critical sensory observations as they contribute to motor function. The Fugl-Meyer Scale (Table 2) has been demonstrated to have a high intratester and intertester reliability and can be completed in 10 to 20 minutes.[6,19] It correlates closely with the severity of spastic tone.[27] Scales with similar purpose have been reported elsewhere, but appear to have no clear advantage.[18,39,48]

Scales such as the Barthel Index[35] provide an accurate and useful parameter of activities of daily living, but do not necessarily reflect spasticity per se. The Barthel Index has been shown in a comprehensive clinical trial to be a valid, reliable, and sensitive method for describing functional abilities and change-over time in any disability.[23] A modified Barthel Index can be used to make the scale more sensitive to the functional improvements of spinal cord patients.[17] Although little change in global functional status should be expected from mild to moderate changes in spasticity secondary to therapeutic intervention, it may prove to be extremely valuable to correlate fluctuations in spastic hypertonia with changes in functional status.

TABLE 1.   Clinical Scale for Spastic Hypertonia

0	No increase in tone
1	Slight increase in muscle tone, manifested by a catch and release or by minimal resistance at the end of the range of motion when the affected part(s) is moved in flexion or extension
1+	Slight increase in muscle tone, manifested by a catch, followed by minimal resistance throughout the remainder (less than half) of the range of motion
2	More marked increase in muscle tone through most of the range of motion, but affected part(s) easily moved
3	Considerable increase in muscle tone; passive movement difficult
4	Affected part(s) rigid in flexion or extension

TABLE 2.   Fugl-Meyer Scale of Functional Return after Hemiplegia

Movement of the shoulder, elbow, forearm, and hand
I	Muscle stretch reflexes can be elicited
II	Volitional movements can be performed within the dynamic flexor/extensor synergies
III	Volitional motion is performed mixing dynamic flexor and extensor synergies
IV	Volitional movements are performed with little or no synergy dependence
V	Normal muscle stretch reflexes

Wrist function—stability, flexion, extension, circumduction
Hand function—mass flexion, mass extension, 5 different grasps
Coordination and speed—assess tremor, dysmetria, speed
    Finger to nose test, heel to shin test
    Balance
    Sit without support
    Parachute reaction—non-affected side, affected side
    Stand—supported, unsupported
    Stand on non-affected side, affected side
Sensation—light touch, position sense
    Passive joint motion, joint pain

BIOMECHANICAL INVESTIGATIONS OF SPASTIC HYPERTONIA

Biomechanical investigations attempt to quantify changes in phasic and tonic reflex activity within the limbs of spastic patients. Quantitative observations can be made of the following variables:

- Joint torque—a measure of the amount of resistance force opposing the movement of the limb over a specified angle,
- Threshold—the angle at which torque or EMG starts to increase significantly during constant velocity joint extension, and
- Electromyography—electrical recordings of muscle activation, often adding rectified signal analysis of EMG from superficial muscle groups.

By definition, spastic limbs demonstrate abnormal resistance to externally imposed joint movement. This resistance is augmented by increasing the angle of joint extension and by increasing the rate at which the limb is moved.

Various investigators have performed biomechanical investigations such as these, using either linear[11,13,24,32,33,36,41,42] or sinusoidal stretch[5,11,12,22,34,38,43,50] of the affected limb. These investigations have yielded conflicting results. For example, earlier studies have shown spastic hypertonia to be strongly dependent upon the rate of stretch,[11-14,24,31,50] and an exaggeration of dynamic (phasic) rather than static (tonic) reflex output.[1,11,13,14,24] These results are somewhat puzzling, as mammalian muscle spindles are only weakly dependent on the rate of stretch, and this sensitivity does not vary significantly with changes in fusimotor input.[16,21,26,37]

CURRENT STUDIES

Recent investigations in our laboratory at the Rehabilitation Institute of Chicago suggest that the reflex response in spastic hypertonia may be quite different than previously believed.[33,41,42] These studies were carried out using a servo-controlled motor, which applied controlled ramp and hold movements to the elbow (Fig. 1). Hemiplegic patients were comfortably seated with shoulder partially abducted and flexed, while the machine produced movements about the elbow joint in a horizontal plane. Angular position and velocity were measured by

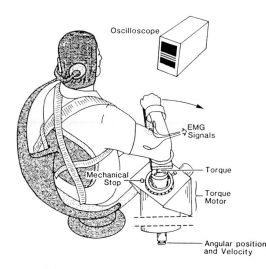

FIGURE 1. A servo-controlled motor that applies ramp and hold movements to the upper extremity. Such apparatus allows measurement of angular position and velocity in the horizontal plane. Electromyographic activity in the biceps brachialis, brachioradialis, and lateral triceps muscles can be measured with surface electrodes. (From Katz RT, Rymer WZ: Spastic hypertonia: Mechanisms and measurement. Arch Phys Med Rehabil 70:144–155, 1989; with permission.)

a potentiometer and tachometer mounted on the motor shaft, and these signals were used as feedback inputs to the controller to produce a position-regulated actuator—a device capable of applying a particular angular deflection regardless of load. Electromyographic activity in the biceps brachialis, brachioradialis, and lateral triceps muscles was measured with surface electrodes.

These studies have generated some novel concepts in the causation of spastic hypertonia. First, spastic hypertonia may be the result simply of a decrease in stretch reflex threshold, i.e., reflexes are elicited with less angular displacement of the extremity. The reflex stiffness covaried in much the same way as that recorded in normal muscle, in which reflex stiffness increases progressively with increasing background force, especially at lower force levels. The magnitude of reduction of this threshold angle proved to be inversely proportional to the clinical severity of hypertonia,[42] which is what would be expected if threshold changes were the predominant source of change in the stretch reflex response.

Second, there was no preferential enhancement of dynamic over static reflex activity.[41] As in normal muscle, reflex torque was relatively insensitive to extension velocity. Moreover, the rather small amount of velocity-dependence of force and EMG output was generated to a large extent by the velocity-related behavior of the reflex threshold rather than by velocity-induced changes in reflex response overall. In other words, the onset of the reflex was greatly advanced as stretch velocity was increased, but once activated the response was not noticeably different in character from the norm.

Third, when initial conditions were matched, stretch reflexes were similar in the hemiplegic limb and non-hemiplegic limb of hemiplegic volunteers; that is, limb reflex "stiffness" was quite similar when the hemiplegic and non-affected sides were compared. Conversely, as stated above, in patients who showed systematic variations in the degree of spastic hypertonia within a given recording session, the changes in tone could be attributed almost entirely to fluctuations in the angular threshold.

GAIN VERSUS THRESHOLD ISSUES

These findings are largely in disagreement with prevailing views about stretch reflexes in spasticity that treat spastic hypertonia as a straightforward velocity-dependent increase in limb resistance. Why do these results differ so markedly from previous investigations?

The main reason is that many earlier investigators failed to dissociate the contributions of changes in stretch reflex threshold from changes in reflex gain. To illustrate this problem further, the application of a stretch to an initially passive muscle in a spastic limb (which is the state recommended for assessment of spasticity) often gives rise to an increased torque and EMG response, which is usually interpreted as reflecting an increase in reflex gain. Such an outcome could equally well arise solely from a change in stretch reflex threshold. For example, if the motoneuron pool innervating a spastic muscle is depolarized by descending spinal input, the introduction of a muscle perturbation will activate motoneurons more readily. However, once activated they would be expected to obey the usual rules for recruitment and rate regulation and would not demonstrate any increase in reflex stiffness.

It follows that in order to dissociate gain and threshold contributions to increased muscle tone in spastic limbs, one must establish a known level of motoneuron excitability against which the responses to increased stretch can be compared. This can be accomplished by establishing a known background force, or "preload" before the muscles are tested. Provided that the patterns of muscle and motoneuron activation are similar in spastic and normal muscles, then setting muscles to the same initial force provides a means to match (approximately) the excitability of the motoneuron pools. Furthermore, this matching of excitability would also imply a matching of a reflex threshold, provided that afferent inflow induced by stretch is comparable in normal and spastic muscles. Even though these various assumptions are not readily confirmed at the present time, the failure to match neuron excitability in spastic and control muscles, even approximately, limits the accuracy of possible quantitative comparisons of reflex gain in spastic and normal muscles.[22,25]

Other investigators also have found substantial static responses to maintained stretch in spastic patients, without a significantly different stiffness than normal muscle. Rack et al. have found muscle stiffness in spastic patients to be set at one end of the normal range of variability.[43] Knutsson et al.[29] noted that spastic reflexes tested in passive limb movements are not identical with those performed by the patients themselves. In some individuals, a low threshold for stetch reflex activation can be found at bedside exam in muscles that are not activated by the stretch imposed by ambulation.[29] Antagonistic restraint of voluntary motion, a previously mentioned component of the upper motor neuron syndrome, becomes much more dramatic as the cadence of gait increases, indicating that spastic reflex mechanisms are not uniformly operational in any particular movement.[28]

These findings may have important implications for evaluating hypotheses about mechanisms of spastic muscular hypertonia. Since reflex stiffness and velocity sensitivity of reflex torque appear to be essentially normal in hypertonic muscles, once the muscle is activated there is no obvious need to invoke mechanisms that require enhanced stretch-evoked synaptic efficacy to spinal motoneurons. These include such hypotheses as enhanced gamma dynamic bias, afferent sprouting, or changes in the level of presynaptic inhibition. Rather, findings in spastic hypertonia may simply be attributed to changes in reflex threshold, which are due in large part to supraspinally mediated increased background levels of depolarization of motoneurons.

Pendulum Test

A pendular model for assessment of spastic hypertonia of the quadriceps and hamstring muscle groups has been proposed and has been evaluated in supine normal and spastic patients.[3,4,7,45,49] Stiffness of the lower limb is assessed by placing patients in a supine position with both legs extending over the edge of a table that supports them only as far as the distal thigh. In this way the knee joint can be easily flexed and extended. When the lower limb segment falls from a fully-extended position, it sways about the vertical like a pendulum, and its movement is dampened or "braked" by the viscoelastic elements of the limb (Fig. 2). Knee movement is assessed by an electrogoniometer and rate of movement by a tachometer. These instruments usually show sinusoidal patterns of angular motion on which a mathematical model has been created to differentiate a spastic from a normal limb.

Although easy to use, the mathematical analysis of the pendulum biomechanical model[3] suffers from the questionable assumption that mechanical properties of knee extensor and flexor musculature are equal and that the model can be treated as a simple linear "second order" system (in which elements can be simulated by various masses, springs, and viscous elements). In fact, muscle stiffness and viscosity vary with the level of muscle excitation and with muscle length. Moreover, the model includes no explanation for threshold and stiffness variation, which is in disagreement with data obtained from mechanical perturbations.[11,13] Despite its flaws, the pendulum test may be performed on commercially available isokinetic exercise equipment, with a high correlation between trials.[9,27]

SUMMARY AND RECOMMENDATIONS

There is not likely to be any useful outcome from measuring angular joint stiffness, since, based on our earlier findings,[33,41,42] stiffness would not be expected to change significantly. In fact, a finding of increased joint stiffness is more likely to indicate contracture than increased stretch reflex response. The major variable that does appear to be worth measuring is the stretch reflex threshold, the angle at which reflex torque and EMG begin to increase in an initially passive muscle.

However, there are some unresolved difficulties with these measurements that make threshold estimates less attractive as an index of the severity of spastic hypertonia. Although measuring the angle at which EMG activity begins during extension of passive muscle is an obvious possibility, estimating the onset angle of low levels of EMG is technically quite difficult, and different muscles typically show quite different reflex thresholds by EMG techniques. Although rigorous quantitative techniques are available for EMG threshold estimation,[42] these are not readily applied in a clinical setting.

An alternative possibility would be to estimate the reflex threshold of the various muscles using mechanical measurements. Mechanical measurements are appealing since they are likely to reflect the contributions of all relevant muscles and have an obvious clinical parallel—the catch point of the reflex response. On the other hand, they require sensitive torque recordings that are not routinely performed in a clinical setting, as well as relatively sophisticated mathematical techniques to allow the active reflex torque to be separated from passive viscoelastic forces that arise during extension of the joint. Commercially available isokinetic systems may serve as a uniform and standard method to assess hypertonia on a clinical basis.

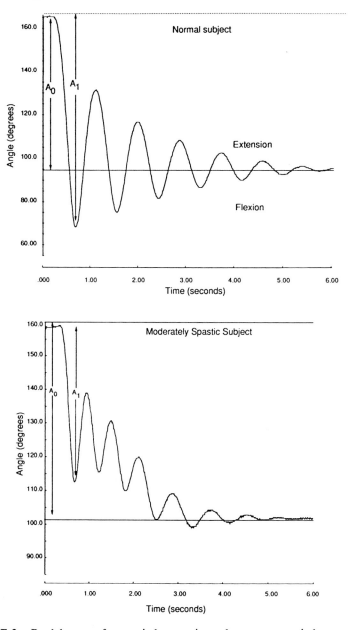

FIGURE 2. Pendulum test for spastic hypertonia used to assess spastic hypertonia of the quadriceps and hamstring muscle groups. Stiffness of the limb is assessed by placing patients in a supine position with both legs extending over the edge of a table, which supports them only as far as the distal thigh. A_0 represents the amplitude of the damped sinusoidal curve as it falls from the extended position to the final resting angle. A_1 represents the amplitude of the plotted waveform from full extension to its first absolute minimum. The upper tracing depicts normal patients. The lower tracing depicts a moderately spastic patient. The initial swing from full extension (A_1) does not reach the vertical, while the normal patient obtains 27° of flexion beyond the vertical. The marked damping of the altered sinusoidal curve is evident in the spastic subject.

The approach we presently favor is simply to measure the torque at some specified joint angle, such as immediately prior to the end of a constant velocity-constant amplitude ramp stretch. Since stiffness is not a reliable variable, the torque measured at a predetermined angle during a specified constant velocity extension is closely dependent on the stretch reflex threshold. (This is because the smaller the threshold angle, the greater the angular range over which muscle stretch produces reflex excitation of spinal motoneurons.) For a given angular extension applied to muscles of one particular spastic subject, variations in torque are then directly attributable to differences in reflex threshold.

The use of torque measurements as an index of spastic hypertonia is certainly not a straightforward matter, especially since most clinicians are inexperienced with mechanical measurements of any kind. Moreover, the torque recorded in limbs of different patients will certainly vary with limb mass, muscle bulk, and the characteristics of the individual's muscular anatomy. This implies that objective quantification of hypertonia in a diverse group of spastic subjects is unlikely to be successful, at least until the range of torque variation in normal passive limbs is documented. A more immediately useful application is the assessment of day-to-day variations in the severity of spastic hypertonia within a given patient. This is because limb inertia, muscle mechanical moments, and passive viscoelastic elements remain constant over relatively long times, so that short-term variations in torque are legitimately attributed to changes in stretch reflex response magnitude.[27]

REFERENCES

1. Ashby P, Burke D: Stretch reflexes in the upper limb of spastic man. J Neurol Neurosurg Psychiatry 34:765–771, 1971.
2. Ashworth B: Preliminary trial of carisoprodol in multiple sclerosis. Practitioner 192:540–542, 1964.
3. Bajd T, Bowman RG: Testing and modelling of spasticity. J Biomed Eng 4:90–96, 1982.
4. Bajd T, Vodovnik L: Pendulum testing of spasticity. J Biomed Eng 6:9–16, 1984.
5. Benecke R, Conrad B, Meinck HM, Hohne J: Electromyographic analysis of bicycling on an ergometer for evaluation of spasticity of lower limbs in man. In Desmedt JE (ed): Motor Control: Mechanisms in Health and Disease. New York, Raven, 1983, pp 1035–1046.
6. Berglund K, Fugl-Meyer AR: Upper extremity function in hemiplegia. A cross-validation study of two assessment methods. Scand J Rehabil Med 18:155–157, 1986.
7. Boczko M, Mumenthaler M: Modified pendulousness test to assess tonus of thigh muscles in spasticity. Neurology 8:846–851, 1958.
8. Bohannon RW, Smith MB: Interrater reliability on a modified Ashworth scale of muscle spasticity. Phys Ther 67:206–207, 1987.
9. Bohannon RW: Variability and reliability of the Pendulum test for spasticity using a Cybex II isokinetic dynamometer. Phys Ther 67:659–661, 1987.
10. Brunnstrom S: Movement Therapy in Hemiplegia. New York, Harper & Row, 1970.
11. Burke D, Gillies JD, Lance J: The quadriceps stretch reflex in human spasticity. J Neurol Neurosurg Psychiatry 33:216–223, 1970.
12. Burke D, Andrews CJ, Gillies JD: Reflex response to sinusoidal stretch in spastic man. Brain 94:455–470, 1971.
13. Burke D, Gillies JD: Hamstrings stretch reflex in human spasticity. J Neurol Neurosurg Psychiatry 34:231–235, 1971.
14. Burke D, Lance JW: Studies of the reflex effects of primary and secondary spindle endings in spasticity. In Desmedt JE (ed): New Developments in Electromyography and Clinical Neurophysiology, Vol 3. Basel, Karger, 1973, pp 475–495.
15. Burry HC: Objective measurement of spasticity. Dev Med Child Neurol 14:508–510, 1972.
16. Crago PE, Houk JC, Hasan Z: Regulatory actions of the human stretch reflex. J Neurophysiol 39:925–935, 1976.
17. Cummens CL, Hough DM: MRSCICS Patient Function Determination Procedure. Chicago, Rehabilitation Institute of Chicago, 1973.
18. DeSouza LH, Langton Hewer R, Miller S: Assessment of arm control in hemiplegic stroke patients. Arm function tests. Int Rehabil Med 2:3–9, 1980.

19. Duncan P, Propst M, Nelson S: Reliability of the Fugl-Meyer assessment of sensorimotor recovery following cerebrovascular accident. Phys Ther 63:1606–1610, 1983.
20. Fugl-Meyer AR, Jaasko L, Leyman I, et al: The post-stroke hemiplegic patient: A method for evaluation of physical performance. Scand J Rehabil Med 7:13–31, 1975.
21. Gielen CCAM, Houk JC: Nonlinear viscosity of human wrist. J Neurophysiol 52:553–569, 1984.
22. Gottlieb GR, Agarwal GC, Penn R: Sinusoidal oscillation of the ankle as a means of evaluating the spastic patient. J Neurol Neurosurg Psychiatry 41:32–39, 1978.
23. Granger CV, Albrecht GL, Hamilton BB: Outcome of comprehensive medical rehabilitation: Measurement by PULSES profile and the Barthel Index. Arch Phys Med Rehabil 60:145–154, 1979.
24. Herman R: The myotatic reflex: Clinicophysiological aspects of spasticity and contraction. Brain 98:272–312, 1970.
25. Herman R, Freedman W, Monster AW, Tamai Y: A systematic analysis of myotatic reflex activity in human spastic muscles. In Desmedt JE (ed): New Developments in Electromyography and Clinical Neurophysiology, Vol 3. Basel, Karger, 1973, pp 556–578.
26. Houk JC, Rymer WZ, Crago P: Dependence of dynamic response of spindle receptors on muscle length and velocity. J Neurophysiol 46:143–166, 1981.
27. Katz RT, Rovai G, Brait C, Rymer WZ: Objective quantification of spastic hypertonia: Correlation with clinical findings. Arch Phys Med Rehabil 73:339–347, 1992.
28. Knutsson E, Martensson A: Dynamic motor capacity in spastic paresis and its relation to prime mover dysfunction, spastic reflexes and antagonist co-activation. Scand J Rehabil Med 12:93–106, 1980.
29. Knutsson E: Analysis of gait and isokinetic movements for evaluation of antispastic drugs or physical therapies. In Desmedt JE (ed): Motor Control: Mechanisms in Health and Disease. New York, Raven, 1983, pp 1013–1034.
30. Lance JW: Symposium synopsis. In Feldman RG, Young RR, Koella WP (eds): Spasticity: Disordered Motor Control. Chicago, Year Book, 1980.
31. Lance JW: The control of muscle tone, reflexes, and movement. Neurology 30:1303–1313, 1980.
32. Leavitt LAS, Beasley WC: Clinical application of quantitative methods in the study of spasticity. Clin Pharmacol Ther 5:918–941, 1964.
33. Lee WA, Boughton A, Rymer WZ: Absence of stretch reflex gain enhancement in voluntarily activated spastic muscle. Exp Neurol 98:317–335, 1987.
34. Long C, Thomas D, Crochetiere WJ: Objective measurement of muscle tone in the hand. Clin Pharmacol Ther 5:909–917, 1964.
35. Mahoney FI, Barthel DW: Functional evaluation: Barthel index. Maryland State Med J 14:61–65, 1965.
36. Nashold BS: An electronic method of measuring and recording resistance to passive muscle stretch. J Neurol Neurosurg Psychiatry 26:310–314, 1964.
37. Nichols TR, Houk JC: The improvement in linearity and the regulation of the stiffness that results from the actions of the stretch reflex. J Neurophysiol 39:119–142, 1976.
38. Norton BJ, Bomze HA, Chaplin H: An approach to the objective measurement of spasticity. Phys Ther 52:15–23, 1972.
39. Parker VM, Wade DT, Langton Hewer R: Loss of arm function after stroke: Measurement, frequency, and recovery. Int Rehabil Med 8:69–73, 1986.
40. Pedersen E: Spasticity: Mechanism, Measurement, and Management. Springfield, IL, CC Thomas, 1969, pp 36–54.
41. Powers RK, Campbell DL, Rymer WZ: Stretch reflex dynamics in spastic elbow flexor muscles. Ann Neurol 25:32–42, 1989.
42. Powers RK, Marder-Meyer J, Rymer WZ: Quantitative relations between hypertonia and stretch reflex threshold in spastic hemiparesis. Ann Neurol 23:115–124, 1988.
43. Rack PMH, Ross HF, Thilman F: The ankle stretch reflexes in normal and spastic subjects. Brain 107:637–654, 1984.
44. Rushworth G: Spasticity and rigidity: An experimental study and review. J Neurol Neurosurg Psychiatry 23:99–118, 1960.
45. Schwab RS: Problems in the clinical estimation of rigidity (hypertonia). Clin Pharmacol Ther 5:942–946, 1964.
46. Twitchell TE: The restoration of motor function following hemiplegia in man. Brain 74:443–480, 1951.
47. Wade DT, Langton Hewer R, Wood VA, et al: The hemiplegic arm after stroke: Measurement and recovery. J Neurol Neurosurg Psychiatry 46:521–524, 1983.
48. Wartenberg R: Pendulousness of the legs as a diagnostic test. Neurology 1:18–24, 1951.
49. Webster DD: Dynamic quantification of spasticity with automated integrals of passive motion resistance. Clin Pharmacol Ther 5:900–908, 1964.

RICHARD T. KATZ, MD

ELECTROPHYSIOLOGIC ASSESSMENT OF SPASTIC HYPERTONIA

From St. Louis University
Medical School and
SSM Rehabilitation Institute
St. Louis, Missouri

Reprint requests to:
Richard T. Katz, MD
Medical Director and Vice
  President of Medical Affairs
SSM Rehabilitation Institute
St. Mary's Health Center
6420 Clayton Road
St. Louis, MO 63117

A wide variety of electrophysiologic reflex studies have been performed to assess spasticity and explore neuronal circuits within the spinal cord.[16] While these reflexes are easily recorded, analyzed, and quantified,[10] the measurements have proven to be of greater pathophysiologic than clinical utility.[15] Other sources offer a full description of these tests[10,11,16,25] and the following discussion provides an overview.

Several standard electrophysiologic tests require definition. The M response is a compound muscle action potential generated by maximally stimulating a peripheral nerve and recording over a muscle innervated by that nerve. The H reflex is not a direct response of muscle to stimulation of its corresponding motor nerve, but a reflex similar to (but not the same as) a muscle stretch reflex. The H reflex is usually elicited by delivering a submaximal stimulus to the tibial neve in the popliteal fossa and recording over the soleus muscle. The generated nerve action potential propagates up to the spinal cord and then, via a predominantly monosynaptic reflex arc, passes down the efferent motor axon. The H reflex is unlike the muscle stretch reflex in that (1) the muscle spindle is bypassed, and (2) the afferent volley is temporally less disperse, and the tendon jerk involves significantly fewer Ib fibers.[8] Although the H reflex is routinely recorded in this manner, it may be similarly recorded from the flexor carpi radialis upon stimulation of the median nerve[23] and vastus medialis upon stimulation of the femoral nerve.[35]

THE H REFLEX

Limitations

Although the H reflex has many theoretically interesting applications, it is riddled with methodologic difficulties in the study of patients with central nervous system symptoms.[24] For example, inexact placement of the recording electrodes allows contamination of the soleus response by gastrocnemius activity. Maryniak et al. have studied the contribution of various deep and superficial muscles to the conventionally recorded H reflex and help explain why amplitudes and latencies may vary significantly between studies using slightly different techniques.[30] H reflex studies may be influenced by changes in stimulation frequency, patient relaxation, limb position, or changes in head and neck position.[19,20] For example, laterally tilting a person results in inhibition of the H reflex ipsilateral to the tilting and facilitation of the contralateral response.[1] The amplitude of the H reflex and the relation between the H reflex and M response change markedly with stimulus duration. H reflexes are brought out to advantage using a stimulus duration between 0.5 and 1 ms.[33] Studies using the H reflex must be cautiously interpreted;[40] Hugon has offered a suggested protocol for H reflex testing.[19]

Electrophysiologic Techniques

A ratio of the maximal H reflex and M response, or H(max)/M(max), has been reported to assess the excitability of the motor nucleus by determining the percentage of motoneurons activated via the H reflex in comparison to direct activation of the motoneurons.[2,31] It assumes that presynaptic inhibition via descending tracts that synapse on the terminal arborizations of Ia afferents remains constant.[22] Increased H(max)/M(max) ratios have been reported in the spastic phase of hemiplegia.[18] Little and Halar studied H(max)/M(max) ratios following spinal cord injury and found both the H-reflex amplitude and H(max)/M(max) ratio increased significantly over a 3-month period following spinal cord injury. They attributed these changes to an increase in central synaptic excitability.[28] Matthews did not find any change in the H(max)/M(max) ratio after administration of intravenous chlorproethazine or diazepam.[31] In contrast, MacDonell et al. found a reduction in the H(max)/M(max) ratio following intrathecal administration of baclofen in 6 patients with severe lower extremity spasticity due to spinal cord injury.[29] Furthermore, there has been little correlation between H(max)/M(max) ratios and the severity of spastic hyperreflexia.[10,24] Similar results have been obtained substituting a mechanically induced muscle stretch reflex for electrical activation of Ia afferent fibers, the so-called T/M ratio.

The effects of reciprocal innervation can be assessed, at least theoretically, by determining the effect of a tibialis anterior contraction on the H reflex. Normal reciprocal inhibitory mechanisms from contraction of the anterior calf muscle should inhibit the reflex response within the triceps surae. Facilitation of Ia interneurons by descending spinal tracts has been demonstrated in humans,[38] and the loss of such descending influences may explain the loss of effectiveness of reciprocal inhibition in spastic subjects. Peroneal nerve stimulation may be substituted for voluntary contraction of the tibialis anterior.

"H reflex recovery curves" claim to reflect polysynaptic changes in motoneuron excitability secondary to segmental and suprasegmental mechanisms. Paired equal stimuli of the tibial nerve are applied in varying temporal arrangement. The resulting H reflexes demonstrate various phases of inhibition and facilitation that are poorly reproducible and of unknown significance.[10] Garcia-Mullin studied acute, subacute, and early chronic hemiplegic patients subsequent to a cerebrovascular accident using the H reflex recovery curve and found changes that suggested a decrease in motoneuron excitability only within the first several days, followed by an increase in excitability thereafter. The changes in motoneuron excitability were not found to be predictive of future motor function or ultimate degree of spastic hypertonia.[18] Similar periods of facilitation and inhibition of the H reflex can be achieved via exteroceptive conditioning, such as stimulating the sural nerve. Alterations in these periods of facilitation and inhibition have been noted in spastic patients.

Paired H reflex studies using a collision technique also may be used to assess Renshaw cell activation and recurrent inhibition. Normally, supramaximal stimulus of a mixed nerve (e.g., tibial) will eliminate the H reflex (e.g., in the gastroc-soleus) due to antidromic cancellation of the efferent volley. However, this is not true when the supramaximal M response is preceded by a conditioning electrical stimulus sufficient to generate an H reflex. The volley of the conditioning H reflex volley collides with the antidromic volley of the M stimulus, which subsequently allows the afferent volley from the supramaximal stimulus to generate an H reflex. On the basis of animal and pharmacological experiments, Pierrot-Deseilligny has argued that Renshaw cells are activated by the conditioning H discharge, and recurrent inhibition is assessed by the subsequent H reflex.[34] This method was used to assess recurrent inhibition in spastic and control patients; spastic patients demonstrated an increase in the second H reflex amplitude. However, these results have been variably interpreted.[34]

H reflexes also have been used to assess short-latency autogenic inhibition, or Ib inhibition in human spasticity. Ib fibers from Golgi tendon organs normally project to the motoneurons of muscle from which they originate and inhibit them. Their activation results in a postsynaptic short-lasting inhibition. Delwaide and Oliver[14] used a technique in which a 1-ms conditioning stimulus was applied to the nerve to the medial head of the gastrocnemius (the gastrocnemius medialis nerve) at the lower part of the popliteal fossa. This particular nerve was selected because it apparently has a considerable number of Ib projections with a relative paucity of Ia afferent fibers. The conditioning stimulus inhibits a subsequent H reflex to varying degrees. In 6 hemiplegics, there was an inhibition of the subsequent H reflex on the normal side and a facilitation on the plegic side. This would suggest that a loss of Ib inhibition may offer an additional mechanism in the development of spastic hypertonia.

Burke and Lance[6] have attempted to differentiate the effects of group Ia versus group II projections on the quadriceps stretch reflex in response to stretch. Using "selective" ischemic blockade of Ia fibers, versus novacaine blockade infiltration into the muscle (which they argue preferentially blocks small fibers such as group II), they have argued that decreased inhibition from group II afferents to extensor muscles does not significantly contribute to increased stretch reflexes in spastics.

F WAVE

The F wave is similar to the H reflex in that it reflects proximal conduction of the peripheral nervous system. It is recorded by supramaximal stimulation of a mixed nerve (in contrast to the submaximal stimulation in performing the H reflex) while recording over a distal muscle innervated by that nerve. Unlike the H reflex, the electrical potential travels antidromically to the spinal cord via motor efferents to activate motoneurons and, after an approximately 1-ms turn-around, travels orthodromically down similar motor fibers to produce a relatively small compound muscle action potential. The F wave seems to be less affected by postural changes than does the H reflex. Eisen and Odusote examined the relationship between the amplitude of the F response, the M response, and the presence of spasticity. While the maximal size (as a percentage of the amplitude of the M wave—F_{av}/M) of the F wave in sequential responses did not increase in amplitude, the averaged amplitude of 32 F responses increased significantly.[15] The F wave is increased in mean and maximal amplitude, duration, and persistence on the spastic side. Fisher similarly found an increase in this ratio—F_{av}/M—which he attributed to a state of central motoneuron excitability. Interestingly, although likely due to different mechanisms, Fisher also found that F_{av}/M ratios were increased in patients with polyneuropathy.[17]

TONIC VIBRATION REFLEX

The tonic vibration reflex (TVR) has been used to assess the status of presynaptic inhibition.[4,9,27] Presynaptic inhibition may act by limiting the magnitude of calcium current moving into primary afferent terminals, which in turn limits neurotransmitter release.[40] Enhanced synaptic excitation could arise if the level of baseline presynaptic inhibition were reduced, because this would result in a greater than normal release of transmitter for each incoming afferent impulse.[39]

Tonic vibration (for example, a vibrator of frequency 100 Hz and excursion of 1 mm) preferentially stimulates Ia (but also group II) afferent nerve fibers. It exerts inhibitory characteristics by way of an interneuron, which is excited by Ia afferent input and then acts on terminal Ia fiber arborisations.[7] This interneuron is strongly modulated by descending pyramidal and extrapyramidal (vestibulospinal, reticulospinal, rubrospinal) tracts;[3,5,9] therefore, the TVR can help to elucidate the role of these descending fibers on the segmental reflex arc.

This is routinely carried out in humans by the application of a tonic vibration to the Achilles tendon, resulting in a strong discharge in triceps surae Ia fibers. Normally, this results in a depression of the soleus H reflex. Since this depression is seen along with a motor discharge (the tonic vibration reflex), reflecting an increased excitability at the motoneuronal level, it was postulated that it was presynaptic in origin. The failure of tonic vibration to suppress the H reflex in spastic patients has been cited as evidence for the loss of presynaptic inhibition in the spastic state.[5,22]

The ratio of the the maximal H reflex during vibration and without vibration, $H(max)_{(vib)}/H(max)$, is increased in the spastic patients, suggesting a loss of presynaptic inhibition.[10,37] Unfortunately, the tonic vibration reflex is of dubious value in the evaluation of spastic hypertonia because there is a wide dispersion of values among patients and poor correlation with the intensity of spasticity. Also, when prolonged vibration is applied, a variety of mechanisms might contribute to suppression of the H reflex, including refractoriness of Ia fibers, transmitter depletion at Ia terminals, postsynaptic reciprocal Ia inhibition due to spread of vibration, activation of muscle spindles in antagonists, and postsynaptic non-reciprocal group I inhibition.[34] In order to address such problems, Iles and Roberts[22] attempted to isolate presynaptic inhibition from a variety of postsynaptic components by studying the effects of the tonic vibration reflex during voluntary contraction of the soleus at constant torque. They argued that the inhibitory action under these conditions should be largely presynaptic. Similarly, they found that spastic patients showed less inhibition than controls at all levels of voluntary torque investigated.

Hultborn et al.[21] have recently developed a technique in which a weak brief vibration is applied over the tibialis anterior tendon in the form of three brief shocks over 10 ms. The resulting Ia volley results in a depression of the H reflex similar to electrical volleys in Ia afferents of the peroneal nerve, as mentioned above. Using this method in a comparison of amyotrophic lateral sclerosis and normal patients, spastic patients demonstrated a smaller presynaptic inhibition of the H reflex than did controls.[34]

FLEXOR WITHDRAWAL RESPONSES

The automatic withdrawal of the lower extremity upon electrically stimulating the sole of the foot—the flexor withdrawl response—is felt to reflect global interneural activities.[11,32,36] Electromyographic recording from the tibialis anterior muscle and other lower extremity flexors record a low-threshold early response (50–60 ms) that disappears with an upper motor neuron lesion and a later (110–400 ms) high-threshold response. Increasing the stimulus strength decreases the latency and increases the amplitude and duration of both components. Flexor withdrawal responses have not proven to be useful due to the variability of their polysynaptic response.[11]

LUMBOSACRAL SPINAL EVOKED RESPONSES

Lumbosacral spinal evoked responses are claimed to be a reflection of presynaptic inhibition in the dorsal horn of the spinal cord. Upon submaximal stimulation of the tibial nerve, an evoked response can be most easily measured over the spinous process of T-12. The evoked response routinely has three peaks: an inconstant positive deflection (P1), a negative deflection (S), and a second larger amplitude positive deflection (P2). Studies in multiple sclerosis patients have demonstrated a reduction of the ratio between the areas of the large positive and negative deflection (P2/S), which strongly correlated with the intensity of spasticity (as measured by the Ashworth scale). Based on previous work in animals, Delwaide has argued that the P2 wave is attributed to presynaptic inhibitory mechanisms and that a diminution of the P2/S reflects a loss of presynaptic inhibition in spastic humans.[11,13] Using this technique, Kofler et al. demonstrated that the administration of intrathecal baclofen in 3 spinal cord injury patients suppressed the P2 wave amplitude and area, and the S wave amplitude was suppressed to a lesser degree.[26]

ELECTROPHYSIOLOGIC TESTING: COMMENTARY

Electrophysiologic testing has been a fascinating tool to examine changes in spinal cord function and segmental reflexes in spastic patients. However, its weakness lies in the poor correlation between various tests as well as etiology of the lesion, location of the lesion, and intensity of spasticity.[11] Delwaide has attempted to demonstrate the usefulness of four such parameters—H(max)/M(max), T(max)/M(max), H(max)$_{vib}$/H(max), and H reflex recovery curves—in assessing the response to single doses of different myorelexant drugs. Diazepam clearly reinforced vibratory inhibition in spastics, causing the index to return to near-normal values. Baclofen did not modify vibratory inhibition at all, but reduced the abnormal facilitation seen in H reflex recovery curves of spastic patients.[12] Unfortunately, because these scales correlate poorly with clinical severity, it is unclear what significance these changes in electrophysiologic parameters reflect.

In summary, a large number of neurophysiologic studies have been performed using a variety of electrophysiologic techniques to assess the mechanisms and to quantify the severity of spastic hypertonia. Often, the premises for use of these techniques were based on animal models, which may or may not be applicable to humans. Most of these studies also assessed the neural circuitry of the spastic individual at rest, ignoring the biomechanic and neurophysiologic features of movement. As any clinician would aptly point out, much of the disability present in a spastic patient is associated with human movement. Thus, in essence, electrophysiologic studies are hampered by taking neural mechanisms out of the milieu of the behavioral motoric complex and studying them as an isolated event.

REFERENCES

1. Aiello I, Rosati G, Sau GF, et al: Modulation of soleus H reflex by lateral tilting in man. Muscle Nerve 15:479–481, 1992.
2. Angel RW, Hoffmann WW: The H reflex in normal spastic and rigid subjects. Arch Neurol 8:591–596, 1963.
3. Ashby P, Verrier M: Neurological changes following spinal cord lesions in man. Can J Neurolog Sci 2:91–100, 1975.
4. Ashby P, Verrier M, Carleton S, Somerville J: Vibratory inhibition of the monosynaptic reflex and presynaptic inhibition in man. In Feldman RG, Young RR, Koella WP (eds): Spasticity: Disordered Motor Control. Chicago, Year Book, 1980.
5. Burke D, Ashby P: Are spinal "presynaptic" inhibitory mechanisms suppressed in spasticity? J Neurolog Sci 15:321–326, 1972.
6. Burke D, Lance JW: Studies of the reflex effects of primary and secondary spindle endings in spasticity. In Desmedt JE (ed): New Developments in Electromyography and Clinical Neurophysiology, Vol 3. Basel, Karger, 1973, pp 475–495.
7. Burke D, Hagbarth KE, Lofstedt L, Wallin BG: The responses of human muscle spindle endings to vibration of non-contracting muscles. J Physiol 261:673–693, 1976.
8. Burke D: Critical examination of the case for or against fusimotor involvement in disorders of muscle tone. In Desmedt JE (ed): Advances in Neurology, Vol 39. New York, Raven, 1983, pp 133–150.
9. Chan CWY: Some techniques for the relief of spasticity and their physiological basis. Physiother Can 38:85–89, 1986.
10. Delwaide PJ: Contribution of human reflex studies to the understanding and management of the pyramidal syndrome. In Shahani BT (ed): Electromyography in Central Nervous System Disorders: Central EMG. Boston, Butterworths, 1984.
11. Delwaide PJ: Electrophysiological testing of spastic patients: Its potential usefulness and limitations. In Delwaide PJ, Young RR (eds): Clinical Neurophysiology in Spasticity: Contributions to Assessment and Pathophysiology. Amsterdam, Elsevier, 1985.
12. Delwaide PJ: Electrophysiological analysis of the mode of action of muscle relaxants in spasticity. Ann Neurol 17:90–95, 1985.
13. Delwaide PJ, Schoenen J, De Pasqua V: Lumbosacral spinal evoked potentials in patients with multiple sclerosis. Neurology 35:174–179, 1985.
14. Delwaide PJ, Oliver E: Short-latency autogenic inhibition (IB inhibition) in human spasticity. J Neurol Neurosurg Psychiatry 51:1546–1550, 1988.
15. Eisen A, Odusote K: Amplitude of the F wave: A potential means of documenting spasticity. Neurology 29:1306–1309, 1979.
16. Eisen A: Electromyography in disorders of muscle tone. Can J Neurolog Sci 14:501–505, 1987.
17. Fisher MA: F/M ratios in polyneuropathy and spastic hyperreflexia. Muscle Nerve 11:217–222, 1988.
18. Garcia-Mullin R, Mayer RF: H reflexes in acute and chronic hemiplegia. Brain 95:559–572, 1972.
19. Hugon M: Methodology of the Hoffman reflex in man. In Desmedt JE (ed): New Developments in Electromyography and Clinical Neurophysiology, Vol 3. Basel, Karger, 1973, pp 277–293.

20. Hugon M: A discussion of the methodology of the triceps surae T- and H-reflexes. In Desmedt JE (ed): New Developments in Electromyography and Clinical Neurophysiology, Vol 3. Basel, Karger, 1973, pp 773–780.
21. Hultborn H, Meunier S, Morin C, Pierrot-Deseilligny E: Assessing changes in presynaptic inhibition of Ia fibers: A study in man and the cat. J Physiol (Lond) 389:729–756, 1987.
22. Iles JF, Roberts RC: Presynaptic inhibition of monosynaptic reflexes in the lower limbs of subjects with upper motoneuron disease. J Neurol Neurosurg Psychiatry 49:937–944, 1986.
23. Jabre JF: Surface recording of the H-reflex of the flexor carpi radialis. Muscle Nerve 4:435–438, 1981.
24. Katz RT, Rovai G, Brait C, Rymer WZ: Objective quantification of spastic hypertonia: Correlation with clinical findings. Arch Phys Med Rehabil 73:339–347, 1992.
25. Katz RT, Rymer WZ: Spastic hypertonia: Mechanisms and measurement. Arch Phys Med Rehabil 70:144–155, 1989.
26. Kofler M, Donovan WH, Loubser PG, Beric A: Effects of intrathecal baclofen on lumbosacral and cortical somatosensory evoked potentials. Neurology 42:864–868, 1992.
27. Lance JW, De Gail P, Neilson PD: Tonic and phasic spinal cord mechanisms in man. J Neurol Neurosurg Psychiatry 29:535–544, 1966.
28. Little JW, Halar EM: H-reflex changes following spinal cord injury. Arch Phys Med Rehabil 66:19–22, 1985.
29. MacDonell RAL, Talalla A, Swash M, Grundy D: Intrathecal baclofen and the H reflex. J Neurol Neurosurg Psychiatry 51:1110–1112, 1989.
30. Maryniak O, Yaworski R, Hayes KC: Intramuscular recording of H-reflexes from muscles of the posterior compartment of the lower leg. Am J Phys Med Rehabil 70:34–39, 1991.
31. Matthews WB: Ratio of maximum H reflex to maximum M response as a measure of spasticity. J Neurol Neurosurg Psychiatry 29:201–204, 1966.
32. Meinck HM, Benecke R, Conrad B: Spasticity and the flexor reflex. In Delwaide PJ, Young RR (eds): Clinical Neurophysiology in Spasticity: Contribution to Assessment and Pathophysiology. Amsterdam, Elsevier, 1985.
33. Panizza M, Nilsson J, Hallett M: Optimal stimulus duration for the H reflex. Muscle Nerve 12:576–579, 1989.
34. Pierrot-Deseilligny E: Electrophysiological assessment of the spinal mechanisms underlying spasticity. Electroencephalogr Clin Neurophysiol Suppl 41:264–273, 1990.
35. Sabbahi MA, Khalil M: Segmental H-reflex studies in upper and lower limbs of healthy subjects. Arch Phys Med Rehabil 71:216–222, 1990.
36. Shahani BT, Young RR: The flexor reflex in spasticity. In Feldman RG, Young RR, Koella WP (eds): Spasticity: Disordered Motor Control. Chicago, Year Book, 1980.
37. Somerville J, Ashby P: Hemiplegic spasticity: Neurophysiologic studies. Arch Phys Med Rehabil 60:145–154, 1978.
38. Tanaka R: Reciprocal Ia inhibition during voluntary movements in man. Exp Brain Res 21:529–540, 1974.
39. Young RR, Delwaide PJ: Drug therapy: Spasticity. N Engl J Med 304:28–33, 96–99, 1981.
40. Young RR, Shahani BT: Spasticity in spinal cord injured patients. In Bloch RF, Basbaum M (eds): Management of Spinal Cord Injuries. Baltimore, Williams & Wilkins, 1986.

RICHARD T. KATZ, MD
DENISE I. CAMPAGNOLO, MD

PHARMACOLOGIC MANAGEMENT OF SPASTICITY

From St. Louis University
    Medical School and
SSM Rehabilitation Institute
St. Louis, Missouri (RTK)
    and
Kessler Institute for Rehabilitation
University of Medicine and
    Dentistry of New Jersey–New
    Jersey Medical School
Newark, New Jersey (DIC)

Reprint requests to:
Richard T. Katz, MD
Medical Director and Vice
    President of Medical Affairs
SSM Rehabilitation Institute
St. Mary's Health Center
6420 Clayton Road
St. Louis, MO 63117

The pharmacologic management of spastic hypertonia is an integral component of the care of many neurologically impaired patients. Before treatment is initiated, however, the physician needs to address several important questions: Is there a functional impairment due to the spastic hypertonia? Is there a disturbance of gait? Do flexor or extensor spasms force the patient from his chair or interfere with transfers? Does the pain that can be associated with "spasms" disturb the patient's sleep? Does the lower extremity extensor tone support the patient during ambulation? A stereotyped therapeutic approach has been proposed[51] but, as in many aspects of rehabilitation, treatment is best individualized to a particular patient.[35] The wide variety of options for treatment from which a practitioner may select has been recently reviewed.[35] This review will be confined to pharmacologic modalities.

ORAL MEDICATIONS

Oral medications for spasticity have been reviewed by several authors.[14,35,79] No medication has been uniformly useful in the treatment of spastic hypertonia. Considering the variety of problems associated with spasticity—flexor spasms in the spinal patient, dystonic posturing in the hemiplegic, spastic diplegia in the child with cerebral palsy—it is unlikely that one agent will be beneficial to all parties. More importantly, all drugs have potentially serious side effects, and these negative features should be carefully weighed when beginning a patient on any drug. Continued use of a drug should be contingent on a clearly beneficial effect. The table describes three drugs that are approved for use in spastic hypertonia.

Baclofen

Baclofen (Lioresal) is an analog of gamma-aminobutyric acid (GABA), a neurotransmitter involved in presynaptic inhibition. Baclofen does not bind to the classical GABA "A" receptor but to a recently discovered and less well characterized "B" receptor. Agonism at this site inhibits calcium influx into presynaptic terminals and suppresses release of excitatory neurotransmitters.[14] Baclofen inhibits both mono- and polysynaptic reflexes and also reduces activity of the gamma efferent.[75] Although therapeutic effects have been shown to occur when plasma levels exceed 400 ng/ml,[49] optimal responses have been obtained at very different plasma and cerebrospinal fluid levels.[40] Baclofen is completely absorbed after oral administration and is eliminated predominantly by the renal route. Half-life is approximately 3.5 hours. Baclofren readily crosses the blood-brain barrier, in contrast to GABA.[19,42]

Baclofen is probably the drug of choice in spinal forms of spasticity. It has been demonstrated to be effective in reducing flexor spasms, increasing range of motion, and decreasing spastic hypertonia.[17,63] Baclofen is equivalent to diazepam in efficacy, but has less sedative effect.[27] The role of baclofen in the treatment of cerebral forms of spasticity remains unsettled;[27,39,75] it may interfere with attention and memory in brain-injured patients.[64] Baclofen may improve bladder control by decreasing hyperreflexive contraction of the external urethral sphincter.[37] It has been shown to be safe and effective in long-term use.[60] Baclofen also has an anxiolytic effect, which probably contributes to its antispasticity actions.[30]

Dosage begins at approximately 5 mg orally two or three times daily and may be slowly titrated upward toward a recommended maximum dose of 80 mg/day. This "recommended maximum dose" may not necessarily be the most effective dose for the patient, however, and higher doses may be well tolerated and therapeutic.[10,38] There is a low incidence of side effects, which may include hallucinations, confusion, sedation, hypotonia, and ataxia.[27,61] Sudden withdrawal of the drug may lead to seizures and hallucinations.[72] Stereospecific L-baclofen has been shown to be more effective than the presently used racemic form in the treatment of pain.[20,66] L-baclofen deserves evaluation for treatment of spastic hypertonia.

TABLE 1.   Approved Drugs for Treatment of Spastic Hypertonia

Agent	Daily Dosage	Half-life (hrs)	Mechanism of Action
Baclofen	10–80+ mg	3.5	Presynaptic inhibitor by activation of GABA "B" receptor
Diazepam	4–60+ mg	27–37*	Facilitates postsynaptic effects of GABA, resulting in increased presynaptic inhibition
Dantrolene	25–400 mg	8.7	Reduces calcium release, interfering with excitation-contraction coupling in skeletal muscle

* Half-life of active primary metabolite is significantly longer.

Diazepam

Diazepam (Valium) facilitates postsynaptic effects of GABA, resulting in an increase in presynaptic inhibition.[13] It has no direct GABA-mimetic effect but exerts indirect mimetic effect only when GABA transmission is functional.[79] In addition to its known effects in the brain,[71] it most likely has effect in patients with demonstrated spinal cord division.[12,77]

Diazepam has been used as a successful treatment for spastic hypertonia in spinal cord injury and is generally well tolerated except for its sedative effect. Diazepam is generally unsuitable in patients with brain injury due to deleterious side effects on attention and memory.[21] Other side effects include intellectual impairment and reduced motor coordination. Evidence of abuse and addiction is rare, but true physiologic addiction may occur. Withdrawal symptoms may appear if diazepam is tapered too rapidly. Some synergistic depression of the central nervous system occurs when it is administered with alcohol. Although the potential for overdose exists, the benzodiazepines, which include diazepam, have an extremely large index of safety.[23] Dosage begins at about 2 mg orally twice daily and may be slowly titrated up to 60 mg or more per day in divided dosages.

Dantrolene Sodium

Dantrolene sodium (Dantrium) reduces muscle action potential-induced release of calcium into the sarcoplasmic reticulum, decreasing the force produced by excitation-contraction coupling.[76] Thus, dantrolene is the only drug that intervenes in spastic hypertonia at a "muscular" rather than a segmental reflex level. It reduces the activity of phasic greater than tonic stretch reflexes.[59] Dantrolene affects fast twitch greater than slow twitch muscle fibers and, for unknown reasons, seems to have little effect on smooth and cardiac muscle tissues. It is metabolized largely in the liver and eliminated in urine and bile. Half-life is 8.7 hours.[59]

Dantrolene is preferred for cerebral forms of spasticity such as hemiplegia or cerebral palsy[36] but may be a useful adjunct to the treatment of spinal forms of spasticity. It is less likely to cause lethargy or cognitive disturbances than baclofen or diazepam.[21] Although dantrolene theoretically "weakens" muscles, the effects on spastic hypertonia are generally without impairment of motor performance. Its most pronounced effects may be a reduction in clonus and muscle spasms resulting from innocuous stimuli.[34]

Dantrolene is mild to moderately sedative and may cause malaise, nausea and vomiting, dizziness, and diarrhea. It has been suggested that the drug may exacerbate seizures in patients with cerebral palsy. The most commonly considered side effect is hepatotoxicity, which may occur in about 1% of patients. Generally, liver function tests are monitored periodically, and the drug can be tapered or discontinued if enzyme elevations are noted. Fatal hepatitis has been reported in 0.1–0.2% of patients treated for longer than 60 days.[10] However, one expert in the use of dantrolene feels that its hepatotoxic effects may have been overstated.[5] Dosage begins at 25 mg/day and may slowly increase up to 400 mg/day.[59] However, clinical results are not clearly related to dose and may plateau at a dosage of 100 mg/day.[52]

Tizanidine

Tizanidine (Sirdalud), an imidazoline derivative, is not available for use in the United States. However, clinical trials of tizanidine for use in the amelioration of spasticity in spinal cord injury as well as other central nervous system impairments are under way. Tizanidine has an agonistic action at central alpha-2 adrenergic receptor sites. It may facilitate the action of glycine, an inhibitory neurotransmitter,[29] and it prevents the release of excitatory amino acids, i.e., L-glutamate and L-aspartate, from the presynaptic terminal of spinal interneurons.[15] It reduces tonic stretch reflexes and enhances presynpatic inhibition in animals. It enhances vibratory inhibition of H reflex and reduces abnormal co-contraction.[80] Tizanidine has the unusual effect of increasing the torque of spastic muscle by increasing the amplitude of the agonist EMG signal.[41] It has been shown to be equivalent to baclofen as an antispastic agent (but may be better tolerated) in both cerebral and spinal forms of spasticity in divided dosages up to 36 mg/day.[31,50,68] It has similarly been shown to be equally efficacious and better tolerated than diazepam in patients with chronic hemiplegia.[9] Multiple sclerosis patients have shown significant benefit in several large double-blind studies.[8,18,31,34] Common side effects include mild hypotension, daytime sleepiness, weakness, and dry mouth.[70] Daytime somnolence may be secondary to nighttime insomnia, which was reported more frequently by patients receiving tizanidine than those receiving baclofen.[8] In two double-blind comparative studies, tizanidine was generally found to be better tolerated than baclofen.[8,50] Both tizanidine and baclofen are more effective in extensor than flexor musculature.[26] Recently a modified release form of tizanidine has been formulated that allows for once or twice daily dosing.[32]

Ketazolam, Clonidine and Others

Ketazolam, a benzodiazepine, has been shown to be equally effective and less sedating than diazepam in spinal forms of spasticity; it may have a similar pharmacologic action. An additional benefit is that ketazolam may be administered in a single dose ranging from 30 to 60 mg/day.[6,7] Unfortunately, it is not presently approved for use in the United States. Tetrazepam (Myolastan), a benzodiazepine derivative, is reported to reduce the tonic component of spastic hypertonia, with little effect on tendon hyperreflexia. No influence on muscle strength has been noted.[53] A benzodiazepine analogue, clorazepate, is transformed into desmethyldiazepam, the major metabolite of diazepam, and has been shown in one study to be effective in normalizing phasic but not tonic stretch reflexes.[45]

Chlorpromazine has been applied to the treatment of hypertonia because of its alpha-adrenergic blocking affect. Clinical and electrophysiologic studies in humans before and after administration of alpha and beta blocking agents suggest that descending adrenergic and noradrenergic pathways may have important modulatory effects on spastic hypertonia.[46] However, the depression of motor function by phenothiazines is thought to be due largely to its effects upon the brainstem reticular formation. A small double-blinded study of chlorpromazine with phenytoin suggests that a combination of these drugs may be beneficial in the treatment of spastic hypertonia. Neither drug alone was as efficacious as the combination of the two, although chlorpromazine alone was nearly as effective. Phenytoin serum levels did not correlate with therapeutic effect as long as this concentration was above 7 μg/ml. The addition of phenytoin lowered the needed optimally therapeutic dose of chlorpromazine, decreasing the sedative effect.[11]

Clonidine, an alpha-2 adrenergic agonist, has been used with fair success in spinal cord injury patients.[48,57] In combination with desipramine, clonidine has improved the vibratory inhibition of the H-reflex after spinal cord injury.[58] Co-activation of antagonist muscle decreased, allowing improved locomotor function in a spastic paraparetic patient with clonidine therapy.[69] Syncope, hypotension, and nausea and vomiting are the most common side effects. One study cited an average dosage of 0.39 mg/day.[48] In a second study, most of the patients who benefitted from the drug noted acceptable relief with dosage of 0.1 mg twice a day or less.[16] Oral clonidine also has been successfully used in one case of spasticity secondary to medullary infarct.[65] Clonidine is now available in an adhesive patch (Catapres-TTs) for week-long transdermal delivery. Initial studies have demonstrated favorable results starting with 0.1 mg patch and titrating up to 0.3 mg patch as needed. Adverse effect rates were similar to those reported with oral clonidine.[78]

Progabide, a systemically active GABA agonist at both the A and B receptors, and THIP (tetrahydroisoxazolopyridin), a second GABA agonist, have been proposed as possible antispasticity drugs.[14,54] Electrophysiologic studies suggest that progabide's likely site of action is spinal interneurons.[55] A median dose of 24.3 mg/kg (1800 mg/day) resulted in satisfactory reduction in spastic hypertonia, tendon reflexes, and flexor spasms without a significant improvement in voluntary strength.[56] The beneficial effects of progabide in higher dosages seems to be limited by serious side effects—fever, weakness, and elevated liver enzymes.[62]

Glycine, a neurotransmitter involved in reciprocal inhibition, has not been thoroughly investigated in the treatment of spastic hypertonia. Glycine passes the blood-brain barrier in amounts sufficient to affect reflex activity, and it has decreased spasticity in small groups of patients.[2] Glycine is rapidly depleted in the spinal cord ventral gray matter after spinal cord transection, and the depletion correlates with spasticity onset in a canine model.[25] Similarly threonine, a glycine precursor, has shown potential efficacy in preliminary investigations.[2,28] Although glycine levels in serum and cerebrospinal fluid did not rise after the administration of threonine, enhancement of glycinergic postsynaptic inhibition of the spinal reflex arc is the hypothesized mechanism of action.[28] Tetrahydrocannabinols (THC), the active agent in marijuana—although not approved for use in the treatment of spastic hypertonia—has occasionally been noted to decrease hypertonia.[47,74] Although various other medications have been forwarded in the treatment of this disorder—cyclobenzaprine, carisoprodol, cyproheptadine, L-acetylcarnitine— there is no consistent evidence to recommend their use.

EXPERIMENTAL DRUGS

GABA and glycine are inhibitory neurotransmitters in the central nervous system. The antispastic effects of the benzodiazepines and baclofen result from agonism at these inhibitory neurotransmitter receptor sites. Spinal excitatory neurotransmitters include glutamate and aspartate, antagonism at their receptor sites would provide another pharmacologic option for management of spastic hypertonia.[1] There are several types of glutamate receptors, which can be broadly categorized as the N-methyl-D-aspartate (NMDA) and non-NMDA types. The NMDA receptors have been implicated in excitotoxic effects after neurologic injury.[1,4,67] A prototype for an NMDA receptor antagonist is the street drug phencyclidine hydrochloride (PCP or "angel dust"). An experimental drug used to block the NMDA receptor is MK-801.[24] As far as the non-NMDA receptor antagonists, the quinoxalinediones (specifically NBQX), have been shown to reduce hind limb extensor tone in genetically spastic rats.[73]

Vigabatrin[22] is an experimental drug specifically designed to increase brain GABA levels by inhibiting catabolism of this neurotransmitter. It replaces GABA as a substrate for GABA transaminase, the enzyme responsible for the first step in GABA breakdown. Vigabatrin was developed as an antiepileptic agent and has shown promise in the treatment of refractory cases of epilepsy. In placebo-controlled trials, vigabatrin in doses of 2–3 g/day improved spasticity in patients with spinal cord injury and multiple sclerosis.[43] The most common adverse reactions were drowsiness, fatigue, and weight gain;[79,80] behavior disturbances have been reported uncommonly.[33]

CONCLUSIONS

The functional impairment due to spasticity must be carefully assessed before any treatment is considered. Baclofen, diazepam, and dantrolene remain the three most commonly used pharmacologic agents in the treatment of spastic hypertonia. Baclofen is generally the drug of choice for spinal cord types of spasticity, and dantrolene sodium is the only agent that acts directly on muscle tissue. Phenytoin with chlorpromazine is potentially useful if sedation does not limit its use. Tizanidine and ketazolam, not yet available in the United States, may be significant additions to the pharmacologic armamenterium.

REFERENCES

1. Anonymous: Spasticity. Lancet 2:1488–1489, 1989.
2. Barbeau A: Preliminary study of glycine administration in patients with spasticity [abstract]. Neurology 24:392, 1974.
3. Barbeau A, Roy M, Chouza C: Pilot study of threonine supplementation in human spasticity. Can J Neurol Sci 9:141–145, 1982.
4. Barry SR: Clinical implications of basic neuroscience research II: NMDA receptors and neurotrophic factors. Arch Phys Med Rehabil 72:1095–1101, 1991.
5. Basmajian JV: Muscle relaxants in multiple sclerosis. Int J Disability Stud 9:90–91, 1987.
6. Basmajian JV, Shankardass K, Russell D, Yucel V: Ketazolam treatment for spasticity: Double-blind study of a new drug. Arch Phys Med Rehabil 65:698–701, 1984.
7. Basmajian JV, Shankardass K, Russell D: Ketazolam once daily for spasticity: Double-blind cross-over study. Arch Phys Med Rehabil 67:556–557, 1986.
8. Bass B, Weinshenker B, Rice GPA, et al: Tizanidine versus baclofen in the treatment of spasticity in patients with multiple slcerosis. Can J Neurol Sci 15:15–19, 1988.
9. Bes A, Eyssette M, Pierrot-Deseilligny E, et al: A multi-centre, double-blind trial of tizanidine, a new antispastic agent, in spasticity associated with hemiplegia. Curr Med Res Opin 10:709–718, 1988.
10. Bianchine JR: Drugs for Parkinson's disease, spasticity, and acute muscle spasms. In Gilman AG, Goodman LS, Rall PW, Murad F (eds): The Pharmacological Basis of Therapeutics, 7th ed. New York, Macmillan, 1985.
11. Cohan SL, Raines A, Panagakos J, Armitage P: Phenytoin and chlorpromazine in the treatment of spasticity. Arch Neurol 37:360–364, 1980.
12. Cook JB, Nathan PW: On the site of action of diazepam in spasticity in man. J Neurolog Sci 5:33–37, 1967.
13. Costa E, Guidotti A: Molecular mechanisms in the receptor action of benzodiazepines. Ann Rev Pharmacol Toxicol 19:531–545, 1979.
14. Davidoff RA: Antispasticity drugs: Mechanisms of action. Ann Neurol 17:107–116, 1985.
15. Davies J, Quinlan JE: Selective inhibition of feline dorsal horn neurons to noxious cutaneous stimuli by tizanidine and noradrenaline: Involvement of alpha-2 adrenoceptors. Neuroscience 16:673–682, 1985.
16. Donovan WH, Carter RE, Rossi D, Wilkerson MA: Clonidine effect on spasticity: A clinical trial. Arch Phys Med Rehabil 69:193–194, 1988.
17. Duncan GW, Shahani BT, Young RR: An evaluation of baclofen treatment for certain symptoms in patients with spinal cord lesions. Neurology 26:441–446, 1976.
18. Eyssette M, Rohmer F, Serratrice G, et al: Multi-centre, double-blind trial of a novel antispastic agent, tizanidine, in spasticity associated with multiple sclerosis. Curr Med Res Opin 10:699–708, 1988.
19. Faigle JW, Keberle H, Degen PH: Chemistry and pharmacokinetics of baclofen. In Feldman RG, Young RR, Koella WP (eds): Spasticity: Disordered Motor Control. Chicago, Year Book, 1980, pp 461–475.

20. Fromm GH, Terrence CF: Comparison of L-baclofen and racemic baclofen in trigeminal neuralgia. Neurology 37:1725–1728, 1987.
21. Glenn MB: Antispasticity medications in the patient with traumatic brain injury. J Head Trauma Rehabil 1:71–72, 1986.
22. Grant SM, Heel RC: Vigabatrin: A review of its pharmacodynamic and pharmacokinetic properties and therapeutic potential in epilepsy and disorders of motor control. Drugs 41:889–926, 1991.
23. Greenblatt DJ, Shader RI, Abernethy DR: Current status of benzodiazepines. N Engl J Med 309:354–358, 410–416, 1983.
24. Hahn JS, Aizenman E, Lipton SA: Central mammalian neurons normally resistant to glutamate toxicity are made sensitive by elevated extracellular Ca2+. Toxicity is blocked by the N-methyl-D-aspartate antagonist MK-801. Proc Natl Acad Sci USA 85:6556, 1988.
25. Hall PV, Smith JE, Campbell RL, et al: Neurochemical correlates of spasticity. Life Sci 18:1467–1472, 1976.
26. Hassan N, McLellan DL: Double-blind comparison of single doses of DS103-282, baclofen, and placebo for suppression of spasticity. J Neurol Neurosurg Psychiatry 43:1132–1136, 1980.
27. Hattab JR: Review of European clinical trials with baclofren. In Feldman RG, Young RR, Koella WP (eds): Spasticity: Disordered Motor Control. Chicago, Year Book, 1980, pp 71–85.
28. Hauser SL, Doolittle TH, Lopez-Bresnahan M, et al: An antispasticity effect of threonine in multiple sclerosis. Arch Neurol 49:923–926, 1992.
29. Hennies OL: A new skeletal muscle relaxant (DS 103-282) compared to diazepam in the treatment of muscle spasm of local origin. J Int Med Res 9:62–68, 1981.
30. Hinderer SR: The supraspinal anxiolytic effect of baclofen for spasticity reduction. Am J Phys Med Rehabil 69:254–258, 1990.
31. Hoogstraten MC, van der Ploeg RJO, van der Burg W, et al: Tizanidine versus baclofen in the treatment of spasticity in multiple sclerosis patients. Acta Neurol Scand 77:224–230, 1988.
32. Hutchinson DR: Modified release tizanidine: A review. J Int Med Res 17:565–573, 1989.
33. Johnston SJ: Vigabatrin and behavior disturbances. Lancet 335:606, 1990.
34. Joynt RL: Dantrolene sodium: Long-term effects in patients with muscle spasticity. Arch Phys Med Rehabil 57:212–217, 1976.
35. Katz RT: Management of spasticity. Am J Phys Med Rehabil 67:108–116, 1988.
36. Ketel WB, Kolb ME: Long-term treatment with dantrolene sodium of stroke patients with spasticity limiting the return to function. Current Medical Research and Opinion 9:161–169, 1984.
37. Khanna OP: Nonsurgical therapeutic modalities. In Krane RJ, Siroky MB (eds): Clinical Neurourology. Boston, Little, Brown & Co., 1979, pp 159–195.
38. Kirkland LR: Baclofen dosage: A suggestion [letter]. Arch Phys Med Rehabil 65:214, 1984.
39. Knutsson E, Lindblom U, Martensson A: Lioresal and spasticity. Acta Neurol Scand Suppl 48:449–450, 1972.
40. Knutsson E, Lindblom U, Martensson A: Plasma and cerebrospinal fluid levels of baclofen (Lioresal) at optimal therapeutic responses in spastic paresis. J Neurol Sci 23:473–484, 1974.
41. Knutsson E, Martensson A, Gransberg L: Antipyretic and anti-spastic effects induced by Tizanidine in patients with spastic paresis. J Neurol Sci 53:187–204, 1982.
42. Koella WP: Baclofen: Its general pharmacology and neuropharmacology. In Feldman RG, Young RR, Koella WP (eds): Spasticity: Disordered Motor Control. Chicago, Year Book, 1980, pp 383–396.
43. Kurlemann G, Palm DG: Vigabatrin in metachromatic leucodystrophy: Positive influence on spasticity. Dev Med Child Neurol 33:179–183, 1991.
44. Lapierre Y, Bouchard S, Tansey C, et al: Treatment of spasticity with tizanidine in multiple sclerosis. Can J Neurol Sci 14:513–517, 1987.
45. Lossius R, Dietrichson P, Lunde PKM: Effect of clorazepate in spasticity and rigidity: A quantitative study of reflexes and plasma concentrations. Acta Neurol Scand 71:190–194, 1985.
46. Mai J: Adernergic influences on spasticity. Acta Neurol Scand 63(suppl):1–143, 1981.
47. Malec J, Harvey RF, Cayner JJ: Cannabis effect on spasticity in spinal cord injury. Arch Phys Med Rehabil 63:116–118, 1982.
48. Maynard FM: Early clinical experience with clonidine in spinal spasticity. Paraplegia 24:175–182, 1986.
49. McLellan DL: Co-contraction and stretch reflexes in spasticity during treatment with baclofen. J Neurol Neurosurg Psychiatry 40:30–38, 1977.
50. Medici M, Pebet M, Ciblis D: A double-blind, long-term study of tizanidine ('Sirdalud') in spasticity due to cerebrovascular lesions. Curr Med Res Opin 11:398–407, 1989.

51. Merritt J: Management of spasticity in spinal cord injury. Mayo Clin Proc 56:614–622, 1981.
52. Meyler WJ, Bakker H, Kok JJ, et al: The effect of dantrolene sodium in relation to blood levels in spastic patients after prolonged administration. J Neurol Neurosurg Psychiatry 44:334–339, 1981.
53. Milanov I: Mechanisms of tetrazepam action on spasticity. Acta Neurol Belg 92:5–15, 1992.
54. Mondrup K, Pedersen E: The acute effect of THIP in human spasticity—a pilot study. In Pedersen E, Clausen J, Oades L (eds): Actual Problems in Multiple Sclerosis Research. Copenhagen, FADL's Forlag, 1983, pp 132–134.
55. Mondrup K, Pedersen E: The effect of the GABA-agonist, progabide, on stretch and flexor reflexes and on voluntary power in spastic patients. Acta Neurol Scand 69:191–199, 1984.
56. Mondrup K, Pedersen E: The clinical effect of the GABA-agonist, progabide, on spasticity. Acta Neurol Scand 69:200–206, 1984.
57. Nance PW, Shears AH, Nance DM: Clonidine in spinal cord injury. Can Med Assoc J 133:41–42, 1985.
58. Nance PW, Shears AH, Nance DM: Reflex changes induced by clonidine in spinal cord injured patients. Paraplegia 27:296–301, 1989.
59. Pinder RM, Brogden RN, Speight TM, Avery GS: Dantrolene sodium: A review of its pharmacological properties and therapeutic efficacy in spasticity. Drugs 13:3–23, 1977.
60. Roussan M, Terrence C, Gromm G: Baclofen versus diazepam for the treatment of spasticity and long-term follow-up of baclofen therapy. Pharmatherapeutica 4:278–284, 1985.
61. Roy CW, Wakefield IR: Baclofen pseudopsychosis: Case report. Paraplegia 24:318–321, 1986.
62. Rudick RA, Breton D, Krall RL: The GABA-agonist progabide for spasticity in multiple sclerosis. Arch Neurol 44:1033–1036, 1987.
63. Sachais BA, Logue JN, Carey MS: Baclofen, a new antispastic drug. Arch Neurol 34:422–428, 1977.
64. Sandy KR, Gillman MH: Baclofen-induced memory impairment. Clin Neuropharmacy 8:294–295, 1985.
65. Sanford PR, Spengler SE, Sawasky KB: Clonidine in the treatment of brainstem spasticity. Am J Phys Med Rehabil 71:301–303, 1992.
66. Sawynok J, Dickson C: D-baclofen is an antagonist at baclofen receptors mediating antinociception in the spinal cord. Pharmacology 31:248–259, 1985.
67. Schwarcz R, Meldrun B: Excitatory aminoacid antagonists provide a therapeutic approach to neurological disorders. Lancet 2:140–143, 1985.
68. Smolenski C, Muff S, Smolenski-Kantz S: A double-blind comparative trial of a new muscle relaxant, tizanidine (DS 103-282) and baclofen in the treatment of chronic spasticity in multiple sclerosis. Curr Med Res Opin 7:374–383, 1981.
69. Stewart JE, Barbeau H, Gauthier S: Modulation of locomotor patterns and spasticity with clonidine in spinal cord injured patients. Can J Neurol Sci 18:321–332, 1991.
70. Stien R, Nordal HJ, Oftedal SI, Slettebo M: Treatment of spasticity in multiple sclerosis: A double-blind clinical trial of a new anti-spastic drug tizanidine compared with baclofen. Acta Neurol Scand 75:190–194, 1987.
71. Study RE, Barker JL: Cellular mechanisms of benzodiazepine action. JAMA 247:2147–2151, 1982.
72. Terrence DV, Fromm GH: Complications of baclofen withdrawal. Arch Neurol 38:588–589, 1981.
73. Turski L, Jacobsen P, Honore T, Stephens D: Relief of experimental spasticity and anxiolytic/anticonvulsant actions of the alpha-amino-3-hydroxy-5-methyl-4-isoxazolepropionate antagonist 2,3-dihydroxy-6-nitro-7 sulfamoyl-benzo(F) quinoxaline. J Pharmacol Exp Ther 260:742–747, 1992.
74. Ungerleider JT, Andyrsiak T, Fairbanks L, et al: Delta-9-THC in the treatment of spasticity associated with multiple sclerosis. In Pharmacological Issues in Alcohol and Substance Abuse. New York, The Hawthorn Press, 1988, pp 39–50.
75. Van Hemert JCJ: A double-blind comparison of baclofen and placebo in patients with spasticity of cerebral origin. In Feldman RG, Young RR, Koella WP (eds): Spasticity: Disordered Motor Control. Chicago, Year Book, 1980, pp 41–49.
76. Van Winkle WB: Calcium release from skeletal muscle sarcoplasmic reticulum: Site of action of dantrolene sodium? Science 193:1130–1131, 1976.
77. Verrier M, Ashby P, MacLeod S: Diazepam effect on reflex activity in patients with complete spinal lesions and in those with other causes of spasticity. Arch Phys Med Rehabil 58:148–153, 1977.
78. Weingarden SI, Belen JG: Clonidine transdermal system for treatment of spasticity in spinal cord injury. Arch Phys Med Rehabil 73:876–877, 1992.
79. Young RR, Delwaide PJ: Drug therapy: Spasticity. N Engl J Med 304:28–33, 96–99, 1981.
80. Young RR, Shahani BT: Spasticity in spinal cord injured patients. In Bloch RF, Basbaum M (eds): Management of Spinal Cord Injuries. Baltimore, Williams & Wilkins, 1986.

MEL B. GLENN, MD

NERVE BLOCKS FOR THE TREATMENT OF SPASTICITY

From the Department of
  Rehabilitation Medicine
Boston University School of
  Medicine and
University Hospital and
Boston City Hospital
Boston, Massachusetts

Reprint requests to:
Mel B. Glenn, MD
Professor and Chairman
Department of Rehabilitation
  Medicine
Boston University School of
  Medicine
80 East Concord Street
Boston, MA 02118-2394

This chapter is excerpted from
Glenn MB: Nerve blocks. In Glenn
MB, Whyte J (eds): The Practical
Management of Spasticity in Chil-
dren and Adults. Philadelphia, Lea
& Febiger, 1990, pp 227–258; with
permission.

Nerve block refers to the application of a chemical agent to a nerve to either temporarily or permanently impair the function of the nerve. The agents most frequently used are phenol, alcohol, and local anesthetics. Phenol and alcohol are used for chemical neurolysis, the physical dissolution of the axon by chemical means. Local anesthetic nerve blocks temporarily block conduction by interfering with the increase in permeability to sodium ions that normally results when the membrane is depolarized, but they leave the nerve intact. When applied to the treatment of spasticity, the intent is to interrupt the various components of the stretch reflex arc. The intramuscular injection of botulinum toxin achieves a similar effect by interfering with neuromuscular transmission.

Chemical neurolysis can be an extremely effective intervention for reducing spasticity. The effects are immediate and often dramatic. Although the effects have not usually been documented in controlled clinical trials, the clinical descriptions of relief of spasticity have frequently been dramatic and explicit. Many authors have described the sustained elimination of clonus beginning immediately following nerve blocks with phenol.[1,5,14,15,17,35,40,43-45,56,62,71] Others have described increases in strength or speed of active voluntary movement in antagonists of muscles blocked and occasionally in the blocked muscle itself.[5,14,15,17,34,44-46] Nerve blocks have also diminished spasticity in opposite extremities or in synergists not innervated by the nerve that was blocked.[45] Passive range of motion often has been improved when spasticity was contributing to contracture formation,[6,12,15,25,34,40,45,48,56] and a reduced need for passive stretching has been seen.[46] In young children who have yet to walk, relief of adductor spasticity by nerve blocks has facilitated crawling, sitting, and standing,[33,71] and nerve blocks to the gluteus maximus have improved sitting or allowed the sitting position for the first time.[75] Improvements in gait have been seen due to a reduction of hip adductor tone, with a resultant decrease in scissoring.[15,60,71,75] Halpern and Meelhuysen reported on 3 children (ages 2, 3, and 6) with spastic diplegia who walked for the first time a few days after nerve blocks or after several weeks of ambulation training following nerve blocks.[33] Chemical neurolysis targeted at spastic ankle plantarflexors have contributed to improved dorsiflexion during gait and, at times, allowed the use of orthotics that could not be previously applied.[1,14,44,46,56,60,62,71,75] Others have found that nerve blocks have facilitated proper fitting of an orthotic device.[35,40] Painful clawing of the toes has been relieved by tibial nerve block.[15,56] Painful spasms have been relieved,[56,60] and spasms have been reduced in patients with spinal cord injury.[35] Reduction of hip flexor spasticity via chemical neurolysis has been reported to reduce the compensatory lumbar lordosis[75] and to facilitate ambulation and sitting.[48] Some authors have reported improvements in activities of daily living following nerve blocks.[1,5,15,17,44-46,56,60,62] Chemical neurolysis has facilitated nursing care, hygiene, positioning, and prevention or healing of pressure ulcers.[15,33,48,71] Perineal nerve block resulted in a significant reduction of postvoid residual urine volumes in a man with a spastic external urethral sphincter following spinal cord injury.[45] Several authors have performed selective sacral rhizotomies with phenol or alcohol to reduce detrusor hyperreflexia or external urethral sphincter spasticity.[68,73,77]

Helweg-Larsen and Jacobsen[35] found that in children with cerebral palsy, 97 of 150 peripheral nerve blocks with 3% phenol resulted in reductions of spasticity. Although improvements in gait were common following lower extremity procedures, upper extremity blocks did not usually result in functional gains.

Khalili et al.[46] rated the degree of spasticity before nerve blocks with 2% or 3% phenol on a scale of 1+ (slight) to 4+ (severe), and after blocks added flaccid and normal to the scale. Spasticity was rated 4+ in all instances before 39 nerve blocks. After blocks, spasticity was rated as normal in 19 patients, 1+ in 5, 2+ in 5, and 3+ in 1. The medial and lateral hamstrings were rated separately after one sciatic nerve block, resulting in 40 postblock ratings. After follow-up intervals varying from 6 to 233 days, 17 of 19 ratings of normal remained at normal or 1+, and 34 of 40 ratings had increased by 1 or less.

Meelhuysen et al.[54] reported that of 31 paravertebral nerve blocks with 3-5% phenol, 20 completely eliminated hip flexor spasticity, and 7 others reduced spasticity. Halpern and Meelhuysen[32] found that of 394 muscles treated with intramuscular neurolysis with 5% phenol in 95 patients, decreased spasticity resulted in functional gains or improved posture in 374. Katz et al.,[40] using 3% phenol, obtained "50% or more" relief of spasticity after 31 of 56 peripheral nerve injections.

C. Tardieu et al.[74] and G. Tardieu et al.[75] published the only controlled study of chemical neurolysis in the literature. They applied 35% alcohol to the right posterior tibial nerve of cats and rendered them decerebrate with a mid-collicular section several weeks later. They then plotted length-tension curves for stretch of both soleus muscles. The tension elicited by passive stretch was significantly lower on the right side when compared to the left. No such difference was found in a group of control animals.

Although nerve blocks can, in some instances, completely eliminate hypertonia, they also can be titrated to a certain extent by adjusting the concentration and quantity of the neurolytic agent injected, by choosing the site along the nerve tree to be injected (and thus the size of the motor branch), and by choosing the numbers of branches to be injected. This impression must be tempered by the poor correlation in the literature between concentration and quantity of phenol and apparent effectiveness, and the lack of controlled data. The effectiveness of a nerve block is related to many variables, not the least of which are the choice of patient and the goals of the treatment.

The effect on spasticity can be localized to the specific muscle or group of muscles that are causing a problem. On the other hand, because the result is not generalized, many blocks may have to be performed to affect a widespread problem with spasticity, and some muscles may be inaccessible or difficult to block.

The duration of effect is widely variable (Table 1). Although most nerve blocks will last from several months to a few years, the effect is usually not permanent. This is in some ways an advantage, because the patient and family, as well as the physician performing the block and the treating team, can be reassured to some degree that if adverse effects result from the block, they are not likely to be permanent. However, the need to repeat nerve blocks multiple times in some individuals can be a disadvantage, although repeating blocks certainly is not always necessary. Nerve blocks can be performed at bedside or in a clinic or office, and general anesthesia is rarely required. Morbidity is not excessive (See Side Effects and Complications, page 489).

TECHNIQUE

Nerve blocks are usually performed using a 22-gauge sterile needle that is Teflon-coated except at the bevel so that a pulsed electrical stimulus will only be transmitted to the nerve when it is in the proximity of the bevel itself. The hub of the needle is connected to a stimulator that delivers a square wave pulse of 0.1 milliseconds once or twice per second and that contains a rheostat to regulate the

TABLE 1. Duration of Effect of Nerve Blocks

Type	Range	Avg. or % >	% Phenol
Peripheral			
(Khalili, 1984)	10–850 days	317 days	2–3%
(Petrillo, 1980)	>9–22 months	Avg. >12.9 months	5%
(Katz, 1967)		29% >1 month	3%
Paravertebral			
(Meelhuysen, 1968)	1½–>10 months	64% >4 months	3–5%
Intramuscular			
(Easton, 1979)	1–36 months		5%
(Halpern, 1967)	1–>14 months	60% >6 months	5%
Endplate			
(Delateur, 1972)	3–6 months		5%
Open Motor			
(Garland, 1982)		6 months	3%
(Braun, 1973)		23% >1 year	3–5%

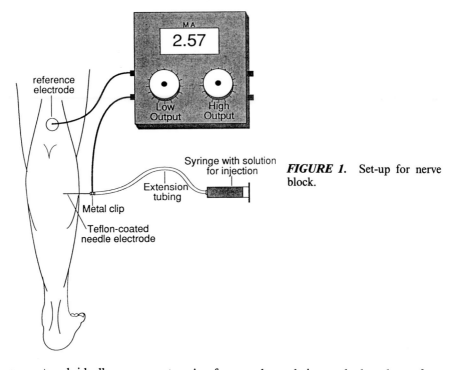

reference electrode

Syringe with solution for injection

Extension tubing

Metal clip

Teflon-coated needle electrode

FIGURE 1. Set-up for nerve block.

current and, ideally, an ammeter. A reference electrode is attached to the surface of the skin (Fig. 1). An assistant is often necessary in order to help position the patient. The needle is inserted in the vicinity of the nerve to be injected, and pulsed stimulation is delivered at a current of 5–10 mA. When a rhythmic response is observed, the physician checks to be sure that the appropriate muscle or group of muscles is contracting. Some practitioners use electromyographic recording equipment to assist in determining that only the target muscle is contracting. The amperage is then reduced and, with the muscle still contracting, but less vigorously so, a search is made by moving the needle in minute increments, in three-dimensions if necessary, until a strong contraction is again observed, indicating that the bevel is now closer to the nerve. This process is continued until 1 mA or less is needed to produce a contraction, at which point the bevel is close enough to the nerve to inject.[1,5,15,19,25,32,33,35,42–46,56,62,71,75] The 1-mA criterion is somewhat arbitrary. Occasionally a more stringent criterion will prove more consistently effective. On the other hand, under difficult circumstances, such as with a combative patient or a patient who is having frequent reflexive movements provoked by the needle, the physician performing the block may have to inject at a higher current and often will be successful nonetheless. If the injection is successful, the contraction will disappear almost immediately or diminish gradually within 1 or 2 minutes. At times this response is preceded by an initial increase in the force of contraction as the solution makes contact with the nerve. The use of flexible extension tubing to connect the syringe to the needle helps to prevent unwanted movement during injection.

The patient can be expected to feel some discomfort during the search; individual tolerance varies greatly. The patient will usually feel a burning sensation when phenol or alcohol is injected, particularly with intramuscular blocks.

Peripheral nerves, their large motor branches, or electrosensitive areas of muscle where small motor branches are entering the muscle can all be located by surface stimulation prior to needle stimulation. It is useful to have a stimulator capable of delivering the current necessary for surface stimulation, generally 10 mA or greater.

NERVE BLOCKS WITH PHENOL

Effects of Phenol on Nerves

Reports that phenol was capable of diminishing spasticity and chronic pain without impairing cutaneous or proprioceptive sensibility or strength generated considerable interest in the differential effect of phenol on nerves of varying fiber size.[7,22,37,52,57] Investigators hypothesized that phenol might selectively affect small gamma motor neurons, leaving alpha motor neurons intact. The sparing of sensibility to pain provoked by cutaneous stimulation was, however, difficult to explain by this theory. Indeed, the weight of the histologic evidence, mostly in animals, and the electrophysiologic evidence in animals and humans, now indicates that phenol destroys axons of all sizes. When phenol is dripped onto a nerve, demyelination and axonal destruction tend to occur in a patchy distribution, moreso on the outer aspect of the nerve bundle (Fig. 2).[8,23,24,27,31,58,66] Lower concentrations of phenol may cause demyelination without axonal destruction.[59,66] In addition, there is a reversible local anesthetic effect lasting at least several hours.[28,66]

Animal studies demonstrate that axons destroyed by phenol do regenerate, with some increase in fibrous tissue at the site of injection.[31] One report on a biopsy in a human with return of spasticity following chemical neurolysis showed fibrous overgrowth felt to be inconsistent with regrowth of axons.[55]

Implications of the Site of Injection

MIXED SENSORIMOTOR PERIPHERAL NERVE BLOCKS

The technique for performing mixed sensorimotor nerve blocks is described above. Surface stimulation can be used prior to percutaneous stimulation, if desired, to facilitate localization of the nerve. If the nerves are deep, surface stimulation is less likely to be helpful. Fascicles containing fibers innervating specific muscles often can be differentially stimulated with the needle electrode, and phenol can be injected in the proximity of the particular fascicles so targeted. Some physicians use electromyographic (EMG) recording electrodes to ensure precise differential localization, although this can usually be adequately assessed by visual inspection and palpation of the contracting muscle and tendon. Most practitioners have used aqueous phenol in concentrations ranging from 2 to 7%, although some authors have found 3% aqueous phenol to be relatively ineffective or to give results of relatively short duration.[27] The quantity injected should depend upon the concentration of solution, the relative size of the nerve, whether the entire nerve or particular fascicles are targeted, and upon the thoroughness of block desired. Quantities of 5% aqueous phenol, for example, injected onto peripheral nerves, usually vary from 1 to 10 mL.[62] The effect of the block can be titrated either within a session or over multiple sessions by injecting smaller

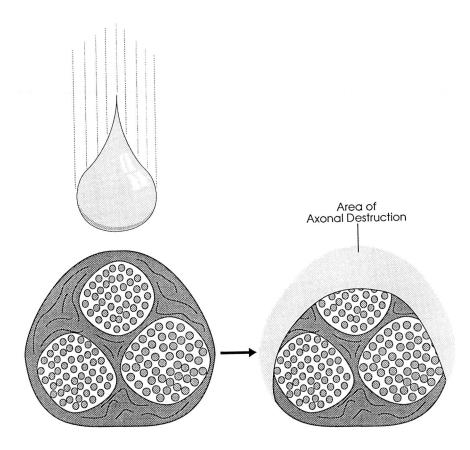

FIGURE 2. Distribution of axonal destruction after dripping phenol onto a peripheral nerve.

quantities, assessing the effectivness, and reinjecting if necessary. If done within a short period of time, the possible confounding effect of the local anesthetic action of phenol upon assessment should be considered.

Other sources address anatomic considerations regarding specific peripheral nerves.[20,28,50,62]

Mixed sensorimotor peripheral nerve blocks offer some potential advantages over motor nerve blocks. Although the issue has never been systematically studied, peripheral blocks probably can provide a more complete block because of the additional blocking of the cutaneous sensory fibers. Although not part of the stretch reflex arc, these fibers do have an excitatory influence on alpha motor neurons and, therefore, on muscle tone. In addition, all motor fibers are available to be blocked in one location, although it is unlikely that this could be accomplished with the quantities of phenol commonly used for neurolysis. One could, in fact, argue that fewer fibers are actually available because the more peripheral fascicles may provide some protection for the centrally located fibers, as noted by Burkel and McPhee.[8] However, peripheral nerve blocks are generally quicker and more easily performed than blocks of the more distal branches of the motor nerve tree, and this can translate into a more thorough block. Although the literature does not necessarily support this assertion (*see* Table 1), some practitioners feel that peripheral nerve blocks last longer than motor branch blocks. If axonal regeneration is the major factor in recurrence of spasticity after neurolysis, this should be the case; however, other factors are probably involved also.[55]

The major disadvantage of mixed sensorimotor nerve blocks is the potential for the development of pain in the distribution of the sensory component of the nerve. Complications of mixed sensorimotor nerve blocks are described beginning on page 489.

MOTOR NERVE BLOCKS

Largely, motor nerves can be blocked at many levels of the peripheral nervous system, and such blocks have been given a variety of names ("intramuscular neurolysis," "motor point blocks," "motor endplate blocks") depending in part upon the anatomic site at which the block takes place. Most frequently, motor nerves are approached within the particular muscle that is targeted. Electrosensitive sites (motor points) can be located by surface stimulation before a needle is inserted. Walthard and Tchicaloff[76] have published charts of the locations of motor points within the various muscles. Motor points are usually thought to correspond to the site at which the nerve enters the muscle or to an area where motor endplates cluster,[76] but can also represent a more proximal motor nerve as it approaches the surface of the muscle. Phenol can be injected at any of these areas, even at the motor endplate, which can be definitively identified by the characteristic pattern of electromyographic activity seen with an EMG needle-recording electrode.[17] Motor endplates cluster at characteristic areas within each muscle ("innervation band"), because the endplate lies in the midpoint of any given muscle fiber.[79] Because of its anatomically imprecise definition, the term "motor point block" might best be avoided in favor of "motor branch block."

The more peripheral into the nervous system one goes, the smaller the branches and, therefore, the more sites that need to be injected for an effective block. The patient then has to suffer more needle sticks and searches, and the physician becomes more fatigued as a result of performing a longer, more tedious procedure. The more proximal the physician moves along the nerve tree, the easier and more effective the procedure becomes. If the practitioner knows the anatomy of the innervation of a particular muscle, he or she can locate large motor branches at the most proximal sites practical after leaving the mixed sensorimotor nerve. Some surgeons perform open nerve blocks to ensure that they are injecting onto the motor branches and not onto the mixed nerve.[6,25,41,61,65] Some nerves, such as the obturator nerve, that are usually considered to be "peripheral nerves" have only a small cutaneous sensory component, and sensory complications from blocking the obturator nerve are rare. Even at the root and plexus level, one can identify motor nerves to such muscles as the iliopsoas, quadratus lumborum, and paraspinal muscles.

The important distinction, then, is not the location of the nerve within the peripheral nervous system, but whether or not the nerve contains cutaneous afferent fibers. If it does not, the risk of dysesthesias following the procedure is eliminated, and the chance of significant complications of the procedure becomes minimal in most anatomic sites commonly injected. "Motor nerves" can contain noncutaneous afferent fibers.

At times, the physician performing the block may choose to lyse multiple small motor branches rather than large ones so that the effect can be finely titrated. This may be a consideration when spasticity or primitive motor behaviors provide some useful function in addition to being problematic. In general, ease of titration is an advantage of motor nerve blocks over mixed sensorimotor nerve blocks. In addition, specific blocking of a single target muscle can be assured.

Practitioners have used concentrations of aqueous phenol ranging from 2–7%. The quantity injected can range from 0.1 to several milliliters, depending upon the size of the motor branch, which is best judged by the strength of contraction observed in the muscle when stimulated by the needle electrode.

Lumbosacral Paravertebral Nerve Block

Lumbar or sacral roots or elements of the lumbosacral plexus can be blocked in the paravertebral area.[43,48,54] Either mixed sensorimotor or motor nerves can be isolated in this area. Paravertebral blocks are discussed separately here because of the special risks and benefits associated with them.

The technique is similar to that used for other nerve blocks with phenol, with the addition of precautions related to the risk of accidental intrathecal injection via the root sleeves, which are an extension of the subarachnoid space.[61] The patient should be placed in the lateral recumbent position with the trunk laterally flexed at an angle of at least 30°. He or she should not be fully reclined until at least 15 minutes after the procedure has been completed. Alternatively, the patient can be sitting upright if feasible. Thus, if phenol were to be injected into the subarachnoid space, only the cauda equina would be affected. If clear fluid is aspirated, the needle should be withdrawn without injecting. As an added precaution, aspiration can be repeated after the injection of a small amount of phenol, in case a small piece of tissue lodged in the lumen of the needle had obstructed the initial aspiration only to be dislodged by the force of the injection.

Caution must also be exercised with regard to needle placement to avoid visceral or vascular puncture. Although the great depth of combined paraspinal muscles and psoas major muscles is adequate to prevent penetration of the peritoneum[28,50] (Fig. 3), needle placement must not veer too far laterally, and needle length should be appropriate to the size and build of the individual. Koyama et al. have used ultrasonic monitoring to guide needle insertion in this area in order to accurately localize the targeted nerves while avoiding visceral or vascular puncture.[48]

The major advantage of lumbosacral paravertebral blocks is that it is only in this location that there is adequate access to the innervation of the iliopsoas muscles. Branches from the lumbar roots to the quadratus lumborum and to the lumbar and sacral paraspinal muscles can also be located in this area. One can also, of course, locate elements of the roots or plexus innervating most of the lower extremity musculature in this area. This is not usually necessary, however, since they can be blocked more distally without the additional risk of bowel, bladder, and sexual dysfunction that could ensue from accidental intrathecal injection. In addition, anatomic specificity is not always completely possible as one moves more proximal in the peripheral nervous system, although one frequently can satisfactorily isolate fascicles even at this level.

Neuropathic pain is, of course, a possibility when mixed sensorimotor nerves are blocked at the paravertebral level as well.

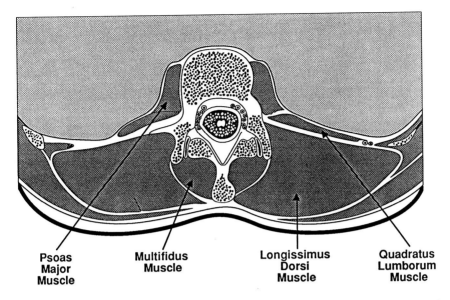

Psoas	Multifidus	Longissimus	Quadratus
Major	Muscle	Dorsi	Lumborum
Muscle		Muscle	Muscle

FIGURE 3. Anatomy of the lumbar paravertebral area. Adapted from Goodgold J: Anatomical Correlates of Clinical Electromyography. Baltimore, Williams & Wilkins, 1974, p 94.

Side Effects and Complications

Despite extensive literature documenting its effectiveness, many physicians remain reluctant to perform neurolytic procedures or to refer their patients to other physicians for nerve blocks for the treatment of spasticity. This is largely due to the fear of side effects or complications. However, serious adverse effects resulting from nerve blocks are not common when performed by physicians who are familiar with the potential side effects and complications and ways to minimize the likelihood of their occurrence.

BOTH MOTOR AND MIXED NERVE BLOCKS

Other than dysesthesias, which only occur when mixed nerves are injected for the treatment of spasticity (see Mixed Sensorimotor Nerve Blocks, page 493), the most common serious side effect of chemical neurolysis is the loss of useful motor function that was based on spasticity or primitive motor behaviors. While spasticity and associated motor behaviors may impair a patient's function to a degree that warrants intervention with nerve blocks, at the same time the patient may be using the increased muscle tone, abnormal posturing, or reflexive behaviors to his or her benefit in some respects. Lysing the nerves that supply the affected muscles, then, may result not only in the benefits that accrue from reducing spasticity but also in functional losses. Instability of the hip and knee during ambulation has been reported following obturator and tibial nerve block, respectively.[56] Loss of "push-off" during ambulation has occurred following tibial nerve block in children with cerebral palsy.[71] Loss of the ability to grasp objects with spastic finger flexors can result from median nerve block.[56] Significant weakness developed following four of 150 peripheral nerve blocks performed in one series.[35] The muscle groups involved included the triceps surae, the quadriceps femoris, and the finger flexors. However, the authors did not specify whether the involved muscle groups had been operating as part of a primitive motor pattern in these children with cerebral palsy. Nerve blocks can affect other aspects of the upper motor neuron syndrome regardless of whether spasticity is problematic. The author observed one patient who, after the last of multiple tibial nerve blocks over many years, lost all motor and sensory function in the distribution of the posterior tibial nerve. Surgical exploration 1 year later found extensive fibrous tissue about the nerve. Surgical neurolysis resulted in considerable return of sensation and partial return of motor function (3+/5 grade).

Any reflex can be affected if either the afferent or efferent components are interrupted. A burn has been reported as a consequence of loss of a withdrawal reflex following multiple upper extremity blocks.[45] Temporary loss of reflex erection has been reported in patients with spinal cord injury following obturator nerve block.[45]

In addition to its direct effect on the muscles that are blocked, a nerve block may have kinesiologic consequences that are not obvious at first glance. For instance, blocking spastic ankle plantarflexors may result in instability at the knee if the extension moment created by the plantarflexion was being used to compensate for weak quadriceps muscles during ambulation (Fig. 4). Difficulty ambulating for several days following tibial nerve blocks is relatively common,[45,71] which may be secondary to the need to adapt to a new kinesiologic dynamic or to a transient weakness that occasionally is seen.[35]

The occurrence of such motor complications is not surprising given that motor and, at times, sensory nerves are interrupted. Most of these effects can be avoided by a careful motor and functional evaluation prior to the block. Diagnostic blocks with local anesthetic agents or alcohol wash can be used to evaluate the functional consequences of a more permanent procedure. However, such diagnostic blocks may not be totally equivalent to a nerve block with phenol. Therefore, a degree of uncertainty is involved in any nerve block in an area in which spasticity and primitive motor behaviors are providing some functional benefits. If the benefits are likely to outweigh the risk involved, the physician might recommend the procedure but must explain the risks to the patient or responsible party before obtaining consent.

Perhaps more surprising is the fact that strong, isolated, voluntary contraction of muscle is usually not significantly weakened by chemical neurolysis, except in the first hours or days after a nerve block, when weakness is not uncommon. The preservation of strength has been documented by numerous clinical observations[14,15,40,46,54,62,75] and in an animal study by Tardieu et al.[75] As described above, they applied 35% alcohol to the right posterior tibial nerves of cats. They then observed that for several weeks before a mid-collicular section, they walked, ran, and jumped normally, despite the fact that the nerve block resulted in a diminution of spasticity after decerebration. Furthermore, an electrical stimulus applied to the nerve evoked a contraction in the soleus that produced tension equal to that of the unblocked side. However, the histologic and chemical studies were at variance with most studies done with phenol in that they were consistent with gamma motor neuron involvement without substantial alpha blocking.

The relative preservation of voluntary, isolated strength in the face of dramatic reductions in spasticity is not the result of a relative immunity of alpha

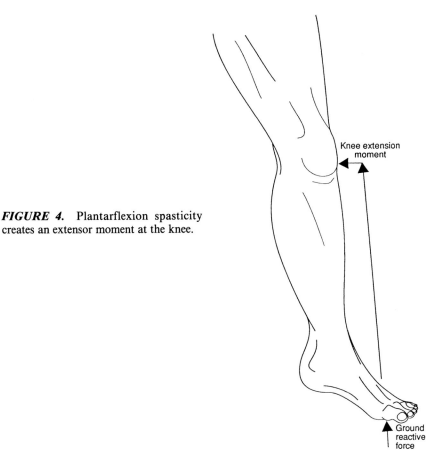

Knee extension
moment

Ground
reactive
force

FIGURE 4. Plantarflexion spasticity creates an extensor moment at the knee.

motor neurons to neurolytic agents. As noted, numerous histologic and electro-physiologic studies have demonstrated that neurons of all sizes are affected when phenol is applied to nerves. Interrupting both efferents (alpha and gamma motor neurons) and afferents (from the muscle spindle), however, may have a synergistic effect upon reflex contractions in comparison to nonreflexive contractions. The nervous system can compensate for loss of motor neurons by recruiting larger motor units and increasing the frequency of firing when increased effort is needed. The loss of motor units may only be significant when the muscle is placed under maximal stress and, even then, other muscles can help to compensate. When cutaneous afferents are also blocked in a mixed nerve, an additional excitatory influence is diminished, perhaps further enhancing the effect. When cutaneous afferents covering large enough sensory areas are blocked, one is more likely to affect the nociceptive reflexes, commonly manifested as flexor spasms after a central nervous system injury. A motor branch block is likely to have a limited effect on flexor spasms. Although primitive motor behaviors such as the synergistic movement patterns seen after cerebral cortical insults seem, for the most part, to be centrally mediated, they also receive a contribution from the muscle spindle afferents, which send facilitory fibers to muscles involved in synergistic movements.[44] In addition, they are often weaker than isolated voluntary contractions and are probably more susceptible on this account as well. The strength of the contraction available in a given situation before a nerve block may be as important a consideration in determining whether it will be preserved as is the extent to which it is free from reflexive or primitive influences.

In two reports, Fischer et al.[22,23] speculate that phenol may have a greater effect on spasticity largely on the basis of its effect on efferents. They point out that partial curarization, which only affects the neuromuscular junction and not the afferents from the muscle spindle, has been shown to reduce spasticity to a much greater degree than voluntary strength.[9] The differential effect, then, would depend largely on the numbers of motor neurons that are lysed, spasticity being affected by a relatively small reduction in motor neurons and voluntary strength being affected only when a relatively large number of fibers were destroyed. Arguing against the destruction of efferents as the predominant factor is the observation of dramatic reductions in spasticity after posterior rhizotomy.[39]

Presumably, there is a slight weakening even of strong, isolated contractions after nerve blocks that is not great enough to have a functional effect under most circumstances, and this should be kept in mind. If unusual demands were to be made upon a muscle after a nerve block, a mild weakening could be significant. A weak muscle is certainly more susceptible to further weakening by a nerve block.[44]

Another potential complication of nerve blocks is an unfavorable reversal of the balance of muscle groups about a joint. This is most likely to occur in the context of severe spasticity that is causing or threatening contracture. The nerve(s) supplying the responsible muscle or group of muscles is blocked, but if the antagonists to those muscles are also severely spastic, a contracture may begin to develop in the opposite direction. In fact, there may be an increase in spasticity in the antagonist due to loss of reciprocal inhibition. In either case, the situation can be remediated by blocking the nerves supplying the antagonist muscle(s). This complication usually can be anticipated during the evaluation preceding the nerve block, and plans can be made either for careful titration of the effect of the block (over more than one session if necessary) or for blocking the antagonist(s) shortly following the first procedure.

Muscle or ligament sprains can occur following nerve blocks, which can be due to loss of reflexive protection against overstretching the muscle in which spasticity has been relieved, changes in the dynamics of ambulation, or loss of reflexive support for other soft tissues.[45] Therapists should anticipate possible difficulties in ambulation and should be careful not to overstretch in the first days and weeks following a nerve block.

Peripheral edema is not uncommon following chemical neurolysis, particularly in the lower extremity. It can be treated with elevation of the extremity and compressive garments or elastic wrapping and usually resolves within a week or two.

Local infection at the site of injection is always a possibility. However, both alcohol and phenol are bacteriocidal at the concentrations used for neurolysis,[78] making infection rare. There has been one report of severe, lancinating pain in the forearm following median nerve block at the level of the elbow.[35]

Overdosage with phenol results in convulsions, central nervous system depression, and cardiovascular collapse. However, the amount of phenol routinely used for nerve blocks is well below the lethal range (8.5 g or more).[78] For instance, 10 mL of 5% phenol contains 0.5 g of phenol. In order to remain well within safe limits, no more than 1 g should be injected on any given day (e.g., 20 mL of 5% phenol).

Routine precautions, such as aspiration prior to injection, make intravascular injection unlikely. Neither overdosage nor accidental intravascular injection has been reported in association with phenol neurolysis. At the time that others were beginning to report on the use of phenol for direct chemical neurolysis, Cooper et al.[13] described the reduction of spasticity by perfusion of an isolated limb with 0.36% aqueous phenol for 10 to 30 minutes. Studies of animals prior to treatment of humans with spasticity had demonstrated that such concentrations could be perfused without damage to large or small vessel walls. However, higher concentrations caused necrosis of the intima of arteries and veins and thrombotic occlusion of small vessels.

Deep venous thrombosis has rarely been reported.[51] It is unclear whether this complication resulted from the direct effect of phenol on the vein, trauma to the vein, or whether the loss of muscle pumping action may have left the extremity in a state of greater susceptibility to thrombosis.

Complications related to arterial occlusion have never been reported with nerve blocks for the treatment of spasticity. However, arterial occlusion resulted in cervical spinal cord infarction in a woman who underwent stellate ganglion block with phenol in glycerine for intractable pain,[72] and a small cerebellar infarct was found at autopsy in a woman with intractable pain related to a Pancoast tumor who was treated with cervical subarachnoid injection of phenol in glycerine.[32] Although the media and elastica of many small arteries on the surface of the spinal cord were affected and some thrombosed, no spinal cord infarcts were found. However, demyelination and Wallerian degeneration were found in the cervical spinal cord. The patient died of complications related to respiratory failure. Nerve blocks with phenol in the vicinity of the cervical spinal cord carry too great a risk to warrant their use in the treatment of spasticity except under extraordinary circumstances.

MIXED SENSORIMOTOR NERVE BLOCKS

Mixed nerve blocks carry many of the same risk factors as the other chemical neurolytic procedures. The major drawback to sensorimotor nerve blocks, when compared with motor nerve blocks, is the additional risk of neuropathic pain, that is, dysesthesias in the sensory distribution of the nerve. The pain usually has its onset from a few days to about 2 weeks following the procedure. It is generally experienced as a continuous burning paresthesia that is exacerbated by light tactile stimulation so that even a draft or a sheet moving across the affected area can be uncomfortable or even intolerable. The pain is generally experienced only in a small portion of the sensory distribution of the nerve that was blocked.[45,62,71]

The incidence of dysesthesias reported following peripheral nerve blocks with phenol has varied from 2 to 32% (Table 2).[5,35,40,43,62,71] This wide variation may to some degree reflect the experience and technique of the individual physician performing the procedure. However, it is probably partly due to variation in the method of follow-up, the frequency with which obturator nerve blocks were included, and the patient population. Dysesthesias following obturator nerve blocks have not been reported, and patients with complete sensory loss do not suffer from this complication.

The majority of patients with neuropathic pain following chemical neurolysis experience a mild to moderate burning sensation that lasts from several days to

TABLE 2.   Incidence of Dysesthesias after Peripheral Nerve Blocks

Author	D/N (%)	N(Obt)	%/mL Phenol
Brattstrom	8/25 (32%)	0	2%/1.5–6 mL
Helweg-Larsen*	4/150 (3%)	58	3%/0.5–2 mL
Khalili	~35/267 (13%)	?	2–3%/0.5–5 mL
Moritz	?/90 (<10%)	11	2–3%/0.5–6 mL
Petrillo	8/33 (24%)	0	5%/2–10 mL
Spira*	7/136 (5%)	40	5%/2–5 mL

D/N = number of blocks resulting in dysesthesias/total number
N(Obt) = number of obturator nerve blocks
*nerve blocks performed on children

greater than 3 months, but several weeks is the most typical.[5,35,44,56,62,71] Helweg-Larsen and Jacobsen[35] reported 12 months of pain and tenderness on the sole of the foot following tibial nerve block in a child with cerebral palsy. The etiology of neuropathic pain following chemical neurolysis is unknown, although some physicians think that it is related to the effects of mechanical trauma to the nerve caused by the needle.[43,45] The lack of such complications from local anesthetic blocks argues against this conclusion. This phenomenon may be similar to that experienced by patients with incomplete sensory neuropathies of other etiologies or regrowth of sensory axons following traumatic lesions. Local inflammation may play a role. Some physicians feel that the incidence of pain has diminished as they have become more experienced with chemical neurolysis.[56] The literature does not reveal a relationship between the concentration or quantity of phenol used and the incidence of dysesthesias, although this has not been studied in a controlled manner. The two studies including only children had an incidence of dysesthesia of 5% or less (see Table 2).

Because this complication is usually temporary, treatment is generally aimed at managing the pain until it disappears of its own accord. Reassurance that the pain is likely to resolve within a few weeks will reduce the patient's concern. A uniformly applied compressive garment such as a sock, glove, or ace wrap will minimize cutaneous stimulation and decrease edema if it is present. Transcutaneous electrical nerve stimulation (TENS) can be effective for reducing dysesthesias in some patients. Acetaminophen or nonsteroidal antiinflammatory drugs sometimes provide some temporary relief, but it is not usually dramatic. Low-dose tricyclic antidepressants can be helpful in more severe cases, and carbamazepine also can be useful. A short course of steroids may help to resolve severe and unremitting pain. If all else fails and the pain is intolerable, reblocking the nerve with phenol usually brings relief.[62] However, both the patient and the physician are likely to experience some trepidation about employing as treatment that which caused the problem to begin with. Braun et al.[6] employed surgical neurolysis to resolve persistent dysesthesias caused by median nerve blocks in two patients.

As with complications related to loss of voluntary, isolated strength, the physician performing the nerve block is likely to be surprised to find that functional loss of sensation is an unusual occurrence following mixed sensorimotor nerve block. Presumably, the number of sensory axons affected by nerve blocks as they are commonly performed is not great enough to have a significant effect. In the first hours or days following the procedure, sensory loss is common,[62] presumably due to the local anesthetic action of phenol or the early inflammatory reaction that occurs. However, this almost invariably resolves. Katz et al.[40] reported that of 56 peripheral nerve blocks performed using 3% phenol, there was one instance of hypesthesia lasting for 2 months following ulnar nerve block and persisting at the time of their writing. Most authors have found that no loss of sensation occurs.[5,14,15,27,46] As noted, this author saw one patient lose all sensation in the distribution of the posterior tibial nerve following the last of multiple tibial nerve blocks over many years. One would have to presume that minor, perhaps subclinical, sensory loss may more commonly occur, but that it is of little significance to most patients. Further studies are needed.

MOTOR NERVE BLOCKS

The only additional side effect involved with the blocking of motor nerves is that, if the block is performed at multiple sites within the muscle itself, local pain, swelling, and induration may be present for a few days or occasionally longer.[25,33] Tender nodules may appear in the muscle 1 to 3 weeks after the injection.[19] Halpern[31] found local necrosis of muscle and an associated inflammatory reaction of the fascia and subfascial tissue in specimens taken from dogs and rats that had undergone intramuscular neurolysis with aqueous phenol. This reaction began within days of the procedure, intensified by 2 weeks, and began to resolve.

The application of ice, acutely, and later, heat; elevation of the extremity; and the administration of analgesic medications can be helpful in instances in which pain, swelling, or nodule formation is prominent. These treatments can be applied prophylactically. The administration of analgesics is warranted as a prophylactic measure in patients who, for physical or cognitive reasons, have difficulty communicating their needs. The injection of larger quantities of phenol is more likely to result in pain and swelling, and the anterior leg, the calf, and the volar forearm are more susceptible.

Intramuscular neurolysis with phenol performed within the calf muscles occasionally causes a local reaction that can mimic deep venous thrombosis: Calf pain and swelling and, at times, peripheral edema may be present, and impedance plethysmography may be consistent with deep vein thrombosis. However, the venogram will be negative.

LUMBOSACRAL PARAVERTEBRAL NERVE BLOCKS

Lumbosacral paravertebral nerve blocks carry the additional risk of accidental intrathecal injection, which could result in cauda equina or even spinal cord injury. Special precautions (described above) are necessary when injecting in this area. Lumbosacral paravertebral blocks should be reserved for treating spasticity in muscle groups that are otherwise inaccessible, such as the iliopsoas, quadratus lumborum, and paraspinal muscles, or when more peripheral approaches have been unsuccessful.

Repeated Nerve Blocks with Phenol

Limited data are available on the effect of repeating nerve blocks with phenol after the recurrence of spasticity. Halpern and Meelhuysen[32] reported that repeating intramuscular neurolysis once in 57 muscles and twice in 14 produced results similar to those achieved on the first occasion. Localization of motor branches by electrical stimulation was more difficult. Helwig-Larsen and Jacobsen[35] achieved similar effects and duration of effect on repeat of peripheral nerve blocks. Awad[1] found that in some patients a permanent reduction in spasticity was achieved after repeating intramuscular neurolysis with phenol three or four times. He speculated that necrosis of muscle leads to fibrosis, which protects against complete reinnervation. After several procedures, a clinically significant cumulative effect occurs.

In one case discussed above, complete loss of posterior tibial nerve motor and sensory function resulted immediately after the last of several tibial nerve blocks over many years. On surgical exploration one year later, excessive fibrosis was found and lysed, with good results. This unusual reaction could have resulted from intraneural injection of phenol on a single occasion. However, it is also possible that cumulative fibrosis over many years left relatively few functional axons, which were then chemically lysed with subsequent further fibrosis after the last injection.

NERVE BLOCKS WITH ALCOHOL

Qualities of Ethanol and Effect on Nerves

Ethyl alcohol, or ethanol, is a potent neurolytic agent, but it has not been used as extensively as phenol for the treatment of spasticity. Ethanol has been used mostly for sympathectomy and for the treatment of pain.

Animal studies of the effect of ethanol on nerves have generally shown destruction of both axons and myelin. The extent of damage has varied widely regardless of the concentration of ethanol used, with the exception of absolute alcohol. In a study by May,[53] absolute alcohol always caused degeneration of neurons with extensive fibrosis and partial regeneration. With lower concentrations, however, May found axonal destruction in some cases but not others. The duration of paralysis varied considerably, but the animals always recovered. With 50% ethanol, no weakness was seen. Gordon[29] found varying degrees of neuronal degeneration and surrounding fibrosis after application of 80% alcohol. Some weakness usually occurred when motor nerves were injected, but none of the animals were completely paralyzed. Labat[49] injected alcohol into the sciatic nerve of dogs. He used 48% alcohol in some animals and 95% in others and found a temporary paralysis with both. The duration of effect did not correlate with the concentration of solution used and was usually less than 2 months. Tardieu et al.[75] found lesions of the myelin, mostly in small fibers, but no axonal damage 3 weeks after application of 35% ethanol to the posterior tibial nerve of cats. Cholinesterase activity was reduced in the endplate of the muscle spindle on the side treated with alcohol, but was normal in the spindle on the untreated side and in the extrafusal muscle fibers bilaterally. The tension produced by the stretch reflex was reduced, but the tension elicited by stimulation of the tibial nerve itself was not, and voluntary movement was normal. These findings suggest a selective effect of the less concentrated solution on small-diameter gamma motor neurons.

Fischer et al.[22] found that 35–47% ethanol had a nonselective effect on the evoked response of fibers of various diameters in the early minutes after exposure. It is unclear whether this represents a nonselective but reversible local anesthetic effect or lasting damage to the nerve, and the finding is therefore not necessarily at odds with the selective small fiber damage seen by Tardieu et al.[75] several weeks after the block. Alcohol can act as a local anesthetic in concentrations as low as 5 or 10% by decreasing sodium and potassium conductance.[64]

Implications of the Site of Injection

Mixed Sensorimotor Blocks

The use of alcohol to perform mixed sensorimotor blocks for the treatment of spasticity has been limited because of the popularity of phenol and by early reports of a relatively high incidence of dysesthesias and hyperesthesias. It is not clear, however, whether the occurrence of this complication is actually any higher than with phenol, and little data exist on the treatment of spasticity by mixed motor and sensory nerve block with alcohol.

Motor Nerve Block with Alcohol

C. Tardieu et al.[74] and G. Tardieu et al.[75] have injected 45% alcohol "in the neighborhood of the motor nerve endings"[75] for the treatment of spasticity in children. They injected 1–1.5 mL at each point. Spasticity was reduced in most cases, with the effect usually lasting from 6 to 12 months, although occasionally as long as 2 or 3 years. Voluntary strength was not reduced.

Intramuscular Alcohol Wash

O'Hanlan et al.[60] modified the technique of G. Tardieu et al.[75] Rather than specifically localizing motor nerves, they injected large quantities of 45% alcohol into multiple locations within the target muscle of patients with a variety of diagnoses resulting in spasticity. In adults, they injected about 20–30 mL of alcohol into three sites in the biceps brachii muscle, 30–40 mL into the gastrocnemius and soleus through six sites, and less into the wrist and finger flexors. In children with cerebral palsy, they injected about 10 mL of alcohol into the hip adductors on each side. A significant reduction of spasticity with functional gains occurred in the 8 adults and 2 children in whom the technique was used. There was no loss of voluntary motor power or sensation. The duration of effect was not reported.

Carpenter and Seitz[11] and Carpenter[10] used a similar procedure and coined the term "intramuscular alcohol wash." A large muscle such as the gastrocnemius was divided into quadrants, and 2–6 mL of 45–50% alcohol was injected into each quadrant. In 130 children with cerebral palsy in whom alcohol was injected into the gastrocnemius-soleus muscles, all but two had a complete elimination of equinus gait for periods lasting 7–20 days. In other muscles, results were not as consistently good. Overall, in 211 children, the effect lasted 1–6 weeks.

If confirmed by other studies, the procedure's limited duration of effect could be useful for diagnostic purposes when a longer period of evaluation is necessary than can be provided by a local anesthetic agent. It could also be used for therapeutic purposes when longer-lasting procedures are unnecessary or undesirable. Another advantage of this procedure is that, because precise localization of nerves is not necessary, it can be performed quickly in situations in which speed is a consideration—for example, in agitated and combative patients and in children. Carpenter and Seitz,[66] however, used general anesthesia nonetheless.

The limited duration of effect of this procedure may be related to the relatively low concentration of ethanol used. Although the literature is inconclusive, it is possible that, as with phenol, lower concentrations result largely in demyelination as opposed to axonal destruction with Wallerian degeneration. The anatomically imprecise nature of the procedure also might play a role in the limited duration of effect. This imprecision could, however, theoretically result in an unpredictable strength and duration of effect.

The only complications noted have been a burning sensation in the muscle usually lasting no more than 24 hours and local hyperemia lasting from 24 to 36 hours. In six patients in whom muscle biopsies were performed at the time of surgery 4 to 6 weeks after the injection, only a small amount of round cell infiltrate was seen in the muscle, but no fibrosis was present. Dysesthesias should not be a problem with an intramuscular procedure. O'Hanlon et al.[60] reported phlebitis after they mixed drinkable alcohol with sterile water. When they began using solutions prepared by the pharmacist, this complication no longer occurred.

Inebriation could result from the injection and subsequent absorption of large amounts of alcohol. This should be considered in patients with a history of untoward reactions to alcohol, with respiratory compromise, in those taking sedating medications, or shortly after a central nervous system injury, when alcohol intoxication might theoretically interfere with neurologic recovery.[70] The possibility of behavioral and motor repercussions should be kept in mind.

NEUROMUSCULAR BLOCKING WITH BOTULINUM TOXIN

Botulinum toxin, when injected into muscle, diminishes spasticity by inhibiting the release of acetylcholine at the neuromuscular junction. Its most frequent uses to date have been for strabismus, torticollis, blepharospasm, and other facial dystonias;[3,4,4a,30,38,67] however, clinicians recently have found it to be helpful in the treatment of spasticity. Published reports demonstrate reductions of spasticity and improvement in range of motion and function in patients with stroke[16] and multiple sclerosis.[2,69]

Like alcohol wash, botulinum toxin injections do not require the rigorous localization of individual nerves that is needed with chemical neurolysis. The area of muscle presumed to house the motor endplates is entered with a needle and the toxin injected in quantities up to 200 units per muscle. The clinical effect is not seen for 24–72 hours, and the reduction in tone lasts up to 4 months.[3]

The possibility of systemic toxicity with generalized weakening limits the application to 400 units in a session. Reported side effects and complications include weakening of the injected muscle and transient fatigue, nausea, and headache.[30] Diffusion to nearby muscles is a potential problem, particularly with small muscles, and may account for the partial ptosis and vertical deviations seen after some injections for strabismus.[4a] Transient dysphagia has resulted from the treatment of cervical dystonia and spastic dysphonia.[38] Some patients develop antibodies to the toxin and become less responsive to subsequent injections.[67] Botulinum toxin is significantly more expensive than phenol or alcohol, with a wholesale price of several dollars per unit.[18]

NERVE BLOCKS WITH LOCAL ANESTHETIC AGENTS

Although both phenol and alcohol have local anesthetic properties, local anesthetic agents are defined here as drugs that, when applied directly to a nerve, reversibly block conduction without causing structural damage to the nerve. They do so by acting on the membrane to decrease the transient increase in permeability to sodium ions that normally results when the membrane is depolarized. In general, they affect small-diameter fibers more rapidly than large ones, and their blocking action lasts longer on small fibers. This is probably due to the smaller internodal distances of small-diameter fibers, which can be covered more rapidly by the diffusing local anesthetic. Once the agent has been allowed to diffuse, however, there may be no differential effect, although this point has not been entirely clarified.[63]

Absorbed systemically in high enough concentrations, local anesthetic agents can result in central nervous system stimulation, manifested by restlessness, tremor, and convulsions, followed by central nervous system depression. With some agents, such as lidocaine and procaine, sedation and subsequent unconsciousness may not be proceeded by stimulation. In addition, myocardial conduction and, therefore, contraction can be depressed, usually only in concentrations that have produced central nervous system effects. Rarely, cardiovascular collapse and death have resulted from infiltration of small amounts of a local anesthetic. Hypersensitivity reactions, including fatal anaphylaxis, do rarely occur, more commonly with agents that have an ester link, such as procaine and tetracaine. The maximal quantities of various local anesthetic drugs without epinephrine that can be safely infiltrated in an adult are presented in Table 3.[63] The amount needed for a diagnostic nerve block to evaluate the effect on spasticity is usually only a few milliliters, well below this limit.

The duration of effect of local anesthetics varies considerably from agent to agent (see Table 3).[63] Lidocaine is commonly used for a relatively short action, as is bupivacaine for a longer duration.

CLINICAL APPLICATIONS

Indications for Nerve Blocks

The decision to perform a nerve block should be based on both a neuromuscular-kinesiologic evaluation and an assessment of the functional or potential functional implications of the disordered muscle tone. The possibility of functional gains resulting from the nerve block must be weighed against the potential for functional losses or other complications and side effects. For the purposes of evaluation, functional considerations can be classified as involving active motor control or passive positioning. Contractures can play an important role in both.

Spasticity most commonly inhibits active motor control when hyperactive stretch reflexes in antagonist muscles resist the motion of the agonists. When it appears that the agonists may be significantly strengthened, with an ultimate functional gain possible if freed from the hyperactive antagonists, nerve blocks are often useful. For instance, if toe drag or a toe-heel gait results from spasticity of the plantarflexors of the ankle in the face of the ability to actively dorsiflex the ankle, either in an isolated fashion or as part of a flexor synergy, blocking the posterior tibial nerve or its branches to the gastrocnemius and soleus can remediate the problem. The effect of the block on other joints should be considered, in particular, the effect of the decreased extension moment on the stability of the

TABLE 3.   Practical Use of Local Anesthetic Agents in Adults

Agent	Maximal Amount	Duration of Action
Procaine 0.5%	1.4 mL/kg	<1 hour
Lidocaine 1%	0.45 mL/kg	1–2 hours
Bupivacaine 0.25%	1 mL/kg	7 hours

knee (Fig. 4). If increased inversion of the foot is also present, an attempt should be made to determine whether this is due to increased tone in the tibialis anterior or tibialis posterior muscle or both. This can be difficult to determine by observation alone, and polyelectromyography or diagnostic nerve blocks can be helpful in this situation. Sometimes inversion during swing phase results from the inability of the tibialis anterior to "fight" spastic or contracted plantarflexors so that all of its contractile force goes toward inversion rather than dorsiflexion. In such cases, nerve blocks affecting the plantarflexors or remediation of contractures will resolve the situation. If a spastic tibialis posterior is felt to be responsible for excessive inversion, the branch or fasicles of the posterior tibial nerve to the tibialis posterior also can be blocked. As the tibialis posterior helps to support the arch of the foot, the possibility of pes planus resulting from such a block should be considered.

Although spasticity itself is the most likely condition to be affected by a nerve block, other motor disorders associated with central nervous system dysfunction, such as rigidity, cocontractions, dystonia, and primitive motor behaviors, can adversely affect function by overpowering an agonist. This may occur with or without the presence of significant spasticity. If increased involuntary muscle contraction is present despite the absence of stretch of that muscle, nerve blocks may still be helpful, although not as consistently. Mooney et al.[55] found that 2 of 8 patients with upper extremity synergy patterns had a weakening of the pattern following phenol neurolysis of motor branches of the median nerve. Easton et al.[19] had less satisfactory results with intramuscular blocks in children with dystonic athetosis, decerebrate rigidity, and hypertonia related to disinhibited vestibular, tonic neck, or spinal reflexes than in children with pure spasticity. Khalili[43] reported on the use of phenol nerve blocks in a patient with dystonia musculorum deformans who developed a superimposed spastic right hemiplegia following a neurosurgical procedure. Although a tibial nerve block relieved ankle clonus, dystonic and voluntary contraction of the plantarflexors were not affected. However, Halpern and Meelhuysen[33] reported reduction in muscle tone in 3 children with tension athetosis.

Rigidity is also less susceptible to the influence of neurolysis with phenol, although Halpern and Meelhuysen[33] also reduced rigidity of the sternocleido-mastoids and hip adductors in 2 patients with Parkinson's disease, with subsequent improvements in posture and ambulation. Similarly, Kjellberg et al.[47] observed improvements in gait in about half of their patients following intrathecal injection of 5% phenol in glycerine. As noted earlier, reductions in abnormal motor responses of any kind can result in functional losses when the motor response is being used for functional purposes. Therefore, the clinician should take an inventory of any such activities when considering a patient for nerve block so that the risk and benefits can be carefully weighed before proceeding.

Less frequently, spasticity masks the voluntary strength of the very muscle in which tone is increased. A nerve block, then, may result in increased strength in the muscle blocked. Such a result is difficult, if not impossible, to predict, except, for instance, by the use of a diagnostic block with a local anesthetic agent. More often, it is the unanticipated by-product of a nerve block performed for other reasons and can be accepted as a gift. It is a particularly pleasant surprise when the innervation of the finger flexors is being blocked to facilitate finger extension and the strength of both improves.

Although the result of a nerve block is likely to have a greater effect on function when active control is at stake, the reduction of passive posturing due to spasticity or primitive motor behaviors also can have significant functional implications. In the case of increased plantarflexion and inversion tone described above, a good result can be obtained even in some instances in which no active dorsiflexion or eversion can be seen. Similarly, if hypertonia of the toe flexors is causing a painful grabbing during the stance phase, blocking the branch of the posterior tibial nerve to the flexor digitorum muscles can be beneficial regardless of whether active toe extension is present. The benefit of an orthosis can be improved by a nerve block that allows it to more effectively do its job—for instance, when plantarflexion or inversion tone prevents proper fitting of an ankle-foot orthosis.

Proper passive positioning in a wheelchair, bed, or other device can result in greater patient comfort and can improve communication, alertness, respiration, upper extremity use, hygiene, skin care, and otherwise facilitate function or nursing care. Thus, obturator nerve blocks that alleviate excessive hip adduction can result in more comfortable sitting or facilitate perineal hygiene. Similarly, hygiene of the axilla, palm of the hand, or anticubital fossa can be improved by nerve blocks that relax the muscle that prevents adequate access. Lower extremity extensor synergies that cause a patient to slide out of even well-constructed wheelchairs can be reduced by blocking the innervation of the primary muscles involved, particularly the gluteus maximus. Ankle clonus that causes positioning problems during transfer, for instance, can be eliminated with blocks of the posterior tibial nerve or its branches. Opisthotonos can be reduced by blocking the innervation of spinal extensor muscles. Hypertonia in any accessible muscle or muscle group that results in discomfort or dysfunctional positioning can be considered for treatment with nerve blocks.

Contractures can prevent active motion or proper passive positioning, and nerve blocks can be used to prevent contractures of potential functional significance when their development is associated with spasticity. If spasticity has already resulted in contracture, remediation of the contracture via range of motion exercises, serial casting, or other means can be greatly facilitated by nerve blocks. Recurrence of contracture can be prevented by prophylactic nerve blocks that allow range of motion exercises to be performed more easily and less painfully and that permit the proper fitting of bivalved casts or other orthoses. Nerve blocks also can be useful for preventing the recurrence of contractures that have been surgically remediated.

The clinician considering a patient for chemical neurolysis as a treatment alternative must consider the time since onset of the upper motor neuron lesion and the diagnosis for improvement. If a nerve block with phenol is performed prematurely, and a patient improves more dramatically than expected shortly after the block, potential function based on primitive motor behaviors may be lost or strength of weak muscles reduced. In addition, if the pattern of hypertonia changes, contracture or loss of function may develop in the direction opposite to that initially anticipated. On the other hand, if a nerve block is avoided because of such risks and the anticipated contractures develop, the consequences are also likely to be significant. Clinicians should make every attempt to prevent contractures if there is even a small possibility of a good outcome.

Alcohol wash represents an alternative approach to nerve blocks with phenol. The literature indicates that the effect is likely to last only for several weeks, at which time longer-lasting blocks with phenol can be considered or alcohol wash repeated if necessary. Even when the physician is confident that enough time has elapsed to warrant the use of phenol, the patient or family member may be unconvinced. In such situations, they may more readily accept an alcohol wash because of the shorter duration of effect and, later, having seen the benefits, consent to a nerve block with phenol. On the other hand, the literature on alcohol wash is limited, and it is an anatomically imprecise procedure. It seems conceivable that, at times, the effect might last longer if a large bolus of alcohol is injected onto one or more larger motor branches.

Botulinum toxin has a more predictable time-limited effect on hypertonia than does phenol or alcohol and therefore presents another alternative when a central nervous system insult is still relatively recent. With a more static disability, the shorter duration of effect is more likely to be a disadvantage. Botulinum toxin is particularly effective for dystonia, at least in small muscles, and might prove to have some advantage over phenol when dystonia is a greater problem than spasticity. Because the onset of its effect is delayed, titration of the effect is not as easily achieved as with phenol.

Local anesthetic blocks also can be used to help prevent contractures early after an injury, but they may need to be repeated frequently, and this can be impractical. The benefit of a local anesthetic block can, however, be stretched by placing the extremity in a cast that inhibits the return of hypertonia and prevents contracture formation.[41] The limb must be carefully observed, because the return of forceful spasticity within the cast could result in skin breakdown.

The usual indication for local anesthetic block, however, is for diagnostic purposes. Local anesthetics can be used to help determine whether there is a component of spasticity at end range in the presence of severe contracture. They can help to determine which muscle is contributing to a pathological posturing, as in the case of inversion of the foot described above. They are probably most useful, however, in situations in which it is uncertain whether a nerve block will cause more harm than good, particularly when significant function based on primitive motor behaviors or spasticity is at stake, or when blocks may affect more than one aspect of a function such as ambulation. However, the local anesthetic block, although frequently helpful, is not likely to exactly reproduce the effect of a nerve block with phenol. This is particularly true when mixed sensorimotor nerves are blocked with local anesthetics, in which case the sensory loss that results may have significant functional consequences. Alcohol wash or botulinum toxin also can be used if several weeks or months may be needed to fully evaluate the potential effects of a block.

Chemical neurolysis must be considered in light of the other treatment alternatives and, when practical, more conservative approaches tried first. In some instances, however, spasticity is so powerful, or contracture is developing so rapidly, that nerve blocks may be required in favor of less invasive treatments. The question of which of two interventions is more conservative can be a matter of subjective opinion, and judgment must be exercised. For instance, medications are generally considered more conservative than nerve blocks; however, in elderly patients or patients with brain damage secondary to trauma, cerebrovascular accident, multiple sclerosis, or other causes, medications that impair cognition can cause significant time lost from a rehabilitation program even when the problem is recognized and, if unrecognized, may permanently impede recovery.

Another important consideration is the possible need to repeat nerve blocks because of the frequently limited duration of their effect. Repetition should not be done reflexively. The possibility that other approaches that were previously unsuccessful might now prove beneficial, or that medications that might previously have been contraindicated might now be acceptable, should be considered. The lack of availability of physicians who perform nerve blocks may make nerve blocks a poor choice for treatment if it appears that the blocks will need to be repeated. Frequent need for repetition of blocks may also make them less acceptable. In such situations, an attempt to find an appropriate systemic pharmacologic alternative should be pursued, and potentially longer-lasting procedures such as radiofrequency rhizotomy, selective posterior rhizotomy, baclofen pump, or musculotendinous releases with neurectomy may be indicated. Nerve blocks can be useful to facilitate the effectiveness of musculotendinous procedures performed in the presence of spasticity.

REFERENCES

1. Awad EA: Intramuscular neurolysis for stroke. Minn Med 8:711–713, 1972.
2. Borg-Stein J, Pine ZM, Miller J, Brin M: Botulinum toxin for treatment of spasticity in multiple sclerosis [abstract]. Am J Phys Med Rehabil 71:251, 1992.
3. Borg-Stein J, Stein J: Update on pharmacology: Pharmacology of botulinum toxin and implications for use in disorders of muscle tone. J Head Trauma Rehabil 8(3):103–106, 1993.
4. Borodic GE, Cozzolino D: Blepharospasm and its treatment, with emphasis on the use of botulinum toxin. Plast Reconstr Surg 83:546–554, 1989.
4a. Botulinum toxin for ocular muscle disorders. Med Lett Drugs Ther 32:100–102, 1990.
5. Brattsrom M, Moritz U, Svantesson G: Electromyographic studies of peripheral nerve block with phenol. Scand J Rehab Med 2:17–22, 1970.
6. Braun RM, Hoffer MM, Mooney V, et al: Phenol nerve block in the treatment of acquired spastic hemiplegia in the upper limb. J Bone Joint Surg 55A:580–585, 1973.
7. Brown AS: The treatment of intractable pain by subarachnoid injection of carbolic acid. Lancet 2:975–978, 1958.
8. Burkel WE, McPhee M: Effect of phenol injection into peripheral nerve of rat: Electron microscope studies. Arch Phys Med Rehabil 51:391–397, 1970.
9. Burman MS: Therapeutic use of curare and erythroidine hydrochloride for spastic and dystonic states. Arch Neurol Psychiatry 41-327:307, 1939.
10. Carpenter EB: Role of nerve blocks in the foot and ankle in cerebral palsy: Therapeutic and diagnostic. Foot Ankle 4:164–166, 1983.
11. Carpenter EB, Seitz DG: Intramuscular alcohol as an aid in the management of spastic cerebral palsy. Dev Med Child Neurol 22:497–501, 1980.
12. Chironna RC, Hecht JS: Subscapularis motor point block for the painful hemiplegic shoulder. Arch Phys Med Rehabil 71:428–429, 1990.
13. Cooper IS, Hirose T, Matsuoka S, et al: Specific neurotoxic perfusion: A new approach to selected cases of pain and spasticity. Neurology 15:985–993, 1965.
14. Copp EP, Harris R, Keenan J: Peripheral nerve block and motor point block with phenol in the management of spasticity. Proc R Soc Med 63:937–938, 1970.
15. Copp EP, Keenan J: Phenol nerve and motor point block in spasticity. Rheum Phys Med 11:287–292, 1972.
16. Das TK, Park DM: Botulinum toxin in treatment spasticity. Br J Cerebral Palsy 43:401–403, 1989.
17. DeLateur BJ: A new technique of intramuscular phenol neurolysis. Arch Phys Med Rehabil 53:179–185, 1972.
18. Drug Topics Red Book: Oradell, NJ, Medical Economics Data, 1992.
19. Easton JKM, Ozel T, Halpern D: Intramuscular neurolysis for spasticity in children. Arch Phys Med Rehabil 60:155–158, 1979.
20. Felsenthal G: Nerve blocks in the lower extremities: Anatomic considerations. Arch Phys Med Rehabil 55:504–507, 1974.
21. Felsenthal G: Pharmacology of phenol in peripheral nerve blocks: A review. Arch Phys Med Rehabil 55:13–16, 1974.
22. Fischer E, Cress RH, Haines G, et al: Evoked nerve conduction after nerve block by chemical means. Am J Phys Med 49:333–347, 1970.
23. Fischer E, Cress RH, Haines G, et al: Recovery of nerve conduction after nerve block by phenol. Am J Phys Med 50:230–234, 1971.

24. Fusfeld RD: Electromyographic findings after phenol block. Arch Phys Med Rehabil 49:217–220, 1968.

25. Garland DE, Lilling M, Keenan MA: Percutaneous phenol blocks to motor points of spastic forearm muscles in head-injured adults. Arch Phys Med Rehabil 65:243–245, 1984.

26. Garland DE, Lucie RS, Waters RL: Current uses of open phenol nerve blocks for adult acquired spasticity. Clin Orthop 165:217–222, 1982.

27. Glass A, Cain HD, Liebgold H, Mead S: Electromyographic and evoked potential responses after phenol blcoks of peripheral nerves. Arch Phys Med Rehabil 49:455–459, 1968.

28. Glenn MB: Nerve blocks. In Glenn MB, Whyte J (eds): The Practical Management of Spasticity in Children and Adults. Philadelphia, Lea & Febiger, 1990, pp 227–258.

29. Gordon A: Experimental study of intraneural injections of alcohol. J Nerv Ment Dis 41:81–95, 1914.

30. Greene P, Kang U, Fahn S, et al: Double-blind, placebo controlled trial of botulinum toxin for the treatment of spasmodic torticollis. Neurology 40:1213–1218, 1990.

31. Halpern D: Histologic studies in animals after intramuscular neurolysis with phenol. Arch Phys Med Rehabil 58:438–443, 1977.

32. Halpern D, Meelhuysen FE: Duration of relaxation after intramuscular neurolysis with phenol. JAMA 200:1152–1154, 1967.

33. Halpern D, Meelhuysen FE: Phenol motor point block in the management of muscular hypertonia. Arch Phys Med Rehabil 47:659–664, 1966.

34. Hecht JS: Subscapular nerve block in the painful hemiplegic shoulder. Arch Phys Med Rehabil 73:1036–1039, 1992.

35. Helweg-Larsen J, Jacobsen E: Treatment of spasticity in cerebral palsy by means of phenol nerve block of peripheral nerves. Dan Med Bull 16:20–25, 1969.

36. Holland AJC, Youssef M: A complication of subarachnoid phenol blockade. Anaesthesia 34:260–262, 1978.

37. Iggo A, Walsh EG: Selective block of small fibres in the spinal roots by phenol. J Physiol 146:701–708, 1959.

38. Jankovic J, Brin MF: Therapeutic uses of botulinum toxin. N Engl J Med 324:1186–1194, 1991.

39. Kasdon D, Abramovitz JN: Neurosurgical approaches. In Glenn MB, Whyte J (eds): The Practical Management of Spasticity in Children and Adults. Philadelphia, Lea & Febiger, 1990, pp 259–267.

40. Katz J, Knott LW, Feldman DJ: Peripheral nerve injections with phenol in the management of spastic patients. Arch Phys Med Rehabil 48:97–99, 1967.

41. Keenan MAE: The orthopedic management of spasticity. J Head Trauma Rehabil 2:62–71, 1987.

42. Kelly RE, Gauthier-Smith PC: Intrathecal phenol in the treatment of reflex spasms and spasticity. Lancet 2:1102–1105, 1959.

43. Khalili AA: Physiatric management of spasticity by phenol nerve and motor point block. In Ruskin AP (ed): Current Therapy in Physiatry. Philadelphia, WB Saunders, 1984.

44. Khalili AA, Benton JG: A physiologic approach to the evaluation and the management of spasticity with procaine and phenol nerve block. Clin Orthop 47:97–104, 1966.

45. Khalili AA, Betts HB: Peripheral nerve block with phenol in the management of spasticity: Indications and complications. JAMA 200:1155–1157, 1967.

46. Khalili AA, Harmel MH, Forster S, Benton JG: Management of spasticity by selective peripheral nerve block with dilute phenol solutions in clinical rehabilitation. Arch Phys Med Rehabil 45:513–519, 1964.

47. Kjellberg RN, Todd DP, Schwab RS, et al: Gait improvement in Parkinsonian patients by gamma motor neuron suppression. Trans Am Neurol Assoc 86:126–130, 1961.

48. Koyama H, Murakami K, Suzuki T, Suzaki K: Phenol block for hip flexor muscle spasticity under ultrasonic monitoring. Arch Phys Med Rehabil 73:1040–1043, 1992.

49. Labat G: The action of alcohol on the living nerve: Experimental and clinical considerations. Curr Res Anesth Analg 12:190–196, 1933.

50. Labib KB, Gans BM: Chemical neurolysis: Technique and anatomical considerations [videotape]. Boston, Department of Rehabilitation Medicine, New England Medical Center, 1984.

51. Macek K: Venous thrombosis results from some phenol injections. JAMA 249:1807, 1983.

52. Maher RM: Neuron selection in relief of pain: Further experiences with intrathecal injections. Lancet 1:16–19, 1957.

53. May O: The functional and histological effects of intraneural and intraganglionic injections of alcohol. Br Med J 465–470, Aug. 31, 1912.

54. Meelhuysen FE, Halpern D, Quast J: Treatment of flexor spasticity of hip by paravertebral lumbar spinal nerve block. Arch Phys Med Rehabil 49:36–41, 1968.

55. Mooney V, Frykman G, McLamb J: Current status of intraneural phenol injections. Clin Orthop Rel Res 63:122–131, 1969.
56. Moritz U: Phenol block of peripheral nerves. Scand J Rehab Med 5:160–163, 1973.
57. Nathan PW: Intrathecal phenol to relieve spasticity in paraplegia. Lancet 2:1099–1102, 1959.
58. Nathan PW, Sears TA, Smith MC: Effects of phenol solutions on the nerve roots of the cat: An electrophysiological and histological study. J Neurol Sci 2:7–29, 1965.
59. Nathan PW, Sears TA: Effects of phenol on nervous conduction. J Physiol 150:565–580, 1960.
60. O'Hanlan JT, Galford HR, Bosley J: The use of 45% alcohol to control spasticity. Va Med Monthly 96:429–436, 1969.
61. O'Rahilly R: Gardner-Gray-O'Rahilly Anatomy: A Regional Study of Human Structure, 5th ed. Philadelphia, WB Saunders, 1986.
62. Petrillo CR, Chu DS, Davis SW: Phenol block on the tibial nerve in the hemiplegic patient. Orthopedics 3:871–874, 1980.
63. Ritchie JM, Greene NM: Local anesthetics. In Gilman AG, Goodman LS, Rall LS, Murad F (eds): Goodman's and Gilman's The Pharmacological Basis of Therapeutics, 7th ed. New York, Macmillan, 1985, pp 302–321.
64. Ritchie JM: The aliphatic alcohols. In Gilman AG, Goodman LS, Rall TW, Murad F (eds): Goodman's and Gilman's The Pharmacological Basis of Therapeutics, 7th ed. New York, Macmillan, 1985, pp 372–386.
65. Roper B: Evaluation of spasticity. The Hand 7:11–14, 1975.
66. Schaumburg HN, Byck R, Weller RO: The effect of phenol on peripheral nerve. A histological and electrophysiological study. J Neuropath Exp Neurol 29:615–630, 1970.
67. Schwartz KS, Jankovic J: Predicting the response to botulinum toxin injections for the treatment of cervical dystonia [abstract]. Neurology 40(suppl 1):382, 1990.
68. Simon DL, Carron H, Rowlingson JC: Treatment of bladder pain with transsacral nerve block. Anesth Analg 61:46–48, 1982.
69. Snow BJ, Tsui JKC, Bhatt MH, et al: Treatment of spasticity with botulinum toxin: A double blind study. Ann Neurol 28:512–515, 1990.
70. Sparadeo FR, Gill D: Effects of prior alcohol use on head injury recovery. J Head Trauma Rehabil 4:75–82, 1989.
71. Spira R: Management of spasticity in cerebral palsied children by peripheral nerve block with phenol. Develop Med Child Neurol 13:164–173, 1971.
72. Superville-Sovak B, Rasminsky M, Finlayson MB: Complications of phenol neurolysis. Arch Neurol 32:226–228, 1975.
73. Susset JG, Zinner N, Archimbaud JP: Differential sacral blocks and selective neurotomies in the treatment of incomplete upper motor neuron lesion. Urol Int 29:236–248, 1974.
74. Tardieu C, Tardieu G, Hariga J, et al: Fondement experimental d'une therapeutique des raideurs d'origine cerebrale. Arch Fr Pediatr 21:5–23, 1964.
75. Tardieu G, Tardieu C, Hariga J, Gagnard L: Treatment of spasticity by injection of dilute alcohol at the motor point or by epidural route. Dev Med Child Neurol 10:555–568, 1968.
76. Walthard KM, Tchicaloff M: Motor points. In Licht S (ed): Electrodiagnosis and Electromyography, 3rd ed. New Haven, Licht, 1971, pp 153–170.
77. Westgate HD: Selective percutaneous sacral root blockade with phenol in neurovesical dysfunction. Can Anaesthesiol Soc J 17:456–463, 1970.
78. Wood KE: The use of phenol as a neurolytic agent: A review. Pain 5:205–229, 1978.
79. Zack SI: The Motor Endplate. Philadelphia, WB Saunders, 1971.

JULIUS P. A. DEWALD, PT, PHD
JOSEPH D. GIVEN, PHD

ELECTRICAL STIMULATION AND SPASTICITY REDUCTION: FACT OR FICTION?

From the Rehabilitation Institute
   of Chicago
Chicago, Illinois

Reprint requests to:
Julius P. A. Dewald, PT, PhD
Sensory Motor Performance
   Program
Rehabilitation Institute of Chicago
Room 1406
345 East Superior Street
Chicago, IL 60611

This research was supported by the Washington Square Foundation grant 357, National Institutes of Health grant NS 19331-11, NIDRR Research and Training Center for Stroke grant H133B30024, and American Paralysis Association grant RB1-9203-1.

All experimental work presented in this chapter was performed in the Sensory Motor Performance Program laboratory at the Rehabilitation Institute of Chicago.

Electrical stimulation in the field of rehabilitation has yielded intriguing observations in which patients and clinicians have reported a substantial reduction of the spastic state. The methodology of studies that have tried to address this issue range from the stimulation of muscles antagonist to the spastic ones,[1] stimulation of the spastic muscle itself,[88] stimulation of dermatomes,[6] to the stimulation of the dorsal columns of the spinal cord.[22,44] All of these authors report reductions in spasticity using subjective clinical scales[3] or the pendulum test.[90] There are also contradictory results in the literature of no changes or even increases in spasticity following electrical stimulation.[34,37,80] How does one explain the wide variation in results of electrical stimulation on spasticity demonstrated in the literature? Is its ability to reduce spasticity fact or fiction? The literature suggests that the diversity of the findings may be due to the design of the individual studies. In addition to variations in patient populations and stimulation protocols, most of these studies did not use rigorous and quantifiable measures of spasticity, few employed a solid experimental design, and fewer still attempted to characterize the nature, origins, and duration of any beneficial effect of electrical stimulation.

Using quantitative biomechanical and electromyographic measures to evaluate spastic hypertonia in a preliminary study, we observed that cutaneous afferent stimulation resulted in significant reductions in spasticity in a hemiparetic stroke test population lasting up to 50 minutes.[19,29] Such reductions could arise because of changes in the effectiveness of synaptic transmission in the involved reflex pathways such as short-term facilitation, short-term depression or long-term potentiation (LTP) and depression (LTD), which will result in short- or long-term changes in motoneuron and interneuron excitability.

BACKGROUND

Spasticity is defined as an enhanced stretch reflex behavior resulting in hypersensitivity of the muscle to elongation, which results in increased resistance of the limb to imposed movements.[52] Spastic hypertonia may be observed in patients who have suffered spinal cord injury due to trauma, demyelinating disorders such as multiple sclerosis, or degenerative disorders such as amyotrophic lateral sclerosis. Spastic hypertonia is both an important physical sign indicating the existence of neurologic damage to the neuraxis and a major source of disability in itself because of flexor spasms and movement-induced activation of muscles when stretched during joint movements. Although hypertonia is readily discernible clinically, the severity of this clinical sign is not readily quantifiable, at least in any uniformly accepted way. As a consequence, the underlying mechanisms are not clearly understood, and a widely accepted quantitative definition of spasticity has not been achieved. In light of the above deficiencies, it is necessary to develop accurate estimates of limb mechanical impedance to help define and constrain the possible mechanisms underlying the increases in muscle tone and to study the effects of electrical stimulation for spasticity reduction.

Electrical Stimulation and Spasticity

The effect of electrical stimulation on spasticity has been examined for more than a century. Clinical observations by Duchenne (1871) showed that stimulating muscles antagonist to the spastic muscle resulted in relaxation of the spastic muscle.[56] Over the last 30 years, interest in the effects of electrical stimulation on spasticity has increased. In the 1950s, studies on the effect of stimulating the spastic muscle with particular current waveforms[54] or the effect of stimulating antagonist muscles[56] were again executed. A renewed interest in the area of functional electrical stimulation during the 1970s yielded further evidence about the therapeutic effects of electrical stimulation on spasticity.[31,58,63,65] The majority of these reports were purely qualitative, but more recent reports, specifically dealing with electrical stimulation and spasticity, use mostly clinical scores[3] in an attempt to quantify changes in muscle tonicity.[1] The first quantitative attempts to assess the effect of electrical stimulation on the spastic state were either electrophysiologic or mechanical. Quantitative electrophysiologic measurements were made using alterations in H-reflex latencies postelectrical stimulation.[38,55] These studies demonstrated increased reflex latencies and increased vibratory H-reflex inhibition after long-term transcutaneous electrical stimulation protocols. Apkarian and Nauman showed a short-term attenuation in electrically measured stretch reflex behavior while stimulating antagonistic muscle groups in the lower extremity.[2] A number of studies used mostly mechanical means to quantify alterations in spasticity following electrical stimulation.[7,75,76,89] This was accomplished by using the pendulum test for the lower extremity.[90] This test, which examines gravity-induced oscillations of the lower leg, is relatively imprecise and not fully substantiated theoretically.[59,85]

All of these studies used some form of transcutaneous stimulation protocol to study the effects of electrical stimulation on spasticity. A large number of studies used invasive surgical means to directly electrically stimulate the spinal cord or nerve roots in cerebral palsy or spinal cord-injured patients.[9,12,20,21,30a,37,44,61,80,86] All of these approaches lacked solid spasticity quantification methods and therefore yielded results that are ambiguous at best.

Finally, the common denominator in the literature we reviewed was the lack of a serious attempt by any of the investigations to determine and/or identify the possible underlying mechanisms responsible for the observed changes in spasticity. This chapter will provide a neuroscientific framework based on preliminary observations and the literature in an effort to compensate for this shortcoming.

The Importance of Proper Quantification of Spasticity

Different experimental paradigms have been used to measure and quantify spastic behavior. These protocols can be roughly separated into either electrical or mechanical perturbations. Several studies have identified reduced electromyogram (EMG) levels in the spastic muscle as an indicator of reduced spasticity.[10,14,38,51,55] However, the inherent variability and high level of noise associated with muscle EMG recordings and poor correlation with intensity of spasticity[18,45] make this approach a suboptimal choice for spasticity quantification. Furthermore, electromyograms are an indirect measure of spasticity and do not provide a quantitative and reliable measure of limb impedance and joint stiffness. The limb's mechanical resistance to movement, the parameter of interest for spasticity reduction, requires an effective experimental methodology for direct measurement of these mechanical properties.

Therefore, we chose to focus on the mechanical methods. Mechanical perturbation techniques can be broken down into gravitational methods, manual methods, controlled position perturbation methods, and controlled torque perturbation methods. **Gravitational methods** involve the use of gravity as the perturbation input. The relaxed limb's impedance to imposed movement due to gravity is called the pendulum test.[5,7,13,59,90] Application and analysis are straightforward; however, the limited, quasi-empirical nature of the information was considered inappropriate for research on the mechanisms of spasticity.[72,85] The second mechanical perturbation category involves **manual stretching of muscle** and subjective measurement of the system response. Although some control over the input was achieved, the higher variability of the input perturbation and limited information gained from this procedure were determined to be unacceptable for this study. **Controlled position perturbation techniques**, such as the ramp and sine wave position perturbations, are considered the optimal choice for identification and quantification of spasticity. The ability to vary the speed, starting angle, range of motion, and background torque levels make the approach adaptable for both normal and spastic muscle. **Controlled torque perturbation methods** are also appropriate; however, the ease of implementation of position, perturbation protocols and simplicity in construction and control of the testing apparatus[72] made the position perturbation approach our preferred initial choice.

The sine wave position perturbation provides a smooth velocity profile that mimics natural movements.[85] However, time varying velocity and position signals make the investigation of the effects of these parameters on spasticity much more complex. The increases in torque attributed to phasic reflex behavior by Stefanovska et al.[85] may simply be a threshold problem in which the required velocity is exceeded and maintained for longer times at the higher sine wave frequencies. A minimum velocity threshold and finite initiation time are required to elicit the stretch reflex behavior. One could argue that the absolute magnitude of the velocity profile is not as important as the time frame of velocities exceeding the reflex threshold and that, therefore, the differences in torque profiles are not due to gain changes in the stretch reflex but to varying ranges of stretch reflex excitation. Plots of torque output versus position and velocity, in addition to time, would help to resolve this problem. The advantages of the slow ramp protocol are that velocity and position can be changed independently of each other and that a constant velocity profile is achieved over a significant time frame providing a steady state velocity condition for the investigation of the stretch reflex response.

Proposed Spasticity Quantification Model

The elbow joint system can be modeled as a second order system comprising agonist and antagonist muscle subsystems with global parameters of elastic stiffness (K), viscous stiffness (B) and inertia (I). Elastic stiffness models the spring-like properties of muscle (i.e., the resistance increases as the muscle is stretched) while viscous stiffness, or viscosity, models the damping properties of muscle (i.e., the velocity-dependent resistance to movement of muscle). A second order angular mechanical system representation is described by the following equation:

$$I\frac{d^2\theta}{dt^2} + B\frac{d\theta}{dt} + K\theta = T \qquad (1)$$

θ is angular position and T is the torque output of system.

The individual contributions from the elbow flexors and extensors can be separated into their respective relative contributions from the passive, intrinsic, and stretch reflex mechanical muscle properties. Previous work at the elbow joint[49] and the ankle[40,92] has demonstrated that this model of the mechanical state of the joint provides reliable and accurate estimation of the system's mechanical response to perturbations in position. Significant differences in system response behavior following electrical stimulation will be reflected by changes in the measured torque response. Discrimination of significant changes in spasticity following electrical stimulation is further enhanced by using the proposed slow ramp protocol since the inertial contribution is removed under constant velocity conditions. The inertial component of this system is significant and can swamp the effects of the viscous and stiffness components to the overall torque response.

EXPERIMENTAL PROTOCOL AND PRELIMINARY RESULTS

Experimental Protocol

A slow ramp position perturbation protocol was applied to the joint in question (elbow) to assess the passive properties (passive muscle, tendon, and connective tissue) and the stretch reflex response. Testees were seated to one side of a computer-controlled motor and positioned such that the axis of rotation of the joint was aligned with that of the motor. The relevant mechanical parameters (torque, velocity, and position) and muscle EMG activities about the elbow were measured. The angular range and velocity were varied for each testee to allow measurement of the joint impedance response of the elbow under passive relaxed conditions alone (very slow ramp perturbation) and then at higher velocities at which the stretch reflex is elicited.

The testee's elbow rested in a shallow cup above the axis of the motor, and the wrist and hand were casted and then attached with a U-bolt in a mid prosupinated position to a lightweight beam coupled to the motor (Fig. 1). EMG activity in the biceps-brachialis, brachioradialis, and lateral triceps muscles were measured using surface electrodes. The test-taker's arm was positioned in 120° of elbow extension or 60° of elbow flexion depending on whether the stiffness in flexors or extensors was estimated (180° is designated as full extension). The arm was moved through an arc of one radian (57.3°) at a constant angular velocity. For all trials, the test-taker was instructed to relax completely and not to intervene. The relaxed state was determined by monitoring relevant EMG activity.

The angular range was varied to assess the presence of any end of range effects, and the range of motion was determined for each testee. The angular velocity was varied for each person to allow measurement of the joint impedance response under passive relaxed conditions alone (very slow ramp pertubation) and then at higher velocities in which the stretch reflex is elicited in spastic patients. Thilmann et al.[87] have reported that angular velocities of greater than 3 radians/ second (175° per second) are required to elicit stretch reflex behavior in normal intact muscle during rotations of the ankle joint. Previous work by the author and others has shown that significantly slower velocities will elicit stretch reflex behavior in hemiparetic and spinal-cord injured patients.[19,30,70,71,78] Spasticity quantification is possible by taking the difference of the combined response of the joint for higher velocities from the estimated response of the passive properties at very slow ramp velocities. The ability to properly distinguish and measure the level of spasticity is essential for the investigation of spasticity reduction using electrical stimulation protocols. The ability to properly quantify the passive response over

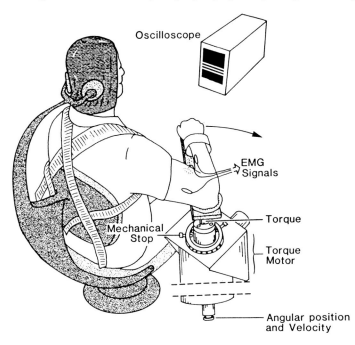

FIGURE 1. Experimental set-up for the elbow joint. (From Katz RT, Rymer WZ: Spastic hypertonia: Mechanisms and measurement. Arch Phys Med Rehabil 70:144–155, 1989; with permission.)

the range in question is required for accurate estimation of the reflex response. The static (angular position) and dynamic (angular velocity) components of the stretch reflex response, and their interaction, in conjunction with peak torque generation and background EMG activity, were used to quantify the level of spasticity present. The level of spasticity was characterized by these static and dynamic parameters relative to normal intact muscle.

Preliminary Results: Evidence for Significant Spasticity Reduction

Prestimulation torque responses of the impaired upper limb were measured during slow ramp perturbations of the elbow in 8 hemiparetic patients and compared with torque responses obtained immediately following stimulation over the antagonistic muscle.[29] In addition, EMG signals of biceps, brachioradialis, and triceps muscles were collected for subsequent analysis. A set of 10–20 position perturbation trials were collected at 1-minute intervals prestimulation and immediately poststimulation. The electrical stimulation was applied to skin over the biceps muscle for 10 minutes at a frequency of 20 Hz, with an intensity level below motor threshold but above sensory threshold.[19] The joint extension protocol was repeated immediately after electrical stimulation. A second set of 10–20 trials was collected a minimum of 30 minutes poststimulation. In some cases, patients were again given electrical stimulation, but at a level that was just above motor threshold, with a duty cycle of 2.5 seconds on and 2.5 seconds off so as to avoid muscle fatigue.

In all patients, cutaneous stimulation over the elbow flexors at submotor levels significantly reduced the torque in both elbow flexors and extensors (Fig. 2),

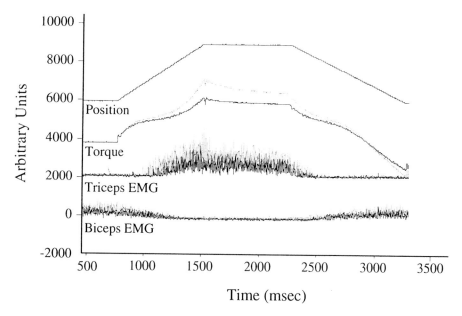

FIGURE 2. Torque and EMG responses of the elbow joint to a slow ramp stretch/ plateau/return of elbow extensors before and after electrical stimulation over the biceps brachii. The prestimulation responses are in gray, and the poststimulation responses are in black. Note the reduction in torque and EMG responses following electrical stimulation at submotor levels.

while stimulation slightly above motor threshold resulted in significant reductions in extensor torques, but significant increases in flexor torques. These effects remained statistically significant for at least 50 minutes following stimulation, but the positive effects diminished with time. The reductions in spasticity were determined to be due primarily to changes in threshold as opposed to gain of the stretch reflex response.

Torque-angle responses for different ramp angular velocities are shown in Figure 3. In the affected limb of hemiparetic stroke patients, the level of stiffness increases with higher angular velocities except for the poststimulation data. In essence, as demonstrated in this figure, the use of low level electrical stimulation has reduced the effective resistance to imposed movement of the spastic limb to equivalent lower angular velocity levels prestimulation. Practically speaking, the spastic arm can be moved at a faster speed (in this case, three times faster) while provoking a lower joint impedance response.

POSSIBLE NEUROPHYSIOLOGIC MECHANISMS OF SPASTICITY-REDUCING EFFECTS OF ELECTRIAL STIMULATION

Modifiability of Spinal Reflexes

In hemiparetic stroke, low levels of cutaneous electrical stimulation over the biceps muscle produced significant reductions in spasticity of the triceps muscle in a study by Dewald et al.[19] The effect of the intervention was determined to be primarily a positive shift in the stretch reflex threshold. It has been postulated that the stimulation intervention modifies the underlying synaptic circuitry to produce this effect.[19]

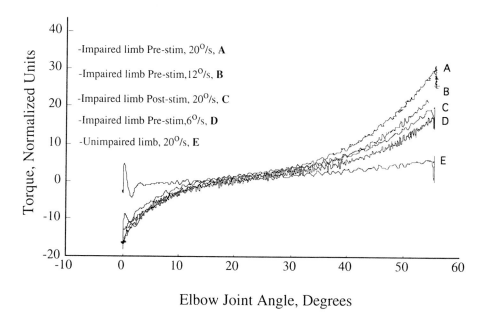

FIGURE 3. Torque responses of the elbow joint for different stretch velocities. The poststimulatory torque responses correspond to a prestimulatory response at a significantly reduced stretch velocity.

In an effort to discuss the spinal circuitry relevant to potential alterations in muscle tonicity, we will use the upper extremity as an example. Figure 4 illustrates the potential locations that may be involved in mediating the electrically induced synaptic facilitations or depressions during a stretch reflex. The underlying circuits are believed to revolve around the Ia inhibitory interneuronal system.[42] For example, electrical stimulation applied to Ia muscle afferents in the biceps would give rise to an afferent volley that would have several destinations. First, there would be an homonymous relay to biceps motoneurons, giving rise to short latency electrical excitation, or an H-reflex.[36,67] The biceps Ia spindle afferents would also induce excitation of Ia inhibitory interneurons located in the intermediate nucleus of the spinal cord gray matter. These Ia interneurons would then project to motoneurons of opposing muscles such as triceps, giving rise to short latency inhibition. Since there is no described capacity for prolonged or repetitive discharge of Ia interneurons following transient stimuli, the Ia inhibitory effects should last for only a few milliseconds, corresponding to single or relatively few Ia interneuron impulses in response to each Ia afferent electrical volley. Other potentially important elements in this network include the Renshaw projection to regional Ia inhibitory neurons,[94] and inhibition of other premotor excitatory interneurons innervating extensor motoneurons also may occur. Finally, Ia afferents also could affect the discharge of antagonist fusimotor neurons, altering spindle afferent discharge from the triceps muscles.[8]

The effects of electrical stimulation on spinal circuits can be subdivided based on their longevity. In classical neurophysiology, effects lasting milliseconds are the most frequently studied. Examples are the facilitation or inhibition of spinal motoneurons, which are studied in the case of Ia,[60] Ib,[53] flexion reflex afferents,[39] and specialized circuits arising from these afferents such as reciprocal inhibition[24] and Renshaw or recurrent inhibition.[74] Because of the short duration of these events, possible effects on the onset of the stretch reflex, as created by elongation

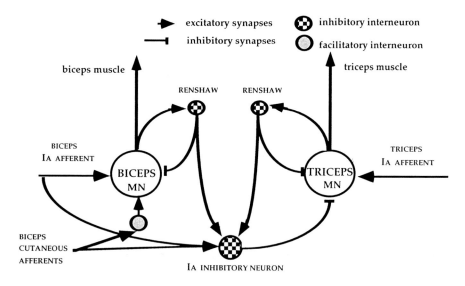

FIGURE 4. Circuitry relevant to the effect of cutaneous and Ia muscle afferents on stretch reflex gain and threshold.

of ankle or elbow muscles, will be hard to capture. Instead of studying the effect of synaptic potentials that last a few milliseconds, this study concentrates on physiologic changes that last seconds or minutes after stimulation. The short-term effects have been studied for homosynaptic events (i.e., synaptic events that result from changes in the presynaptic neuron) in processes such as synaptic facilitation, augmentation and potentiation due to posttetanic potentiation (PTP), and synaptic depression. Long-term synaptic changes, lasting hours to days, are found in the form of long-term potentiation (LTP) and depression (LTD) and have mostly been studied in heterosynaptic events (i.e., synaptic events in which synaptic changes are mediated by other neurons that converge on the synapse).

SHORT-TERM SYNAPTIC PLASTICITY: HOMOSYNAPTIC EVENTS

Short-term Synaptic Facilitation.   Short-term synaptic facilitation is often displayed after the application of high-frequency stimulation (100–500 Hz) of the presynaptic neuron. When the high frequency is applied for a short time the synaptic *facilitation* occurs for an equally short time (1 second or less[96]). Enhanced synaptic transmission with a lifetime of several seconds is sometimes called ***augmentation***. Both forms of synaptic facilitation are proposed to be related to transient saturation of various Ca^{2+} buffering systems in the synaptic terminals, primarily at the level of smooth endoplasmic reticulum and mitochondria. The excess of Ca^{2+}, called ***residual Ca^{2+}***, builds up after the relatively large influx of Ca^{2+} accompanying many action potentials. According to the residual calicum hypothesis,[46,68] increases in the resting concentration of free Ca^{2+} presumably acts on Ca^{2+}-dependent mobilization steps, which enhances neuro-transmitter release for many minutes depending on the length of preceding tetanic stimulation. Synaptic ***potentiation*** is an increase in efficacy of transmission requiring minutes of stimulation and lasts for minutes up to an hour after stimulation. Potentiation appears to arise from two sources. It is reduced but not abolished by stimulation in a Ca^{2+}-free medium,[26,77,91] which suggests that potentiation is at least partially dependent on the presence of residual calcium. It has been proposed that sodium that accumulated presynaptically during a tetanus potentiates transmitter release by displacing calcium from intracellular stores[73] or reducing calcium extrusion by Na/Ca exchange.[64]

Short-term Synaptic Depression.   The simplest form of synaptic modification that occurs as a result of repeated stimulation is ***habituation***, which refers to a decrement in synaptic response that occurs as the stimulus train proceeds.[45] A number of spinal synapses exhibit this property, including those interposed in the flexion reflex pathway synapses in cats.[81,82] The depression occurs over several minutes of repeated stimulation at a low frequency (0.1–5 Hz), with recovery occurring with a time constant of minutes.[25,93] The habituation shows rapid recovery after a strong stimulus delivered to some other convergent pathway.[81] The ***homosynaptic depression*** model is defined as reduced transmission across the activated synapse or synaptic fatigue during repetitive stimulation.[81] The mechanisms underlying homosynaptic depression might exhibit similar mechanisms as observed in *Aplysia californica*.[15] In this invertebrate, neurotransmitter release seems to be decreased due to a slow inactivation of Ca^{2+} conductance[50] so that Ca^{2+} entry into the presynaptic terminals diminishes, resulting in a reduction of transmitter release. A similar correlation has been observed at synapses between cultured spinal cord neurons.[43] Also, in vitro studies in neonatal rat spinal cords show prolonged synaptic depression using 5 Hz stimulus trains.[57] The duration of short-term synaptic depression is seconds to minutes and is likely to be dependent on the duration of the preceding low frequency stimulation, as in the case of synaptic facilitation discussed previously.

In quantitative experiments in humans concerning the effect of electrical stimulation on stretch reflex characteristics, homosynaptic circuits cannot be isolated; however, the effect of stimulation frequencies, intensities, and durations on heterosynaptic events can be studied. The preceding forms of short-term homosynaptic plasticity are calcium-based and play a significant role in heterosynaptic circuits.

Long-term Synaptic Plasticity: Homosynaptic Events

Long-term Facilitation and Habituation. Repeated exposure to the stimulus protocol can lead to long-term facilitation or habituation (depending on the frequency of the applied stimulus) lasting from hours to days. This form of facilitation, studied in *Aplysia californica*, involves synthesis of proteins that prolong the facilitatory response and synthesis of proteins important for the growth of new synaptic connections.[28] In long-term habituation, morphological changes in the form of a loss in synapses has been reported.[4]

Only during repeated stimulation sessions can possible morphological changes at the cellular level be considered with respect to long-term synaptic plasticity. Only a few studies have attempted to look at longitudinal effects of electrical stimulation on spasticity in humans. Robinson et al.[76] found no evidence for spasticity reduction as a consequence of chronic electrical stimulation in spinal cord-injured patients. Alternatively, chronic electrical stimulation has been shown to alter stretch reflex behavior in patients with hemiparetic stroke.[84] Further investigations using the quantitative methods discussed in this chapter are required to better understand the role of long-term homosynaptic events in spasticity modification.

Long-term Synaptic Plasticity: Heterosynaptic Events

Long-term Potentiation. This form of long-term facilitation has been most extensively studied at the hippocampus and requires a brief, intense, high-frequency train (1 second, 100–500 Hz) of stimuli to a single afferent system. The resulting excitatory synaptic potential in the postsynaptic neuron can last for hours and, in the intact animal, for days and even weeks.[11] LTP as observed at the hippocampus has several interesting properties: (1) more than one afferent fiber needs to be activated to obtain LTP, (2) the afferent fibers and the postsynaptic cell need to be active together, in an associative fashion, and (3) LTP is specific to the active pathway.[66] The induction of LTP is postsynaptic; it can be facilitated greatly when postsynaptic inhibition is blocked by picrotoxin and reduced by properly timed inhibitory inputs.[32] These properties can be explained by the neurotransmitter-receptor system believed to be responsible for LTP. Action of the neuro facilitatory ligand glutamate on N-methyl-D-aspartate (NMDA) receptor-channel is postulated for the induction of LTP because it requires depolarization of the postsynaptic membrane. This occurs during a high frequency tetanus, which activates nonNMDA (quisqualate/kainate) receptor-channels depolarizing the postsynaptic membrane, thus relieving the blockade of the NMDA channel.[32] The fact that NMDA receptor channel, once activated, allows for the flow of CA^{2+} in addition to Na^+, K^+ results in a rise of Ca^{2+} at the postsynaptic level triggering Ca^{2+}-dependent kinases that lead to the induction of LTP. Although a significant portion of the current knowledge concerning LTP has been gathered at the level of the hippocampus, evidence for LTP has also been noted at the level of the spinal cord in the dorsal horn in monkeys[23] and rats[95] and in the ventral horn in neonatal mice[33] and in the rat.[79]

Long-term Depression.   Long-lasting depression of synaptic transmission follows short-duration, high-intensity, low-frequency (0.1–5 Hz) stimulatory trains and has been most extensively studied at the hippocampus[16,17,35,69,83] and in the cerebellum.[41] These studies have shown the associative activation requirements for LTD (as in LTP), its heterosynaptic nature, and its dependence on Ca^{2+} and quisqualate-specific glutamate receptor-channels. It is postulated that increased inflow of Ca^{2+} at the postsynaptic cell may directly facilitate desensitization of glutamate receptor-channels, thus promoting LTD. The duration of LTD has been reported to last for hours to days.[16,69] LTD as defined here has not been studied at the level of the spinal cord. However, the presence of glutamate and nonNMDA receptors at the level of the cord do not rule out its existence.

The unique feature of LTP and LTD is that short-term stimulatory events (1 second or less) create long-term effects (hours to days). In the heterosynaptic circuits prevalent in human experimentation, different stimulation durations can be used to determine the minimal stimulus duration time required for seconds to minutes of circuit depression. Preliminary data have shown reductions of the stretch reflex response lasting at least 50 minutes following 5–10 minutes of stimulation.[19,29] These observed reductions could be due to a number of short-term or long-term synaptic plasticity mechanisms, all of which are dependent on the spinal circuits involved. Future investigations with variations of the stimulation parameters such as intensity, duration, frequency, and location are needed for the investigation and separation of the primary circuits and synaptic plasticities involved.

Possible Sources of Synaptic Plasticity in Stretch Reflex Circuitry

The principal parameters of the proposed general electrical stimulation protocol (intensity, frequency, duration, and location) will permit the investigation of the long-term effects observed in the preliminary results and identification of possible underlying mechanisms. By careful examination of the changes in the mechanical and electromyographic responses of the spastic muscles, it should be possible to determine whether the effects are mediated directly at the motoneuron level or whether they take place at premotoneuronal sites. Specifically, changes of motoneuronal excitability alone, which would emerge because of direct projections from Ia interneurons to motoneurons, would produce primarily increases in the threshold of the stretch reflex, which is the angle at which the stretch reflex is initiated in initially quiescent muscle. On the other hand, changes in the excitability of premotoneuronal elements such as premotor interneurons could emerge as changes in reflex gain or its mechanical equivalent, the reflex stiffness.

STIMULATION OF MUSCLE AFFERENTS

Based on the neural circuitry and types of synaptic plasticity discussed previously, electrical stimulation of the Ia muscle afferents could produce the following scenarios:

- *Possible facilitation effects*
  Facilitation of the biceps motoneuron pool from direct stimulation of its Ia afferents with a corresponding facilitation of the Ia inhibitory interneuron

resulting in a depression of the antagonistic motoneuron pool. These facilitatory effects are expected with higher stimulatory frequencies. The experimental result of these changes will be measured by an increase in the stretch reflex threshold of the antagonistic muscle with the inverse effect on the agonist.

• *Possible depression effects*
Depression of the biceps motoneuron pool and its corresponding Ia inhibitory interneuron is possible with low frequency electrical stimulation. The result of these effects will be seen as a decrease in the antagonistic stretch reflex threshold (more excitable) along with the opposite effect on the agonist (biceps).

Due to stimulation of Ia afferents, alterations in the excitability of antagonistic fusimotor neurons or neurons in polysynaptic Ia circuits (as opposed to mono-synaptic ones) may also occur, which may affect the stretch reflex gain.

STIMULATION OF LOW THRESHOLD CUTANEOUS AFFERENTS

Stimulation of cutaneous afferents could also affect the agonistic motoneuron pool via facilitory interneurons (*see* Fig. 1) and its Ia inhibitory interneuronal system and would thus influence the same circuitry.[27]

• *Possible facilitation effects*
Cutaneous stimulation at higher frequencies is expected to result in the facilitation of the agonistic motoneuron pool with corresponding depression of the antagonistic motoneuron pool through facilitation of the Ia inhibitory interneuron. This behavior would result in an increase in the stretch reflex threshold of the antagonist with a corresponding inverse effect on the agonist.

• *Possible depression effects*
Low frequency cutaneous stimulation should have an opposite effect on the same circuitry discussed above. The agonistic motoneuron pool will be depressed while the antagonistic motoneuron pool will be facilitated via the respective interneuronal systems. This behavior will be identified by changes in the stretch reflex threshold of the muscles.

In addition, interneuronal circuits (cutaneous interneuron, Ia inhibitory interneuron, and others) could also be modified by the use of cutaneous stimulation. Cutaneous afferents affect gamma motoneurons in cats, which infers that reflex gain changes are possible.[65a]

CLINICAL IMPLICATIONS AND CONCLUSION

Clinically, a need exists for noninvasive rehabilitation interventions such as electrical stimulation for the reduction of spasticity. Other means to reduce spasticity are pharmacologic therapies, which present side effects such as generalized weakness,[18,62] or surgical interventions, which are invasive procedures whose positive results are questionable at best.[47] As presented in this chapter, the main obstacle for determination of the effects of electrical stimulation on spasticity is the lack of proper quantification techniques for the detection of changes in spasticity levels. With the methodology discussed here, an evaluation of the appropriate stimulation parameters for consistent and effective spasticity reduction can be realized and is in progress by the authors. Results to date are encouraging.

Most studies have used vastly different stimulation protocols and spasticity measurements. The lack of a consensus on proper spasticity quantification and a solid neuroscientific framework for the understanding and interpretation of results is evident throughout the literature. The first ingredient required to understand the effect of electrical stimulation on spasticity is the use of electromechanical measurements, which allow for the quantification of alterations in stretch reflex gain and threshold. Subsequently, the determination of optimal stimulation parameters for spasticity reduction should be determined for various afflictions. Based on encouraging preliminary results reported by our laboratory at the Rehabilitation Institute of Chicago, we believe this to be an achievable goal that will provide both relevant clinical and scientific information.

REFERENCES

1. Alfieri V: Electrical treatment of spasticity. Scand J Rehabil Med 14:177–182, 1982.
2. Apkarian JA, Naumann S: Stretch reflex inhibition using electrical stimulation in normal subjects and subjects with spasticity. J Biomed Eng 13:67–73, 1991.
3. Ashworth RW: Preliminary trial of carisoprodol in multiple sclerosis. Practitioner 192:540–542, 1964.
4. Bailey CH, Chen M: Morphological basis of long-term habituation and sensitization in aplysia. Science 220:91–93, 1983.
5. Bajd T, Bowman B: Testing and modeling of spasticity. J Biomed Eng 4:90–96, 1982.
6. Bajd T, Gregoric M, Vodovnik L, Benko H: Electrical stimulation in treating spasticity resulting from spinal cord injury. Arch Phys Med Rehabil 66:515–517, 1985.
7. Bajd T, Vodovnik L: Pendulum testing of spasticity. J Biomed Eng 6:9–16, 1984.
8. Baldissera F, Hultborn H, Illert M: Integration in spinal neuronal systems. In Brooks VB (ed): Handbook of Physiology. Motor Control, Vol 2, Sec 1. Bethesda, MD, American Physiological Society, 1981, pp 509–595.
9. Barolat-Romana G, Myklebust JB, Hemmy DC, et al: Immediate effects of spinal cord stimulation in spinal spasticity. J Neurosurg 62:558–562, 1985.
10. Benecke R, Conrad B, Meinck HM, Hohn J: Electromyographic analysis of bicycling on a ergometer for evaluation of spasticity of lower limbs in man. Adv Neurol 39:1035–1046, 1983.
11. Bliss TVP, Lomo T: Long-lasting potentiation of synaptic transmission in the dentate area of the anaesthetized rabbit following stimulation of the perforant path. J Physiol (Lond) 232:331–356, 1973.
12. Broseta J, Garcia-March G, Sanchez-Ledesma MJ, et al: High frequency cervical spinal cord stimulation in spasticity and motor disorders. Acta Neurochir Suppl (Wien) 39:106–111, 1987.
13. Brown RA, Lawson DA, Leslie GC, Part NJ: Observations on the applicability of the Wartenberg pendulum test to healthy elderly subjects. J Neurol Neurosurg Psychiatry 51:1171–1177, 1988.
14. Burke DD, Gilliels JD, Lance JW: The quadriceps stretch reflex in human spasticity. J Neurol Neurosurg Psychiatry 33:216, 1970.
15. Castelluci V, Kandel ER: A Quantal Analysis of the synaptic depression underlying habituation of the gill-withdrawal reflex in aplysia. Proc Natl Acad Sci USA 71:5004–5008, 1974.
16. Christie BR, Abraham WC: Priming of associative long-term depression in the dentate gyrus by theta frequency synaptic activity. Neuron 9:79–84, 1992.
17. Desmond NL, Colbert CM, Zhang DX, Levy WB: NMDA receptor antagonists block the induction of long-term depression in the hippocampal dentate gyrus of the anesthetized rat. Brain Res 552:93–98, 1991.
18. Delwaide PJ: Electrophysiological analysis of mode of action of muscle relaxants in spasticity. Ann Neurol 17:90–95, 1985.
19. Dewald JPA, Given JD, Rymer WZ: Significant reductions in upper limb spasticity in hemiparetic stroke using cutaneous levels of electrical stimulation. Soc Neurosci Abstr 19:990, 1993.
20. Dimitrijevic MM, Dimitrijevic MR, Illis LS, et al: Spinal cord stimulation for the control of spasticity in patients with chronic spinal cord injury: Clinical observations. Central Nervous System Trauma 3:129–144, 1986.
21. Dimitrijevic MR, Illis LS, Nakajima K, et al: Spinal cord stimulation for the control of spasticity in patients with chronic spinal cord injury: Neurophysiologic observations. Central Nervous System Trauma 3:145–152, 1986.
22. Dimitrijevic MR, Faganel J: Spinal cord stimulation for the treatment of movement disorders. In Lazorthes Y, Updon AR (eds): Neurostimulation: An Overview. New York, Futura Publishing, 1985, p 147.
23. Dougherty PM, Willis WD: Enhancement of spinothalamic neuron responses to chemical and mechanical stimuli following combined micro-iontophoretic application of N-methyl-D-aspartic acid and substance P. Pain 47:85–93, 1991.

24. Eccles RM, Lunberg A: Integrated pattern of Ia synaptic actions on motorneurons of hip and knee muscles. J Physiol (Lond) 144:271–298, 1958.

25. Egger MD: Sensitization and habituation of dorsal horn cells in cats. J Physiol (Lond) 279:153–166, 1978.

26. Erulkar SD, Rahamimoff R: The role of calcium ions in tetanic and posttetanic increase of miniature end-plate potential frequency. J Physiol 278:501–511, 1978.

27. Fedina L, Hultborn H: Facilitation from ipsilateral primary afferents of interneuronal transmission in the Ia inhibitory pathway to motoneurons. Acta Physiol Scand 86:56–81, 1972.

28. Frost WN, Castellucci VF, Hawkins RD, Kandel ER: Monosynaptic connections from the sensory neurons participate in the storage of long-term memory for senitization of the gill- and siphon-withdrawal reflex in aplysia. Proc Natl Acad Sci USA 82:8266–8269, 1985.

29. Given JD, Dewald JPA: Changes in stretch reflex threshold in spastic muscle as a result of electrical stimulation. Soc Neurosci Abstr 17:1033, 1991.

30. Given JD, Dewald JPA, Rymer WZ: Evidence for changes in muscle mechanical properties and stretch reflex characteristics in spastic hemiparetic stroke. Soc Neurosci Abstr 18:1411, 1992.

30a. Gottlieb GL, Myklebust BM, Stefoski D, et al: Evaluation of cervical stimulation for chronic treatment of spasticity. Neurology 35:699–704, 1985.

31. Granat MH, Ferguson AC, Andrews BJ, Delargy M: The role of functional electrical stimulation in the rehabilitation of patients with incomplete spinal cord injury—observed benefits during gait studies. Paraplegia 31:207–215, 1993.

32. Gustafson B, Wigström H: Physiological mechanisms underlying long-term potentiation. Trans Neurosci 11:156–162, 1988.

33. Hernandez P, Elbert K, Droge MH: Spontaneous and NMDA evoked motor rhythms in the neonatal mouse spinal cord: An in vitro study with comparisons to in situ study. Exp Brain Res 85:66–74, 1991.

34. Hines AE, Crago PE, Billian C: Functional electrical stimulation for the reduction of spasticity in the hemiplegic hand. Biomed Sci Instrum 29:259–266, 1993.

35. Hirsch JC, Crepel F: Blockade of NMDA receptors unmasks a long-term depression in synaptic efficacy in rat prefrontal neurons in vitro. Exp Brain Res 85:621–624, 1991.

36. Hoffman P: Untersuchungen uber die Eigenreflexe (Sechnenreflexe) Menschlicker Muskeln. Berlin, Spinger, 1922.

37. Hugenholtz H, Humphreys P, McIntyre WM, et al: Cervical spinal cord stimulation for spasticity in cerebral palsy. Neurosurgery 22:707–714, 1988.

38. Hui-Chan CW, Levin MF: Stretch reflex latencies in spastic hemiparetic subjects are prolonged after transcutaneous electrical nerve stimulation. Can J Neurol Sci 20:97–106, 1993.

39. Hultborn H, Illert M, Santini M: Convergence on interneurones mediating the reciprocal Ia inhibition of motoneurones. II. Effects from segmental flexor reflex pathways. Acta Physiol Scand 96:351–367, 1976.

40. Hunter IW, Kearney RE: Dynamics of human ankle stiffness: Variation with mean ankle torque. J Biomech 15:747–752, 1982.

41. Ito M: Long-term depression. Ann Rev Neurosci 12:85–102, 1989.

42. Jankowska E: Interneuronal relay in spinal pathways from proprioceptors. Prog Neurobiol 38:335–378, 1992.

43. Jia M, Nelson PG: Calcium currents and transmitter output in cultured spinal cord and dorsal root ganglion neurons. J Neurophysiol 56:1257–1267, 1986.

44. Kanaka TS, Kumar MM: Neurostimulation for spinal spasticity. Paraplegia 28:399–405, 1990.

45. Kandel ER: Neuronal plasticity and the modification of behavior. In Kandel ER (ed): Handbook of Physiology. The Nervous System, Cellular Biology of Neurons, Vol 1, Sec 1. Bethesda, MD, American Physiological Society, 1977, pp 1137–1182.

46. Katz B, Miledi R: The role of calcium in neuromuscular facilitation. J Physiol 195:481–492, 1968.

47. Katz RT: Management of spasticity. Am J Phys Med Rehabil 67:108–116, 1988.

48. Katz RT, Rymer WZ: Spastic hypertonia: Mechanisms and measurement. Arch Phys Med Rehabil 70:144–155, 1989.

49. Kirsch RF: Neural mechanisms mediating compensation for muscle fatigue in cat and man [PhD dissertation], Chicago, Northwestern University, 1990.

50. Klein M, Shapiro E, Kandel ER: Synaptic plasticity and the modulation of the calcium current. J Exp Biol 89:117–157, 1980.

51. Knutsson E, Martenson A: Dynamic motor capacity in spastic paresis and its relation to prime mover dysfunction, spastic reflexes and antagonistic co-activation. Scand J Rehabil Med 12:93–106, 1980.

52. Lance JW: Pathophysiology of spasticity and clinical experience with baclofen. In Feldman RG, Young RR, Koella WP (eds): Spasticity: Disordered Motor Control. Chicago, Year Book, 1980, pp 185–203.

53. Laporte Y, Lloyd DPC: Nature and significance of the reflex connections established by large afferent fibers of muscular origin. Am J Physiol 169:609–621, 1952.

54. Lee WJ, McGovern JP, Duval EN: Cutaneous tetanizing (low voltage) currents for relief of spasm. Arch Phys Med Rehabil 31:766–770, 1950.

55. Levin MF, Hui-Chan CW: Relief of hemiparetic spasticity by TENS is associated with improvement in reflex and voluntary motor functions. Electroencephalogr Clin Neurophysiol 85:131–142, 1992.

56. Levine MG, Knott M, Kabat H: Relaxation of spasticity by electrical stimulation of antagonist muscles. Arch Phys Med Rehabil 33:668–673, 1952.

57. Lev-Tov A, Pinco M: In vitro studies of prolonged synaptic depression in the neonatal rat spinal cord. J Physiol 447:149–169, 1992.

58. Liberson WT, Homquest HJ, Scott D, Dow M: Functional electrotherapy: Stimulation of peroneal nerve synchronized with swing phase of gait of hemiplegic patients. Arch Phys Med Rehabil 42:101–105, 1961.

59. Lin DC, Rymer WZ: Quantitative analysis of pendular motion of the lower leg in spastic human subjects. IEEE Trans Biomed Eng 38:906–918, 1991.

60. Lloyd DPC: Conduction and synaptic transmission of the reflex response to stretch in spinal cats. J Neurophysiol 6:317–326, 1943.

61. Maiman DJ, Mykleburst JB, Barolat-Romana G: Spinal cord stimulation for amelioration of spasticity: Experimental results. Neurosurgery 21:331–333, 1987.

62. Memin B, Pollak P, Hommel M, Perret J: Treatment of spasticity with botulinum toxin. Rev Neurol (Paris) 148:212–214, 1992.

63. Merletti R, Andina A, Galante M, Furlan I: Clinical experience of electronic peroneal stimulators in 50 hemiparetic patients. Scand J Rehabil Med 11:111–121, 1979.

64. Mistler S, Falke L, Martin S: Cation dependence of posttetanic potentiation of neuromuscular transmission. Am J Physiol 252:C55–C62, 1987.

65. Mooney V, Wileman E, McNeal DR: Stimulator reduces spastic activity. JAMA 207:2199–2200, 1964.

65a. Murphy PR, Hammond GR: The role of cutaneous afferents in the control of gamma moto-neurons during locomotion in the decerebrate cat. J Physiol 434:529–547, 1991.

66. Nicoll RA, Kauer JA, Malenka RC: The current excitement in long-term potentiation. Neuron 1:97–103, 1988.

67. Paillard J: Reflexes et Regulations d'Origine Proprioceptive chez l'Homme Etude Neurophysiologique et Psychophysiologique. Paris, Arnette, 1955.

68. Parnas H, Dudel J, Parnas I: Neurotransmitter release and its facilitation in crayfish. I. Saturation kinetics of release, and of entry and removal of calcium. Pfluggers Arch 393:1–14, 1982.

69. Pockett S, Brookes NH, Bindman LJ: Long-term depression at synapses in slices of rat hippocampus can be induced by bursts of postsynaptic activity. Exp Brain Res 80:196–200, 1990.

70. Powers RK, Campbell DL, Rymer WZ: Stretch reflex dynamics in spastic elbow flexor muscles. Ann Neurol 25:32–42, 1989.

71. Powers RK, Marder-Meyer J, Rymer WZ: Quantitative relations between hypertonia and stretch reflex threshold in spastic hemiparesis. Ann Neurol 23:115–124, 1988.

72. Price R: Mechanical spasticity evaluation techniques. Crit Rev Phys Rehabil Med 2:65–73, 1990.

73. Rahamimoff R, Lev-Tov A, Meiri H: Primary and secondary regulation of quantal transmitter release: Calcium and sodium. J Exp Biol 89:5–18, 1980.

74. Renshaw B: Influence of discharge of motoneurons upon excitation of neighboring motoneurons. J Neurophysiol 4:167–183, 1941.

75. Robinson CJ, Kett NA, Bolam JM: Spasticity in spinal cord injured patients: Short term effects of surface electrical stimulation. Arch Phys Med Rehabil 69:598–604, 1988.

76. Robinson CJ, Kett NA, Bolam JM: Spasticity in spinal cord injured patients: Initial measures and long term effects of surface electrical stimulation. Arch Phys Med Rehabil 69:862–868, 1988.

77. Rosenthal J: Post-tetanic potentiation at the neuromuscular junction of the frog. J Physiol 203:121–133, 1969.

78. Sinkjaer T, Toft E, Larsen K, et al: Non-reflex and reflex mediated ankle joint stiffness in multiple sclerosis patients with spasticity. Muscle Nerve 16:69–76, 1993.

79. Smith DO, Franke C, Rosenheimer JL, et al: Glutamate-activated channels in adult rat ventral spinal cord cells. J Neurophysiol 66:369–378, 1991.

80. Speelman JD: Cervical epidural spinal cord stimulation in infantile encephalopathy. Ned Tijdschr Geneeskd 134:1732–1735, 1990.

81. Spencer WA, Thompson RF, Neilson DR: Response decrement of the flexion reflex in the acute spinal cat and transient restoration by strong stimuli. J Neurophysiol 29:221–239, 1966.

82. Spencer WA, Thompson RF, Neilson DR: Decrement of ventral root electrotonus and intracellularly recorded PSPs produced by iterated cutaneous afferent volleys. J Neurophysiol 29:253–274, 1966.

83. Stanton PK, Chattarji S, Sejnowski TJ: 2-amino-3-phosphonopropionic acid, an inhibitor of glutamate-stimulated phosphoinositide turnover, blocks induction of homosynaptic long-term depression, but not potentiation, in rat hippocampus. Neurosci Lett 127:61–66, 1991.

84. Stefanovska A, Gros N, Vodovnik L, et al: Chronic electrical stimulation of the modification of spasticity in hemiplegic patients. Scand J Rehabil Med Suppl 17:115–121, 1988.

85. Stefanovska A, Rebersek S, Bajd T, Vodovnik L: Effects of electrical stimulation on spasticity. Crit Rev Phys Med Rehabil 3:59–99, 1991.

86. Steinbok P, Langill L, Cochrane DD, Keyes R: Observations on electrical stimulation of lumbosacral nerve roots in children with and without lower limb spasticity. Childs Nerv Syst 8:376–382, 1992.

87. Thilmann AF, Fellows SJ, Garms E: The mechanisms of spastic muscle hypertonus variation in reflex gain over the time course of spasticity. Brain 114:233–244, 1991.

88. Vodovnik L, Bowman BR, Winchester P: Effects of electrical stimulation on spinal spasticity. Scand J Rehabil Med 19:29–34, 1984.

89. Vodovnik L, Stefanovska A, Bajd T: Effects of stimulation parameters on modification of spinal spasticity. Med Biol Eng Comput 25:439–442, 1987.

90. Wartenberg R: Pendulousness of the leg as a diagnostic test. Neurol 1:18–24, 1951.

91. Weinreich D: Ionic mechanism of post-tetanic potentiation at the neuromuscular junction of the frog. J Physiol 212:431–446, 1971.

92. Weiss PL, Hunter IW, Kearney RE: Human ankle joint stiffness over the full range of muscle activation levels. J Biomech 21:539–544, 1988.

93. Wickelgren BG: Habituation of spinal motoneurons. J Neurophysiol 30:1404–1438, 1967.

94. Windhorst U: Activation of renshaw cells. Prog Neurobiol 35:135–179, 1990.

95. Yamamoto T, Yaksh TL: Studies on the spinal interaction of morphine and the NMDA antagonist MK-801 on the hyperesthesia observed in a rat model of sciatic neuropathy. Neurosci Lett 135:67–70, 1992.

96. Zucker RS: Short-term synaptic plasticity. Ann Rev Neurosci 12:13–31, 1989.

ALBERTO ESQUENAZI, MD
BARBARA A. HIRAI, BS

ASSESSMENT AND MANAGEMENT OF GAIT DYSFUNCTION IN PATIENTS WITH SPASTIC STROKE OR BRAIN INJURY

Gait and Motion Analysis
  Laboratory
MossRehab Hospital (AE, BH)
  and
Department of Rehabilitation
  Medicine
Temple University School of
  Medicine (AE)
Philadelphia, Pennsylvania

Reprint requests to:
Alberto Esquenazi, MD
Director
Gait and Motion Analysis
  Laboratory
MossRehab Hospital
1200 West Tabor Road
Philadelphia, PA 19141-3099

This chapter is adapted from Esquenazi A, Hirai B: Assessment of
Gait and Orthotic Prescription.
Phys Med Rehabil Clin North Am
2:473–485, 1991; with permission.

Most survivors of brain insult or a stroke have the potential for the return of significant function and the resumption of useful lives. The average life expectancy for patients who survive the first month after a stroke is approximately 6 years;[8] after traumatic head injury, survival is even longer.[10] At least 70% of hemiplegic patients regain the ability to walk. This article discusses the factors affecting ambulation and possible interventions in patients with a brain insult.

Normal gait is a cyclic, highly automatic, stereotypic movement pattern that involves rhythmic, alternating motion of the trunk and extremities. In a normal individual, cycle-to-cycle variation of the movement is relatively low.[15] In healthy people, gait is a skill that is performed in a relatively uniform way. The three main functional goals of human ambulation are (1) to move from one place to another, (2) to move safely, and (3) to move efficiently.[6]

The gait of patients with spastic hemiparesis is frequently not safe or energy efficient. Compensatory movements necessary for ambulation produce abnormal displacement of the center of gravity, resulting in increased expenditure of energy. Cardiopulmonary fitness is impaired because of decreased intensity and frequency of ambulation. Impaired balance, sensory deficits, and foot drag all contribute to loss of balance, falls, and increased anxiety regarding ambulation.[13]

NORMAL LOCOMOTION

From the clinical standpoint, one must understand the events of the walking cycle so that pathologic locomotion can be correlated as to cause and effect during gait. From the perspective of one limb, the gait cycle has two basic components: the stance phase, during which the limb is in contact with the ground, and the swing phase, during which the limb is off the ground. The stance phase includes the following event and functional subphases: (1) initial contact, (2) loading response, (3) mid-stance, (4) terminal stance, and (5) preswing. The swing phase includes three functional subphases: (1) initial swing, (2) mid-swing, and (3) terminal swing[2] (Fig. 1).

A stride is one complete gait cycle. The stride period is the time from the initial contact of one foot until the next initial contact of the same foot. The stride period is useful for the purpose of comparison between patients. It is also useful to temporally normalize to this interval for the purpose of averaging strides within and between patients. The stride period (100%) is the sum of the stance period (60%) and the swing period (40%). These percentages have been calculated from normal patients walking at comfortable speed, and they vary greatly with changes in walking velocity. The stride length is equal to the distance covered during one stride period and should be equal for left and right strides. The stride also can be analyzed according to whether one or both feet are in contact with the floor. The double support is the period of time during which both feet are in contact with the ground. With increasing cadence, the double support period steadily decreases, and it disappears during running. Single support is the period when only one foot is in contact with the ground and is the swing period of the contralateral limb.

The step period is the time measured from an event in one foot to the subsequent occurrence of the same event in the other foot. The step period is useful for measuring asymmetry between left and right sides. Step length is the distance covered in the direction of progression during one step. Step time and length are fairly symmetric in normal individuals, and they are important parameters in patients. The cadence is the number of steps per minute. Gait velocity is the average horizontal speed of the body along the plane of progression.

Gait can be studied through the collection of a wide range of information. The variables that can be recorded can be grouped into the following categories: (1) temporal and stride measures, (2) kinematics, (3) kinetics, and (4) electromyography.[5]

Temporal and Spatial Descriptive Measures

In order to characterize gait, some basic output variables that concern the temporospatial structure and sequencing of the stance and swing phases can be

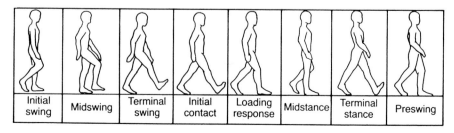

FIGURE 1.   The gait cycle.

measured. These data can be obtained by measuring the distances and timing involved in the floor contacts of the feet. In our laboratory, a device called the Electronic Gait Mat is used to extract this type of information. A left and right "footprint record" is obtained, and a printout is generated that provides information about walking velocity, cadence, stance, and swing times for each side as well as stride lengths and step lengths. Comparison of right and left parameters can be used to determine the extent of unilateral impairment.

Kinematics

Kinematics provides a description of movements without regard to the forces generating them. Early techniques to assess kinematics included the use of photographs and cinematographs. Other techniques have used accelerometers and electrogoniometers. Modern systems involve the use of high-speed video/film recording or, as in our laboratory, specialized optoelectronic apparatus in which active optical sources (infrared emitting diodes) attached to the patient serve as markers. Video and film (passive systems) are unique in their capacity to record events when instrumenting the patient is unacceptable. Their liability is the subsequent need to process the film and to convert the findings into quantitative data by manual or semiautomatic digitization, which is time consuming and prone to error; individual marker identification usually requires manual intervention. Automatic digitization is possible when few markers are used and no crossing of trajectories occurs. Other problems include the limited sampling rates available and the need for enhanced lighting for high-speed cinema and video. With active optoelectronic systems, the coordinates of the diodes are generated directly by computer once the system has been set up and calibrated. Time coincidence between controller illumination and camera reception uniquely identifies each light-emitting diode. Once the kinematic information is available as coordinate data, it can be processed and displayed as stick figures that demonstrate the gait sequence in the imaged plane (Fig. 2). Joint angles can be computed and displayed as a function of time or as a percentage of the stride period. Velocities and accelerations also can be calculated.

Kinetics

Kinetic analysis deals with the forces, moments, and mechanical energies that develop during walking. Ground reaction forces are generally measured using a triaxial force platform. Two platforms should be placed adjacent to each other so that the forces transmitted through the contact surface for each foot can be recorded independently and simultaneously. The measured ground reaction forces are often normalized to body weight or expressed in newtons. In our laboratory, the ground reaction force vector is visualized and superimposed in real time on the video image of the walking subject using laser optics.

Electromyographic Patterns in Human Gait

The electromyographic (EMG) signal can be used as an indication of the neurologic control of muscle activation. Superficial muscles can be studied using surface electrodes. For underlying muscles, indwelling wire electrodes are necessary to record EMG activities.

In order to assess patient EMG profiles, the patterns obtained from the patient can be superimposed on normative data (including both a mean and

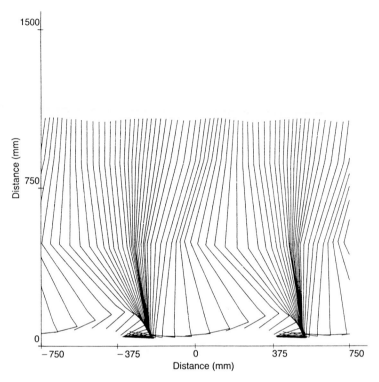

FIGURE 2.   Computer-generated stick figure representing human walking. (Information generated with Selspot II Multilab.)

variation measure) to identify how the patient's pattern deviates from the normal pattern. A particular muscle may be either over- or underactive during a given segment of the cycle. When such deviations are observed, they should be carefully correlated with the patient's kinematics. If there is clinical correlation between the EMG pattern and the observed kinematics, a fairly confident diagnostic conclusion may be drawn regarding the basis for an observed gait deviation. One should keep in mind that the EMG patterns are very sensitive to gait velocity and that it is not correct to compare a patient walking at slow speeds to an able-bodied person walking at a higher velocity with natural cadence.

LOWER LIMB ORTHOSES

Orthoses are devices that are applied to the external surface of a body part to achieve one or more of the following: (1) relief of pain, (2) immobilization of musculoskeletal segments by limiting/directing joint motion, (3) reduction of axial load, (4) prevention or correction of deformity, and (5) improvement of function. Overall, orthotics can be divided into two major categories: corrective and accommodative devices. Corrective devices are meant to improve the position of the limb segment, whether it be by stretching a contracture or correcting the alignment of skeletal structures.[1] Accommodative devices are meant to provide additional support to an already deformed tissue, to prevent any further deformity, and ultimately to improve function.

Orthoses can be further classified as static (resting) or dynamic, the latter permitting the movement of the involved joint(s) while controlling the direction or alignment of the movement and, at times, providing a substitute power source for weak muscles. The spectrum of orthotic devices available is quite broad, ranging from a simple plastic or leather device applied across one joint to a much more complex device made of a variety of materials and crossing multiple joints.[1]

Knowledge of the disease or disorder in question, functional anatomy, biomechanics, orthotic componentry, materials, and, finally, recognition of the anticipated functional outcome are essential for a proper prescription of an orthotic device. To achieve some universal terminology, orthotic devices are named in correct sequence by the joints they encompass, followed by the word "orthosis," as outlined in the early 1970s by the International Committee on Prosthetics and Orthotics. For example, an orthosis that crosses the ankle and the foot is named an AFO for ankle-foot orthosis. One that crosses the knee, ankle, and foot is called KAFO. More elaborate names or eponyms are typically given to such devices,[1] but universal language should be used whenever possible.

The orthotic components chosen depend on which functions they fulfill, but most orthoses consist of three basic elements: interface components, structural components, and joints. In orthoses of newer design it may be impossible to differentiate the joints from the structural and interface components, e.g., plastic AFO.[15]

The shoe is an integral part of any lower limb orthosis that includes the foot, because it serves as the foundation for the device and directly impacts its function. Correct shoe size must take into consideration fit while standing, because the foot configuration changes with weightbearing and spasticity.

The choice of materials in the fabrication of orthotics is expanding rapidly; the reader is referred to Redford[15] for a more comprehensive review. The two primary materials are plastics and metals. Plastics have the benefits of light weight, total contact, adjustable flexibility, the ability to reshape or remold, and a more cosmetic appearance than that provided by metal implants.

Metal orthoses often have the advantage of increased durability and, in the hands of a skilled orthotist, built-in adjustability. With the advent of new materials such as carbon graphite and extruded plastic, the advantages of maximal tension strength, light weight, and ease of adjustability are available. Factors that dictate the type of material used in orthotic fabrication include the length of time the orthosis will be used, the amount of forces applied across the orthosis, and the amount of axial weight loading.

A complete orthotic prescription should include the joints it encompasses and suggest the desired biomechanical alignment and materials of fabrication. When the orthosis is ready, it should be evaluated off and on the patient to ensure proper fit and function. When these characteristics are achieved, appropriate training of the patient and family should begin.

Orthotic management is best accomplished in the majority of hemiplegic patients with the use of plastic molded orthoses. They provide more intimate contact with better distribution of the controlling/corrective forces over a larger area. These devices tend to be more cosmetic and, hence, better accepted. Patients are permitted to exchange shoes as long as constant heel height is maintained to avoid altering the dynamic alignment. Plastic materials are lighter and easier to maintain. The recent availability of adjustable ankle joints that can be attached to plastic orthoses has eliminated a major disadvantage of these devices. Adjustments to the biomechanical alignment and fit require an orthotist.

Lack of sensation and fluctuating edema are relative contraindications to the prescription of plastic molded orthoses. If the patient has adequate visual perception and cognition and good social support, he or she can compensate for these deficits and receive the added benefits provided by plastic braces.

Metal/leather orthoses continue to have a definite place in the treatment of hemiplegic patients. Patients are being transferred to rehabilitation programs much earlier than in the past, and the length of stay in the rehabilitation programs has decreased significantly. Predicting the final rehabilitative outcome of these patients so early in their recovery may be difficult. The ability to adjust the biomechanical alignment of the orthosis with simple tools or to convert a controlling force into an assistive one in order to respond to the patient's needs is an important advantage.

Proper biomechanical alignment of any orthosis is critical to the maximization of the patient's ability to ambulate. Malalignment can and does prevent patients from becoming functional ambulators; patients with better recovery may be able to compensate for inadequate orthotic alignment. In patients in whom free joint motion is required, close correlation between the orthotic and the anatomic joint centers of rotation is mandatory to avoid a discrepancy in motion that ultimately will produce pain, skin breakdown, and other preventable problems.

PATHOLOGIC GAIT IN SPASTIC HEMIPLEGIA

The disturbances of the temporal, spatial, kinematic, and EMG patterns of hemiplegic gait are well documented[7] and can be extended to brain-injured patients. Although differences occur from patient to patient, some generalities have been demonstrated, including a decrease in walking velocity with a shorter stride length, shorter stance phase, and increased swing time for the involved limb.[14] A decrease in weightbearing on the involved limb is noted, as well as a decrease in single support time. The unaffected limb has increased stance time.

The stance phase abnormalities include forefoot first or flat foot initial contact rather than heel first; in addition, ankle inversion may occur, causing the medial border of the foot not to contact the ground. In this phase of the gait cycle, incomplete knee extension may be noted. Hyperextension of the knee is common, with continued equinovarus deformity of the ankle during mid-stance. During terminal stance, heel-off can occur early or late, and the pelvis may drop on the contralateral side.[12] Inadequate hip and knee flexion during the initial swing may result in toe drag. During mid-swing, a major problem is insufficient dorsiflexion. Inability to perform coordinated hip flexion and knee extension during terminal swing produces a shortened step length, which may be further complicated by insufficient ankle dorsiflexion.

From the functional perspective, one can categorize gait deficiencies on the basis of their timing with respect to the gait cycle. During the stance phase an abnormal base of support and limb instability may make walking unsafe, energy-inefficient, and possibly painful. Inadequate limb clearance and limb advancement during the swing phase interfere with safety and energy efficiency. A comparison of normal gait patterns to those exhibited by individuals with hemiplegia demonstrates differences in temporal, kinetic, and kinematic factors and muscle activation patterns across multiple joints.

In order to properly identify and evaluate the gait problems of patients with stroke or brain injury, the clinician must be able to understand what the problem is, where *and* when it is present, and why it occurs. Knowledge of the available orthotic devices and other interventions to correct the problem and the anatomic limitations of the patient as well as a thorough medical, cognitive, and social history are needed to determine the most appropriate intervention.[5]

Abnormal Base of Support

The lack of adequate base of support results in instability of the whole body. For this reason, the correction of abnormal ankle-foot posture by conservative means or, if these fail, by invasive or surgical methods, is essential. Equinovarus deformity is the most common pathologic lower limb posture in patients with stroke on brain injury. This abnormal posture results in an unstable base of support during the stance phase. The contact with the ground occurs with the forefoot first, and weight is borne primarily on the lateral border of the foot. This position is maintained during the stance phase. Limitation in dorsiflexion prevents forward progression of the tibia over the stationary foot, causing knee hyperextension and interference with terminal stance and preswing where lack of the propulsive phase is noted. During the swing phase there is a sustained plantar-flexed and inverted posture of the foot resulting in a limb clearance problem. Dynamic polyEMG demonstrates that prolonged activation of the gastrocnemius-soleus complex is the most common cause of plantar flexion. Inversion is the result of the abnormal activities of the tibialis posterior and/or anterior in combination with the gastrocnemius-soleus group. Other causes of an abnormal base of support include toe flexion or extension during the stance phase, particularly the hallux. This can produce significant pain and interference with weightbearing.

The use of an AFO to control the abnormal posture of the ankle during the stance and swing phase should be attempted. An ankle inversion strap or pad should be used to assist in controlling the inversion deformity. The orthosis should be attached to an orthopedic shoe and should include a plantar flexion stop to prevent ankle plantar flexion. If ankle clonus is triggered during the stance phase, a dorsiflexion stop should be used to prevent the stretch response. When cognition and sensation are not impaired or adequate social support exists for supervision, the use of a molded plastic ankle-foot orthosis (MAFO) with inversion control build-up is preferred. A long plastic foot-plate with soft padding in combination with a toe strap and an extra-depth shoe with high toe box can be used to accommodate the abnormal toe posture (Fig. 3).

Phenol motor point blocks to the hyperactive musculature can provide selective relief of spasticity with decreased deformity and improvement in function for 1–10 months.[9]

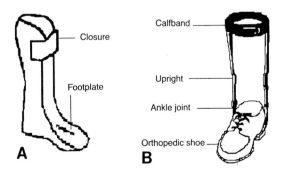

FIGURE 3.   *A*, molded ankle-foot orthosis and *B*, ankle-foot orthosis.

Abnormal Limb Stability

Knee flexion during the early stance phase produces limb instability. In patients with stroke or brain injury this problem is more commonly observed in the early phase of recovery, with flaccidity and weakness affecting the involved limb. The patient is unable to control the knee flexion moment during the early stance phase and is unable to walk. The dynamic polyEMG demonstrates shortened or uncoordinated activities of the quadriceps musculature. Occasionally, increased activities of the knee flexors also can be seen. If external means of knee control are provided through a KAFO, knee orthosis, or MAFO during early stance, the patient most likely will be able to maintain limb stability and to ambulate.

A KAFO with off-set knee joints, a rigid MAFO set in a few degrees of plantar flexion, or a shoe with a solid ankle-cushion heel (SACH)—a soft wedge in the heel of the shoe—provides knee stability by positioning the ground reaction force anterior to the knee mechanism. It is critical in this phase of the rehabilitation program that a knee extensor strengthening program be encouraged and maintained, as knee weakness is promoted by the muscle disuse that the orthotic intervention causes, as demonstrated in a 1989 study.[6]

Knee hyperextension present during the stance phase is the result of spasticity of the ankle plantar flexors, a plantar flexion contracture, or, less likely in stroke patients, compensation for knee weakness. This abnormal posture of the knee prevents adequate contralateral limb advancement. Orthotic management of this problem includes the use of an AFO with limited plantar flexion or, in the case of ankle plantar flexion contracture, the combination of an AFO and a heel lift (Fig. 4). These two options limit the knee hyperextension, while knee collapse is prevented if the alignment is appropriate. Correction of the deformity also can be obtained by decreasing the ankle plantar flexor spasticity, if present, with oral antispasticity agents, phenol motor point blocks, or surgery.

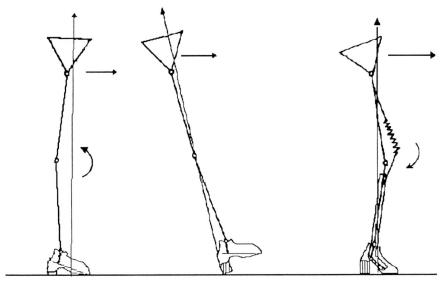

FIGURE 4. Effect of heel lift or ankle-foot orthosis in combination with a heel lift to control knee hyperextension.

Hip flexion during the stance phase is a less common gait deviation. When it occurs, trunk instability and significant interference with ambulation are produced. This problem is common in the early stage of recovery with flaccidity or in patients with significant flexor spasticity. In the latter group, dynamic polyEMG demonstrates an increase in the activity of the iliopsoas and possibly the rectus femoris. The use of a locked external hip joint, attached proximally to a pelvic belt and distally to a thigh corset, can be useful to control this gait deviation.[5] Hip hiking and contralateral trunk lean are needed as a compensation for limb advancement and clearance in swing.

Limb Clearance

During the swing phase, limb clearance and advancement occur. When limb clearance is inadequate, limb advancement is usually compromised. In patients with stroke or brain injury, the most common causes of limb clearance problems are lack of adequate hip flexion, knee flexion, and ankle dorsiflexion. The clinician needs to recognize the importance of coordinated lower limb motion during the swing phase. Not only the total joint displacement, but the synchronization of motion between the involved joints is essential to produce adequate limb clearance.

Stiff knee gait pattern is most commonly seen in patients with spastic hemiplegia. Patients are unable to flex the knee adequately, creating a large moment of inertia that increases the energy required to initiate the swing phase of the involved limb.[16] This requires patients to use ipsilateral hip and trunk and contralateral limb compensatory motions. Even if the ankle-foot system has an appropriate position, early swing toe drag is evident and can be corrected only by generating knee flexion or increasing the contralateral limb length.

One explanation for this problem can be found in the dynamic polyEMG, which demonstrates increased activities in the quadriceps muscles as a group or preferentially in the rectus femoris and vastus intermedius, with or without hamstring co-contraction. Lack of momentum because of decreased walking speed is another possible cause of this problem. Quadriceps phenol motor point blocks or surgical intervention may be useful. The application of electrical stimulation directly to the hamstrings or in the form of a nociceptive stimulus delivered to the sural nerve in the preswing phase when maximal hip extension occurs has been attempted for research purposes[3] (Fig. 5).

Inadequate hip flexion is also a cause of abnormal limb clearance. This problem effectively prevents physiologic "shortening" of the limb, producing a swing phase toe drag. The use of compensatory techniques such as hip adduction to advance the limb should be attempted. The use of a shoe lift to cause functional lengthening of the contralateral limb or the use of thigh corset with a waist belt to prevent lengthening of the affected limb by gravity can be attempted. The use of electrical stimulation directly to the iliopsoas has many problems with existing technology. Stimulation of the hamstrings or the sural nerve of the foot to elicit a flexor withdrawal has been attempted for research purposes, with improvement in some cases.

Increased hip adduction can interfere with ipsilateral and contralateral limb advancement and with other activities of daily living. Overactivity of the adductor musculature or imbalance of the abductor and adductor muscle groups is the main cause of this problem. Since many hemiplegic patients use the adductors to compensate for hip flexion in limb advancement, the clinician needs to be certain

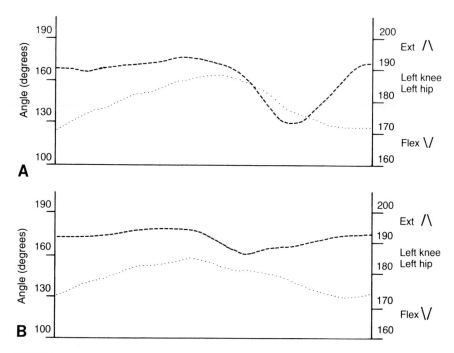

FIGURE 5. *A*, normal knee and hip range of motion during slow walking. The knee curve is dashed, and the corresponding axis is on the left. The hip curve is dotted, and the axis is shown on the right. *B*, stiff knee gait pattern. (Information generated with Selspot Multilab.)

that elimination of adductor activities does not render the patient nonambulatory. Percutaneous phenol obturator nerve block is the least invasive approach to this problem. Open phenolization and surgery are other available treatment options (see chapter 6).

Another common gait deviation in hemiplegic patients is limited knee extension during the late swing and early stance phases resulting from hamstring spasticity. This problem interferes with ipsilateral limb advancement, because the knee is flexed and is not able to easily "reach" the ground. Contralateral limb clearance is also affected, because a decrease in functional height requires increased hip and knee flexion to avoid foot drag.

Pelvic retraction affecting the involved limb during the gait cycle interferes with limb advancement, resulting in a shortened step. These two problems are not amenable to intervention with orthotics.

In adults and children with traumatic brain injury, bilateral problems can occur. The pattern of abnormality frequently will be common to both legs; in some cases an asymmetrical brain injury may result in extensor spasticity on one side and flexor spasticity on the other with resulting complex gait abnormalities.

SUMMARY

The basics of ambulation, gait analysis, and orthotic intervention as they apply to patients with hemiplegia and brain injury are reviewed here. The potential use of surgical and pharmacologic intervention is also discussed. The majority of patients surviving a stroke and other brain insults achieve limited ambulation, and the use of orthoses or other types of interventions is indicated in an attempt to optimize patients' functional capabilities and encourage improved functional level and quality of life.

REFERENCES

1. American Academy of Orthopaedic Surgeons: Atlas of Orthotics. St. Louis, Mosby, 1985.
2. Bampton S: A Guide to the Visual Examination of Pathological Gait. Philadelphia, Temple University-Moss Rehabilitation Hospital, 1979.
3. Craik R, Cozzens B, Miyazaki S: Enhancement of swing phase clearance through sensory stimulation. Proceedings of the Fourth Annual Conference on Rehabilitation Engineering. Chicago, Rehabilitation Engineering Society of North America, 1981, pp 217–219.
4. De JB, Saunders MB, Inman VT, Eberhart HD: Major determinants in normal and pathological gait. J Bone Joint Surg 35A:543–558, 1953.
5. Esquenazi A, Hirai B: Assessment of gait and orthotic prescription. Phys Med Rehabil Clin North Am 2:473–485, 1991.
6. Esquenazi A, Wikoff E, Hirai B, et al: Effects of a plantar flexed plastic molded ankle foot orthoses on gait pattern and lower limb muscle strength. Proceedings of the Sixth World Congress of the International Society for Prosthetics and Orthotics, Kobe, Japan, 1989, p 208.
7. Finch L, Barbeau H: Hemiplegic gait: New treatment strategies. Phsyiother Can 38:36–40, 1986.
8. Garraway WM, Whisnant JP, Drury I: The changing pattern of survival following stroke. Stroke 14:699, 1983.
9. Glenn MB: Nerve blocks. In Glenn MB, Whyte J (eds): The Practical Management of Spasticity in Children and Adults. Philadelphia, Lea & Febiger, 1990, pp 227–258.
10. Heiden JS, Small R, Canton W, et al: Severe head injury and outcome: A prospective study. In Popp AJ, Bourke RS, Nelson LR, et al (eds): Neural Trauma. New York, Raven, 1979, pp 181–183.
11. Inman VT, Ralston HJ, Todd F: Human Walking. Baltimore, Williams & Wilkins, 1981.
12. Montgomery J: Assessment and treatment of locomotor deficits in stroke. In Duncan W, Badke M (eds): Stroke Rehabilitation: The Recovery of Motor Control. Chicago, Year Book, 1987, pp 223–257.
13. Olney S, Monga T, Costigan P: Mechanical energy of walking of stroke patients. Arch Phys Med Rehabil 67:92–98, 1986.
14. Peat M, Dubo H, Winter D, et al: Electromyographic temporal analysis of gait: Hemiplegic locomotion. Arch Phys Med Rehabil 57:421–425, 1976.
15. Redford JB: Orthotics: General principles. Phys Med Rehabil State Art Rev 1:1–10, 1987.
16. Winter DA: Pathologic gait diagnosis with computer-averaged electromyographic profiles. Arch Phys Med Rehabil 65:393–398, 1984.

MICHAEL S. PINZUR, MD

UPPER EXTREMITY SURGERY FOR THE SPASTIC PATIENT

From the Loyola University Stritch
  School of Medicine
Maywood, Illinois

Reprint requests to:
Michael S. Pinzur, MD
Professor of Orthopaedic Surgery
Department of Orthopaedic
  Surgery
Loyola University Medical Center
2160 South First Avenue
Maywood, IL 60153

In a 1991 editorial in the *Journal of Hand Surgery,* Brian Roper reminded hand surgeons that surgery does have a role in the management of adult patients with upper motor neuron lesions.[26] While a small amount of literature exists for surgical treatment of acquired spasticity in the lower extremities of adults, even less information deals with the upper extremities. This is probably related to the complexity of the objective evaluation of functional disability, rehabilitation potential, and outcome analysis in this heterogenous population. Keenan[4] has been able to show that balance is the best predictor of a patient's ability to walk following a stroke. There is no similar simple predictor of upper extremity function.

In order to evaluate the rehabilitation potential of such patients and to develop a reasonable rationale for surgical intervention, one must possess a simple model for adult acquired spasticity due to stable, nonprogressive upper motor neuron deficit.

MODEL OF SPASTICITY

The deformities seen in patients with spasticity are either dynamic, static, or, more often, a combination of both. Dynamic deformity is produced by unbalanced muscle hypertonicity. Under anesthesia, or following a diagnostic anesthetic nerve block, the spastic deformity can be fully corrected by passive movement. Static deformity is the result of fixed contracture produced by connective tissue cross-linking within muscles, ligaments, and joints. Static contracture cannot be passively corrected, even under anesthesia. With the combination of dynamic and static deformity, only the dynamic component can be passively corrected under anesthesia.

Spasticity is a complex disorder characterized neurologically by loss of descending inhibition, afferent excitation, and uncovering of more primitive motor patterns. The newborn has reflexic activity but lacks the higher brain inhibitory centers to modulate these activities, as evidenced by the "startle" response. As the child grows and matures, he or she develops integration and modulation of these primitive motor patterns, which gradually mature into gross and, eventually, selective motor control. Traumatic brain injury damages these inhibitory pathways by diaschisis or shear and uncovers the characteristic synergic patterns of muscle activity associated with spasticity. Rehabilitation strives to re-educate and unmask alternative inhibitory modulatory controls, both during spontaneous recovery and when the neurologic recovery stabilizes.

When planning intervention, we use a simple agonist-antagonist motor imbalance model. In normal movement, smooth balance is assumed between the muscles on both sides of a joint, i.e., agonist and antagonist muscles. For example, when grasping an object, balanced muscle activity occurs between wrist and finger flexor and extensor muscle groups, with relatively greater activity of the flexors during grasp activities. The spastic patient has a loss of this balance between opposing muscle groups. Due to the imbalance, patients will co-contract and assume an unbalanced, poorly functional position. Consequently, they will not be able to perform tasks.

In our model for intervention, we use the length-strength characteristics of the involved muscle groups—the so-called Blix curve. There is an optimal muscle length for achieving the greatest force of contraction. If the muscle is surgically lengthened, it is placed at a less advantageous position in its length-strength relationship, thus weakening its force of contraction. By lengthening the agonist muscle that is producing the dynamic deformity, the deforming motor force and the stretch reflex are weakened. Motor balance across the joint is thus achieved by weakening the agonist deforming motor force and potentially augmenting the antagonist with a tendon transfer.

Intervention: Timing and Goals

Invasive intervention is generally avoided during the acute recovery phase. Standard functional rehabilitation is used during the acute period, which lasts approximately 6 months following stroke and up to 18 months following traumatic brain injury. Invasive intervention is delayed until the patient's recovery clearly reaches a plateau or until deformities impair the rehabilitation effort. Early intervention, when necessary, should be reversible. Early intervention generally is limited to percutaneous nerve blocks with long-acting anesthetics. Phenol nerve blocks should be avoided in the upper extremity to avoid potentially disabling anesthesia or the dysesthesia frequently seen when phenol nerve blocks are performed on mixed motor and sensory nerves of the upper extremity. When a phenol nerve block is indicated to overcome a severe early spasticity pattern, an open phenol block can be used to obtain strictly a motor block.[13]

Invasive intervention can be considered for both functional or nonfunctional goals. Surgical release of static contracture is generally performed to assist nursing care or hygiene when the fixed contracture, with or without a spasticity component, produces skin maceration or breakdown. Static contracture release has a functional use when it is performed to improve upper extremity "tracking," i.e., arm swing, during walking.

Most of the upper extremity surgery performed in spastic patients has the goal of increasing function. The goal may be simply to improve placement, enabling use of the hand as a "paperweight," or to achieve improved fine motor control. In patients with prehensile potential, surgery may be entertained to make the "one-handed" patient "two-handed" by increasing involved hand function from no function to assistive, or from assistive to independent.

When the goal of surgery is to improve function, patients must first be screened for cognitive capacity, motivation, and body image awareness. Patients must have the cognitive skills and learning capability to participate in therapy following surgery and to functionally use their newly acquired skills at the completion of their rehabilitation program. If not motivated, they will not participate in the prolonged effort necessary to achieve meaningful functional improvement. Patients with poor stereognosis or neglect, such as those with a poor body image, will find that their involved hand will "drift" in space and not be "available" for use if they have not been carefully trained in visual compensation techniques.

EVALUATION

Once it has been determined that the patient has the potential to make functional upper extremity gains with surgery, one must obtain a semi-objective functional grading score, within the constraints of upper extremity spasticity variability.[26] Patients are initially screened for cognitive capacity, motivation, and body image awareness. Appropriate consultation with providers specializing in neurology, physical medicine, psychology, occupational therapy, or social work is frequently beneficial. Patients who pass the initial screen are graded on the basis of hand placement, proprioception and sensibility, and voluntary motor control.

Trunk and shoulder stability is a prerequisite for placing the limb in space. Shoulder abduction and forward flexion combined with graded elbow extension place the hand in position for task performance.[28] Spastic synergy patterning limits prepositioning of the hand. A median nerve block at the mid arm is performed with 10 ml of 0.5% bupivacaine hydrochloride (Marcaine) to evaluate the dynamic and static components of the deformity and the magnitude of the dynamic deformity limiting hand pre-positioning.

Grading of hand placement is outlined in Table 1. Moberg has used two-point discrimination as a measure of sensibility and rehabilitation potential in quadriplegic

TABLE 1.   Hand Placement/Pre-Positioning

Grade	Characteristics
0	Severe spastic synergy patterning at the shoulder and elbow; volitional elbow extension is absent
1	Shoulder internal rotation and adduction overpowering does not greatly limit forward placement of the limb; volitional elbow flexion is present in extension but weak; median nerve block may enhance forward positioning
2	Forward limb placement is not hindered; volitional elbow extension is present but is greatly overpowered by the flexors; median nerve block improves positioning, but the spastic pattern remains present
3	Shoulder limitation is minimal; dynamic elbow flexor overpowering persists but can be overcome; median nerve block may eliminate the spastic pattern
4	Forward hand placement and active shoulder motion are virtually normal; a small amount of elbow spasticity may be present when the patient is anxious

TABLE 2.   Sensibility: Two-Point Discrimination

Grade 1	11+ mm
Grade 2	6–10 mm
Grade 3	1–5 mm

patients.[11,12] We have had similar experience and thus use his scale as a measure of sensibility and stereognosis (Table 2). Voluntary motor control tends to fall into six groups (Table 3). By combining these measures of evaluation, patients can be grouped into eight functional grade levels (Table 4). Patients in functional levels 0, 1, and 2 show no functional prehensile capacity; those in levels 3, 4, and 5 possess increasing assistive function; and patients in levels 6 and 7 have the capacity for independent hand function.[16] Dynamic electromyography is only used when delineation of phasic motor activity is essential for surgical planning.[18,19]

SURGERY

Shoulder

Shoulder deformities are characterized as dynamic (spastic), static (contracture), and flail. Tendon transfer does not play a role in reconstruction of adult acquired spastic shoulder disorders, due to the absence of available motors, much as in brachial plexus palsy and other acquired paralytic disorders. In addition to the absence of available motors, patients with both the dynamic and static disorder exhibit adduction and internal rotation deformity.

Dynamic or static adduction/internal rotation deformity may restrict hygiene or produce skin maceration in the axilla. The first line of treatment is passive stretching. If a program of daily passive stretching is unsuccessful and the shoulder cannot externally rotate to neutral, release of the pectoralis major and subscapularis tendons is indicated. This procedure can be performed through a 5–8 cm incision in the deltopectoral groove. The pectoralis major tendon is transected, and the

TABLE 3.   Voluntary Motor Capacity

Grade	Characteristics
0	Primarily a static deformity, with the wrist and fingers clasped tightly in a pronated fist; no volitional motor capacity is seen in flexion or extension; median nerve block provides little improvement in volitional release, but clasp may be slightly decreased
1	The resting position remains a pronated clasp; this deformity is primarily dynamic; volitional grip is present but not released; volitional wrist extension is absent or weak; and finger extension is absent; release is improved with nerve block; finger extension is absent
2	Position assumes a tight clasped posture with initiation of volitional activity; release is accomplished through tenodesis action; wrist extension is present with finger extension absent or weak; median nerve block enhances extensors and may "uncover" apparently absent finger extensors
3	Grasp and release can be initiated with flexors dominating; wrist extension is accomplished with fingers flexed and finger extension with wrist flexed; prehension is accomplished in a flexed position; median nerve block enhances positioning, dynamic balance, and functional capacity
4	Patients possess gross dynamic balance but are not able to perform fine motor tasks
5	Patients can perform fine motor tasks with generally more "motor planning" than can normal patients

TABLE 4. Hand Functional Levels

Functional Level	Hand Placement	Two-point Discrimination	Volitional Motor Control
No functional prehensile capacity			
0	0	1	0
1	1	1	1
2	2	1–2	2
Increasing assistive function			
3	3	2	2
4	3–4	2	3
5	3–4	2	4
Independent hand function			
6	4	2–3	4–4+
7	4	3	5

subscapularis muscle is freed from the anterior shoulder joint capsule and then transected. Any other offending muscle units can be released through the same or additional small incisions. A simple sling is attached and a passive stretching program is begun immediately following surgery.[15]

Painless inferior subluxation of the shoulder joint is common in spastic patients. It usually occurs in the paralyzed, or weakened, upper extremity, due to the absence of counterbalancing muscle tone maintaining the shoulder in the joint. The capsuloligamentous complex attenuates and the shoulder subluxes inferiorly. This situation is generally painless, and a sling is recommended only if the flail limb gets "in the way." When painful, any of a number of commercially available arm slings will usually resolve the symptoms. If symptoms persist, the biceps tendon can be used as a static sling to reduce the subluxation. The biceps tendon is identified in the deltopectoral groove. It is looped over the coracoid process of the scapula, reducing the shoulder joint, and then secured to the coracoid process with a bone stable or nonabsorbable suture[20] (Fig. 1).

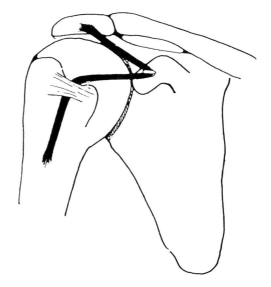

FIGURE 1. Biceps tenodesis. The biceps tendon is looped over, and secured to, the coracoid process of the scapula, reducing the inferiorly subluxed humeral head.

Elbow

Dynamic deformities of the elbow are generally due to spasticity of the brachioradialis, biceps, and brachialis muscles.[5] This overpowering of the elbow flexors limits the patient's ability to place the hand in space. The dynamic component of the deformity can be assessed by median nerve block performed at the mid arm from a medial approach in the interval between biceps and triceps muscles. When motor balance about the elbow is limited by increased muscle tone in the elbow flexors, improved balance and, hence, hand placement can be achieved by step-cut lengthening of the biceps and fractional musculotendinous lengthening of the brachialis, as described by Mital.[10,16]

One occasionally sees a patient with the reverse dynamic deformity, which is due to increased muscle tone in the triceps. These patients can place their hands in space but have difficulty bringing the involved hand from the periphery to the center of their functional sphere. Diagnostic motor nerve block is accomplished by motor nerve block at the point of entry of the motor nerve to the triceps muscle. When the dynamic deformity is sufficient to limit the patient's functional activities, V-Y lengthening of the triceps can be performed.[21]

Occasionally, severe static contracture cannot be adequately corrected by simple muscle lengthening or release. In these situations, a more extensive release, combined with joint capsule release when necessary, can be accomplished through a lateral incision, releasing the lateral intermuscular septum.[1]

Wrist and Hand

Surgery to increase functional prehension is performed in patients with some functional capacity. Using our functional grading system, the goal of surgery is to upgrade a patient from no function (levels 0, 1, 2) to assistive prehensile hand function (levels 3, 4, 5), or from assistive to independent (levels 6 and 7) functional prehension. The predominant deformity is wrist and finger flexion and pronation. Elbow flexor spasticity frequently accompanies this deformity, so elbow flexor lengthening is often performed at the same time.

When flexor spasticity is not too severe, or in older patients in whom surgery requiring extensive dissection is not warranted, fractional musculotendinous lengthening of flexor digitorum sublimis and profundus, combined with step-cut lengthening of the flexor pollicis longus and overlengthening of the flexor carpi radialis and flexor carpi ulnaris, is sufficient to balance the deformity (Fig. 2). Patients are splinted in the neutral position following surgery, with active motion beginning 48 hours postoperatively. This early active motion is initiated in order to achieve optimal agonist-antagonist muscle balance.[6,16]

When patients have voluntary control of both wrist and finger flexors and extensors, with overpowering of the flexors, the hand is pre-positioned in a nonfunctional flexed position. Improved pre-positioning can be obtained without weakening the agonist deforming flexors by flexor-pronator origin release. First described by Page in 1923[14] and resurrected by Braun[2] and Sakellarides,[27] it changes the arc of motion of the spastic hand to a more functional arc without sacrificing strength. The surgery is more extensive than simple musculotendinous lengthening, involving surgical dissection about the origin of the flexor muscle mass at the elbow with an extensive dissection about the course of median and ulnar nerves[22] (Fig. 3).

Patients who do not have voluntary control of the finger extensors are incapable of opening their involved hand. They can grasp but not release. While

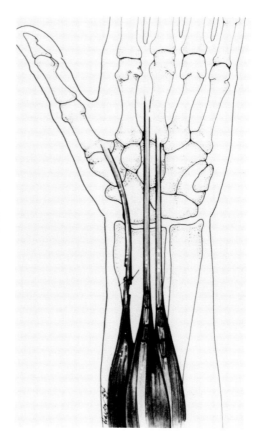

FIGURE 2. Fractional musculotendinous lengthening of the finger flexors is combined with step-cut lengthening of the flexor pollicis longus and overlengthening of the wrist flexors.

improved with fractional musculotendinous lengthening, they do not achieve the gains seen in patients with voluntary finger extensor control. Many of these patients also possess out-of-phase electrical activity of the brachioradialis, showing electrical activity during elbow extension, as opposed to its normal period of action during elbow flexion (Fig. 4). This allows the brachioradialis to be used as an "in-phase" tendon transfer to the extensor digitorum communis to accomplish hand opening, i.e., grip release (Fig. 5).

We recently have collected a small group of patients with a combination of static and dynamic deformity of such magnitude that the above procedures were not sufficient to accomplish adequate hand positioning to achieve functional prehension. In these patients, we have achieved relative flexor muscle "lengthening" by removing the carpal bones and surgically fusing the radius to the third metacarpal (Fig. 6).[24]

Rarely, patients will have voluntary grasp and release but will be poorly pre-positioned due to isolated wrist flexor spasticity. This is difficult to differentiate from combined wrist and finger spasticity. With the wrist positioned at neutral or in slight dorsiflexion, the patient should be able to easily open and close his or her hand. If so, step-cut overlengthening (so the wrist flexor hypertonicity will not recur) of flexor carpi radialis and ulnaris is performed. If the patient is not able to open and close the hand easily, the finger and thumb flexors will need to be lengthened.

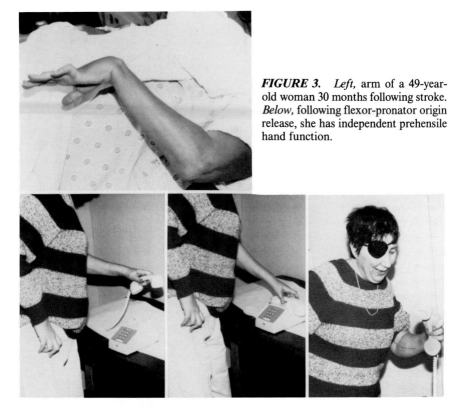

FIGURE 3. *Left,* arm of a 49-year-old woman 30 months following stroke. *Below,* following flexor-pronator origin release, she has independent prehensile hand function.

In patients with no voluntary control who are not candidates for functional reconstructive surgery, severe spasticity and contracture may be painful, may produce skin maceration, or may restrict hygiene. In these patients, contracture release without risk for the development of reverse extension contracture can be accomplished by sublimis-to-profundus (STP) tendon transfer. In this procedure, the flexor carpi radialis and ulnaris tendons are released or overlengthened and a

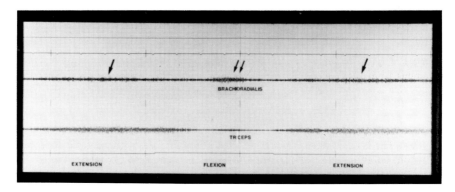

FIGURE 4. Dynamic electromyogram exhibiting "out-of-phase" activity of the brachioradialis muscle during elbow extension, allowing its use as an "in-phase" tendon transfer to accomplish hand opening.

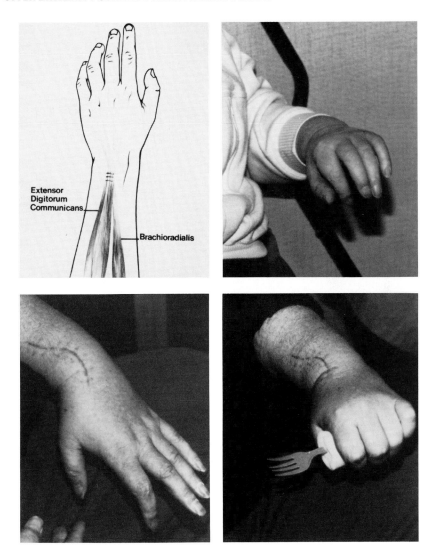

FIGURE 5. *Upper left,* operative schematic of brachioradialis to extensor digitorum communis tendon transfer used to achieve hand opening in patients with no voluntary finger extension. *Upper right,* preoperatively, the patient was not able to open her hand. *Lower left,* postoperative hand position. *Lower right,* functional prehension.

step-cut lengthening of the flexor pollicis longus is performed in combination with the STP. The STP is performed by suturing together then transecting the flexor digitorum sublimis tendons just proximal to the transverse carpal ligament, i.e., carpal tunnel, which is released. The flexor digitorum profundus tendons also are sutured together and transected at the musculotendinous junction. The sutures are tied together, releasing the deformity.[3] To prevent the development of an intrinsic plus deformity, the motor branch of the ulnar nerve is transected just after splitting from the sensory branch.[7]

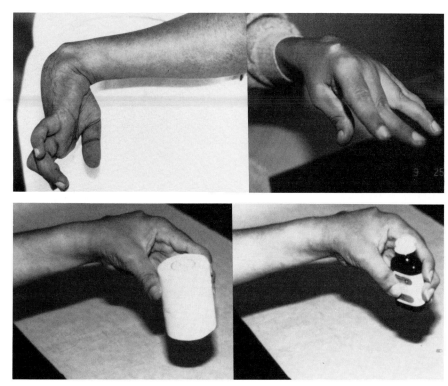

FIGURE 6. *Upper left,* hand prior to carpectomy and wrist fusion. *Others,* hand function 5 years following surgery.

A thumb-in-palm deformity may be a dynamic deformity due to absence of opponens muscle activity, or it may be static due to contracture of the muscles of the thenar eminence. The dynamic type, due to loss of active thumb opposition, can be improved with release of the tendon sheath of the flexor pollicis longus. This allows the tendon to bowstring and act as a substitute opponens, improving pinch grip[25] (Fig. 7).

Contracture with or without spasticity of the first dorsal interosseous muscle leads to narrowing of the space between the first and second metacarpals. Correction is obtained by release of the muscle from the radial shaft of the second metacarpal and release of the muscle insertion into the proximal phalanx of the thumb. If the deforming force is due to thenar muscle contracture, with or without spasticity, correction is obtained by palmar release of the involved muscles from their origins about the periphery of the thenar eminence.[9]

Sterling Bunnell frequently stated that "…when you have nothing, a little is a lot." That statement is true in spastic patients. Surgery does not replace, but only augments, a carefully planned rehabilitation program following the development of acquired spasticity in an adult. When patients reach a plateau in functional recovery, or when deformity impairs the rehabilitation effort, a surgical intervention should be considered.

FIGURE 7. *Above,* before and *Below,* after release of the flexor pollicis longus tendon sheath to accomplish improved functional prehension.

REFERENCES

1. Botte MJ, Keenan MA: Reconstructive surgery in the upper extremity in the patient with head trauma. J Head Trauma Rehabil 2:34–45, 1987.
2. Braun RM, Mooney V, Nickel VL: Flexor-origin release for pronation-flexion deformity of the forearm and hand in the stroke patient. J Bone Joint Surg 52A:907–920, 1970.
3. Braun RM, Vise GT, Roper B: Preliminary experience with the superficialis-to-profundus tendon transfer in the hemiplegic upper extremity. J Bone Joint Surg 56A:466–472, 1974.
4. Keenan MA, Perry J, Jordan C: Factors affecting balance and ambulation following stroke. Clin Orthop 182:165–171, 1984.
5. Keenan MA, Haider TT, Stone LR: Dynamic electromyography to access elbow spasticity. J Hand Surg 15A:607–614, 1990.
6. Keenan MA, Adams RA, Garland DE, Waters RL: Results of fractional lengthening of the finger flexors in adults with upper extremity spasticity. J Hand Surg 12A:575–581, 1987.
7. Keenan MA, Korchek JI, Botte MJ, et al: Results of transfer of the flexor digitorum superficialis tendons to the flexor digitorum profundus tendons in adults with acquired spasticity of the hand. J Bone Joint Surg 69A:1127–1132, 1987.
8. [Reference deleted.]
9. Matev I: Surgery of the spastic thumb-in-palm deformity. J Hand Surg 16B:127–132, 1991.
10. Mital MA: Lengthening of the elbow flexors in cerebral palsy. J Bone Joint Surg 61A:515–522, 1979.
11. Moberg E: Reconstructive hand surgery in tetraplegia, stroke, and cerebral palsy: Some basic concepts in physiology and neurology. J Hand Surg 1B:29–34, 1976.
12. Moberg E: Criticism and study of methods for examining sensibility in the hand. Neurology 12:8–19, 1962.
13. Moore TJ, Anderson RB: The use of open phenol blocks to the motor branches of the tibial nerve in adult acquired spasticity. Foot Ankle 11:219–221, 1991.
14. Page CM: An operation for the relief of flexion-contracture in the forearm. J Bone Joint Surg 5A:233–234, 1923.
15. Perry J, Waters RL: Orthopaedic evaluation and treatment of the stroke patient. Instr Course Lect 24:40–44, 1975.
16. Pinzur MS: Surgery to achieve dynamic motor balance in adult acquired spastic hemiplegia: A preliminary report. J Hand Surg 10A:547–553, 1985.

17. Pinzur MS: Functional surgery in stroke and head injury. Complications in Orthopaedics May/June:73–77, 1990.
18. Pinzur MS, Wehner J, Kett N, Trilla M: Brachioradialis to finger extensor tendon transfer to achieve hand opening in acquired spasticity. J Hand Surg 13A:549–552, 1988.
19. Pinzur MS, Sherman RS, Dimonte-Levine P: Triceps spasticity in traumatic hemiplegia: Diagnosis and treatment. Arch Phys Med Rehabil 68:446–449, 1987.
20. Pinzur MS, Hopkins GE: Biceps tenodesis for painful inferior subluxation of the shoulder in adult acquired hemiplegia. Clin Orthop 206:100–103, 1986.
21. Pinzur MS, Sherman RS, Dimonte-Levine P: Triceps spasticity in traumatic hemiplegia: Diagnosis and treatment. Arch Phys Med Rehabil 68:446–449, 1987.
22. Pinzur MS: Flexor origin release and functional prehension in adult spastic hand deformity. J Hand Surg 16B:133–136, 1991.
23. Pinzur MS: Brachioradialis to finger extensor tendon transfer to achieve hand opening in acquired spastcity. J Hand Surg 13A:549–552, 1988.
24. Pinzur MS: Carpectomy and wrist function in severe spasticity of the hand. Orthopedics (in press).
25. Pinzur MS: Modified Moberg opponensplasty in acquired spastic hemiplegia. Orthopedics 8:1151–1152, 1985.
26. Roper B: Surgical treatment for upper motor neurone lesions [editorial]. J Hand Surg 16B:123, 1991.
27. Sakellarides HT, Mital MA, Lenzi WD: Treatment of pronation contractures of the forearm in cerebral palsy by changing the insertion of the pronator radii teres. J Bone Joint Surg 63A:645–652, 1981.
28. Sarrafin SK: Kinesiology and functional characteristics of the upper limb. In Bowker J, Michael J (eds): Atlas of Limb Prosthetics. St. Louis, Mosby-Year Book, 1992, pp 83–106.

CRAIG J. ANMUTH, DO
ALBERTO ESQUENAZI, MD
MARY ANN E. KEENAN, MD

LOWER EXTREMITY SURGERY
FOR THE SPASTIC PATIENT

From The Department of
  Orthopaedic Surgery
  and
The Department of Physical
  Medicine and Rehabilitation
Albert Einstein Medical Center and
MossRehab Hospital
  and
The Department of Physical
  Medicine and Rehabilitation
Temple University School of
  Medicine
Philadelphia, Pennsylvania

Reprint requests to:
Mary Ann E. Keenan, MD
Department of Orthopaedic
  Surgery
Albert Einstein Medical Center
5501 Old York Road
Philadelphia, PA 19141

Muscle spasticity is frequently encountered after disruption of motor pathways in the brain or spinal cord. Spasticity is a velocity-dependent increase in muscle tone that indicates that the muscle stretch reflex has become separated from the supraspinal inhibitory-modulation system. Some important disorders in which spasticity is seen include traumatic or anoxic brain injury, cerebrovascular accident, spinal cord injury, multiple sclerosis, and cerebral palsy. When spasticity affects the musculature of the upper and lower extremities, one can expect deficits in ambulation and activities of daily living. This chapter will concentrate on the surgical management of spasticity in the lower extremities. The general principles of treatment can be applied to the upper extremity as well.[12]

Muscle spasticity disrupts the functioning of an ordinarily balanced limb by creating unequal forces that act on the joints. When severe enough, these forces create muscle imbalance and may lead to deformity and ambulation dysfunction. It is important to assess motor recovery if one is considering surgical intervention to improve function. Surgery can be used to facilitate motor recovery, such as lengthening a tendon to change the point at which the muscle stretch reflex is triggered.[15]

In the surgical management of the spastic lower extremity, careful evaluation is necessary to determine how the forces acting on muscles and joints can be changed or manipulated to improve function. With surgery one can eliminate the deforming forces entirely by performing a tenotomy or neurectomy. With appropriate planning, the forces can be redirected to produce a different moment such as with a tendon transfer. The forces acting on a joint can be diminished by tendon lengthening procedures. Depending on the clinical picture, one method may be followed alone or may be combined with any of the others for a result that will promote balance of the forces acting on a joint. Correcting the deforming forces may allow a patient to bear weight on the lower extremity, sit, or perform activities of daily living. Surgical management also can be considered, with the goal of correcting fixed contractures in a nonfunctional limb. Lastly, fusion can be carried out to stabilize a joint if it is determined that the forces acting on the joint cannot be fully controlled using soft tissue procedures alone.

The surgical approach to treating muscle spasticity involves acting on the peripheral level. By manipulating muscle tone, the desired rehabilitation goals may be more easily obtained. The timing of a surgical intervention should depend on the neurologic situation. Surgery should be performed when the neurologic status is stable and not improving or deteriorating.

PREOPERATIVE EVALUATION

Determination of Goals

Extremity function requires that complex and highly organized mechanisms work together in unison. Surgical goals must be practical and clearly understood by the patient, the family, and the rehabilitation team. The initial assessment should include an evaluation of cognition and communication skills, which is done during the physical examination of the patient.[8,24] Ideally, the patient should be capable of following simple commands and should also be able to cooperate with a postoperative therapy program. The patient also should have sufficient cognition to incorporate the improved motor function into the use of the extremity during ambulation or activities of daily living. Adequate memory is useful for the patient to retain what is taught postoperatively, but lack of necessary cognition or communication skills is not an absolute contraindication to surgery if clear rehabilitation goals are identified prior to performing the procedure. A simple example would be performing a hip adductor release to allow adequate nursing and hygiene care in a nonambulatory patient, thereby preventing further complications such as skin breakdown.

Evaluation of Joint Mobility

During the preoperative evaluation it is essential to determine the range of motion at each joint and ascertain whether the forces acting on the joints are from increased tone, myostatic contracture, or a bony deformity.[7] When testing range of motion, the examiner should use slow motions to avoid activating the stretch response, which will exacerbate the spasticity. When uncertainty remains regarding whether a restriction in joint motion is secondary to spasticity or contracture, a diagnostic nerve block can be performed with lidocaine to give temporary muscle relaxation. It is also necessary to rule out a bony deformity that could be causing limited range of motion. The clinician should have a high index of suspicion for fractures, dislocations, heterotopic bone formation, and arthritis.[6,21]

The spasticity associated with traumatic brain injury is often seen in combination with multiple trauma. The presence and healing status of fractures and peripheral nerve injury must be evaluated on admission to the rehabilitation facility.[6,21] It is not uncommon for a fracture or peripheral nerve injury to be missed while other more obvious or life-threatening injuries are being treated. With peripheral nerve injury, lower motor neuron findings should exist rather than the upper motor neuron finding of spasticity. Hence, the pattern of involvement seen clinically will distinguish between neurologic deficits secondary to peripheral nerve injury versus those resulting from central nervous system lesions.[2,3] Fractures also should be suspected in a stroke patient who had an associated fall.

Standard radiographic examination will detect most fractures or dislocations. When radiographs fail to detect fracture and index of suspicion remains high, a bone scan may be useful. The bone scan also can be used to detect heterotopic bone formation, which can significantly decrease joint range of motion. The forming bone is often palpable around the joint, and attempted range of motion is painful. A bone scan will be an aid to diagnosing heterotopic bone formation earlier than standard radiographs and will show areas of increased metabolic activity as well as increased blood flow.

Evaluation of Sensory Function

Sensory function is important to evaluate during the preoperative examination. The ability to maintain balance and ambulate depends on adequate sensation in the foot and ankle and knowing where the ankle-foot complex is in space. Proprioception sense is essential in the ankle joint for good balance reactions. If proprioception at the ankle is impaired, a molded ankle-foot orthosis may be needed during ambulation to prevent a compensatory knee extension thrust.[5,9]

Clinical Evaluation of Motor Function

An assessment of motor function also should be made during preoperative evaluation. The degree of muscle tone or spasticity can be judged by slow passive motion of the extremity and by observing the positioning of the extremity during various functional activities. A quick stretch test may elicit spasticity that was not previously appreciated in a mildly impaired muscle. Since the vestibular system can influence the amount of tone present, a patient may exhibit more tone while standing than while sitting.[18] Tone will be increased further while attempting to perform an activity such as transferring or walking; therefore, it is important to observe the patient performing a variety of different functional activities.

The amount of motor control present in an extremity can be more difficult to determine. Spasticity may have negative effects by masking underlying motor control. Synergistic mass pattern movement may have positive effects in the lower extremity by providing support of the lower extremity for transfers or ambulation. Synergistic motion involves the mass action of muscles in an all-or-none type of response.[18] For example, a patient who attempts to extend the knee will also extend the hip and plantarflex the ankle. When the patient flexes the hip, the knee will flex and the ankle dorsiflex. The patient can often initiate the synergistic pattern of mass motion volitionally but cannot deviate from the pattern. As volitional motor control returns, it usually follows a proximal to distal pattern. Motor control in the extremity can be graded using a clinical scale (Table 1).

In assessing motor control, attention should also be directed to adequacy of balance reactions. Independent ambulation is a frequent rehabilitation goal and intact balance reactions correlate highly with the ability to regain ambulatory status after a neurologic event has occurred. Balance reactions should be tested both in the sitting and standing positions. The factors that correlate most closely

TABLE 1. Clinical Scale of Motor Control

	Motor Control	Clinical Finding
Grade 1	Flaccid	Hypotonic, no active motion
Grade 2	Rigid	Hypertonic, no active motion
Grade 3	Reflexive mass pattern (synergy)	Mass flexion or extension in response to stimulation
Grade 4	Volitional mass pattern	Patient-initiated mass flexion or extension movement
Grade 5	Selective with pattern overlay	Slow volitional movement of specific joints Physiologic stress results in mass action
Grade 6	Selective	Volitional control of individual joints

with intact balance reactions are the degree of motor control in the extremity and intact proprioception.[13]

Laboratory Assessment of Motor Control

The most useful preoperative test in assessing motor control is gait analysis with the dynamic poly-electromyogram (EMG). Surface electrodes can be used to study superficial muscles in the lower extremity while deeper muscles can be studied by inserting a thin wire electrode into the muscle.[1,4,9,10,12,19,22–25] The electromyographic data obtained can be compared to normative data obtained during walking and can be used to provide a complete picture of what each muscle is doing during each phase of the gait cycle.[5] With this data in hand, the appropriate surgery can be planned. The level of EMG activity is described as none, slight, moderate, or marked based on the potentials that are seen and their relationship to the baseline of the tracing (Table 2). The timing of EMG activity can be classified along a continuum from normal phasic activity to absent activity (Table 3).[12]

COMMON CLINICAL PROBLEMS AND THEIR SURGICAL MANAGEMENT

This section will discuss five common functional deformities that are a result of muscle spasticity in the lower extremity: limb scissoring, crouched gait, stiff-knee gait, equinovarus foot, and spastic valgus foot. The clinical problem and findings, the rationale for surgery for each situation, and a discussion of postoperative management will be presented.

Limb Scissoring

A spastic hip adduction deformity causes excessive limb scissoring and a narrow-based gait during attempted transfers and ambulation in a patient with active function. In a nonambulatory patient, excessive adduction can interfere with bed positioning, hygiene, and seating. Depending on the extent of fixed contracture, this problem can be surgically corrected by either obturator neurectomy

TABLE 2. Definitions for EMG Activity Levels

None	No potentials seen
Slight	Individual potentials and baseline seen
Moderate	Individual potentials can be distinguished but baseline is not seen
Marked	Individual potentials and baseline are not distinguishable

TABLE 3.   Classification of EMG Activity

Class I	Normal phasic activity
Class II	Premature prolonged activity
Class III	Phasic prolonged activity
IIIA	Mild prolongation activity
IIIB	Moderate prolongation activity
IIIC	Severe prolongation activity
Class IV	Continuous activity
Class V	Stretch response activity
Class VI	Absent activity

From Keenan MAE, Haider T, Stone LR: Dynamic electromyography to assess elbow spasticity. J Hand Surg 15A:607–614, 1990; with permission.

or hip adductor release. The spastic hip adductors cause limb scissoring during attempted ambulation and result over time in a myostatic adduction contracture. A preoperative anesthetic block of the obturator nerve will eliminate the adductor spasticity and allow assessment of the extent of hip adduction contracture. When there is no significant adduction contracture, an obturator neurectomy will eliminate the spasticity and improve the base of support. When a significant myostatic contracture is present, a hip adductor release is required to correct the deformity (Fig. 1).

In a severely spastic patient, a flexion contracture of the hip and knee commonly occurs in conjunction with an adduction contracture. As with any contracture, preoperative radiographs should be obtained prior to performing soft tissue releases in order to rule out the presence of heterotopic ossification or an underlying bony deformity that would prevent correction.

Postoperative management following obturator neurectomy involves removing the drain within 48 hours after surgery. No immobilization or abduction splinting is needed following obturator neurectomy. Early gait training with weightbearing as tolerated is instituted postoperatively.

Postoperative care after hip adductor release involves daily wound care to prevent infection in this potentially contaminated area and careful examination for hematoma formation. A drain is used for 24–48 hours after surgery. The hips

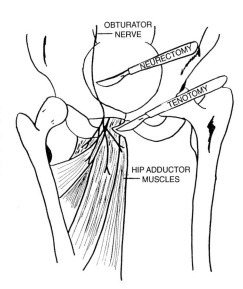

FIGURE 1.   When there is spasticity of the hip adductors but no fixed myostatic contracture, a neurectomy of the anterior branch of the obturator nerve will eliminate the spasticity and correct limb scissoring. If a contracture is present, it is necessary to release the hip adductor tendons.

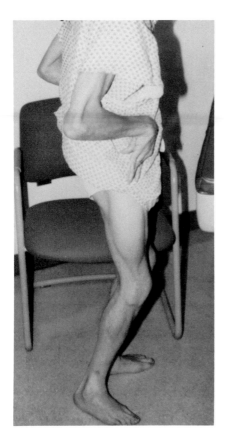

FIGURE 2. Spasticity of the hip and knee flexor muscles causes a crouched posture, which severely limits a person's ability to walk any distance because of the excessive energy that walking requires.

should be kept in abduction for 4 weeks using casts or an abduction pillow splint to prevent recurrence of the deformity during wound healing.

Crouched Gait

Spasticity of the hip flexors can result in a crouched gait with compensatory knee flexion and lumbar hyperlordosis for maintenance of balance (Fig. 2). Gait analysis with dynamic EMG is useful to elucidate the offending muscles (Fig. 3). The hip and knee flexion posture causes an increased demand on the hip and knee extensors during standing and walking. This deformity is very costly from an energy point of view since it requires constant use of the hip extensors and quadriceps muscles to maintain an upright posture. The energy requirements for the continuous firing of the quadriceps are extremely high. Hence, few patients are able to remain ambulatory with this deformity.

The hip flexor muscles are needed to advance the limb during gait. Therefore, complete release of the hip flexors should be avoided in any patient with the potential to ambulate. Removing the iliopsoas tendon from the lesser trochanter of the femur does not provide a complete release since the iliopsoas has capsular insertions. When the iliopsoas tendon is released from the lesser trochanter, the muscle recesses proximally, thereby diminishing its pull while also retaining its function as a hip flexor (Fig. 4).

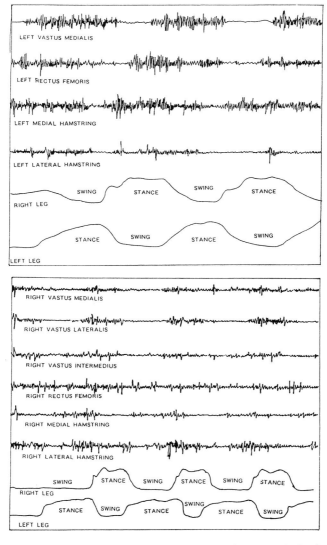

FIGURE 3. A dynamic electromyogram from a patient with a crouched gait reveals that the medial and lateral hamstring muscles in both legs have prolonged activity during both the swing and stance phases. There is also increased activity in the rectus femoris muscles, which causes the patient to stand with flexed hips and knees.

Postoperative management after iliopsoas recession does not require immobilization. Physical therapy should be initiated early for range of motion. Active and passive hip range of motion can be performed while gait training resumes. The patient can ambulate and bear weight as tolerated. If a residual hip flexion contracture is present following surgery, a program of prone positioning should be instituted to correct the deformity.

Another problem usually seen in combination with hip flexion that can cause a crouched gait is excessive hamstring spasticity causing a dynamic knee flexion

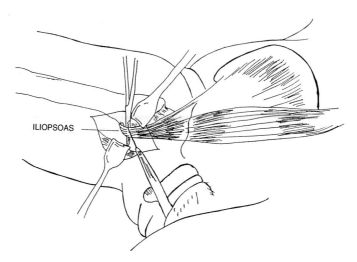

FIGURE 4. Excessive hip flexion can be corrected by release of the iliopsoas tendon from its insertion on the lesser trochanter of the femur. This allows the tendon to migrate a short distance proximally, where it attaches to the anterior hip joint capsule.

deformity. This deformity prevents adequate knee extension during the stance phase of the gait cycle, thereby interfering with ambulation. With severe spasticity of the hamstring muscles or a knee flexion contracture of greater than 40°, attempts to correct the knee position with serial casting or bracing may result in posterior subluxation of the tibia. Distal release of the hamstring tendons does not prevent a patient from becoming ambulatory.[14]

The rationale for hamstring lengthening surgery in the ambulatory patient is that the flexed knee position during stance increases the quadriceps requirement necessary to stabilize the knee in order to maintain an upright posture. This decreases the efficiency of the gait and increases the energy consumption during ambulation. Surgical lengthening of the hamstring muscle corrects the dynamic knee flexion deformity while preserving hamstring function (Fig. 5). An approximate 50% correction of the knee flexion deformity can be expected at the time of surgery. Further correction is limited due to tethering of the neurovascular structures.

Postoperative management after this surgery requires that the extremity be immobilized in a long leg cast. The extremity is casted in the position of knee extension that it assumes while being supported under the heel. Forced extension should not be attempted because it could result in limb ischemia. The long leg cast should be changed weekly until full knee extension has been obtained. A night splint can then be used for an additional 4 weeks to maintain the correction. A knee-ankle-foot orthosis (KAFO) may be necessary to prevent recurrence. Transfer activities and gait training can be started immediately after surgery with weightbearing as tolerated.

Stiff-knee Gait

A stiff-knee gait is the result of inadequate knee flexion during the swing phase of the gait cycle.[16,23] Spastic patients who have this gait deviation have inappropriate firing of the quadriceps during the terminal stance phase. This

HAMSTRING LENGTHENING

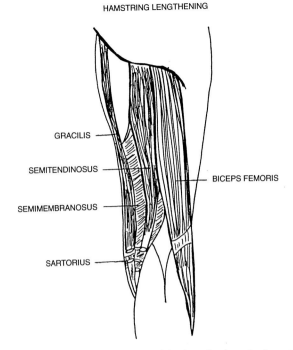

GRACILIS

SEMITENDINOSUS

BICEPS FEMORIS

SEMIMEMBRANOSUS

SARTORIUS

FIGURE 5.   Excessive knee flexion is corrected by lengthening the hamstring tendons distally at their myotendinous junction.

prevents the passive knee flexion needed to clear the foot during the swing phase because it causes the patient to hike the hip and circumduct the leg during swing. A stiff-knee gait is also a very energy-consuming gait deviation.

The rationale for surgery with this deformity is that knee flexion during the swing phase is a passive event that occurs by the forward momentum of the swinging limb. The knee normally begins to flex during terminal stance (the preswing period) when the opposite limb contacts the ground. If the quadriceps muscle contracts inappropriately during this preswing period, the knee is unable to flex and the patient walks with a stiff-knee gait. Selective quadriceps release can correct the problem (Fig. 6).

A dynamic EMG is mandatory to study which muscles are the offenders in the quadriceps group. Previous studies demonstrate that about 25% of patients with a stiff-knee gait have premature activity limited to either the rectus femoris alone or the rectus femoris and the vastus intermedius muscles together during the swing phase.[16,23] These are the individuals who are candidates for selective release of the offending quadriceps muscles to improve knee flexion. The remaining 75% of patients are not candidates for surgery. Their dynamic EMG will demonstrate inappropriate swing phase activity in all four quadriceps muscles, and release of the entire quadriceps complex would result in postoperative knee instability. Figure 7 is a dynamic EMG recording obtained from selected muscles in the right lower extremity in a patient with a stiff-knee gait.

Distal release of the quadriceps requires no postoperative casting. A knee immobilized splint is applied to the knee for approximately 5 days to control pain.

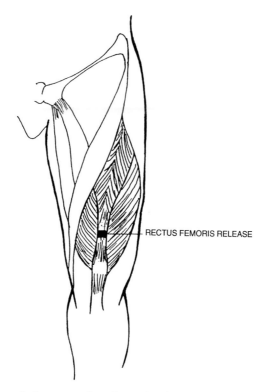

RECTUS FEMORIS RELEASE

FIGURE 6. Release of the rectus femoris tendon just proximal to the knee allows improved knee flexion during the swing phase.

Ambulation training with the splint can be begun immediately postoperatively with weightbearing as tolerated. Active and passive knee range of motion are begun with quadriceps strengthening exercises on the fifth day after surgery.

Equinovarus Foot

The spastic equinovarus foot is the most common deformity seen in spastic patients (Fig. 8). This clinical problem usually is seen in a triad constellation that includes an equinus deformity, a varus deformity, and a toe curling deformity. The varus deformity is the result of spasticity in the tibialis anterior muscle. The equinus deformity of the foot is secondary to spasticity of the gastrocnemius and soleus muscles. The toe curling is secondary to spasticity of the extrinsic and intrinsic toe flexor muscles.[10,11,19,22]

Gait analysis with dynamic electromyography is used to supplement the physical examination and to delineate the spastic muscle groups. Figure 9 shows a dynamic electromyographic tracing obtained from selected muscles in the right lower extremity in a patient with an equinovarus foot. Clinically the patient had an abnormal base of support evidenced by inversion and plantar flexion of the ankle-foot system and toe curling. This equinovarus deformity was the result of abnormal activities of the gastrocnemius soleus complex, lack of phasic activity of the tibialis anterior muscle, and spasticity of the extrinsic and intrinsic toe flexors.

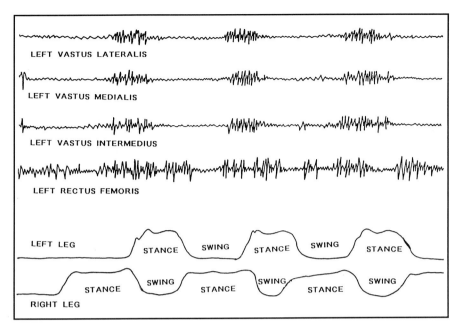

LEFT VASTUS LATERALIS

LEFT VASTUS MEDIALIS

LEFT VASTUS INTERMEDIUS

LEFT RECTUS FEMORIS

LEFT LEG   STANCE   SWING   STANCE   SWING   STANCE

                STANCE   SWING   STANCE   SWING   STANCE   SWING

RIGHT LEG

FIGURE 7. A dynamic electromyogram from a patient with a stiff-knee gait. The tracings from the vastus medialis, vastus intermedius, and vastus lateralis show phasic activation. The rectus femoris muscle demonstrates prolonged activation. During the preswing period when the right foot contacts the floor, the rectus femoris muscle is firing, thereby preventing early flexion of the left knee. Since the abnormal activity is limited to the rectus femoris muscle, selective release of this tendon will allow improved knee flexion while maintaining knee stability.

An equinus deformity may be static secondary to contracture or dynamic secondary to spasticity of the gastrocnemius soleus muscles. This deformity hinders both the swing and stance phases of the gait cycle by making limb

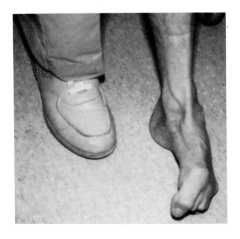

FIGURE 8. An equinovarus deformity of the foot results in an abnormal base of support and causes a severe gait abnormality. Severe spasticity interferes with wearing shoes and braces.

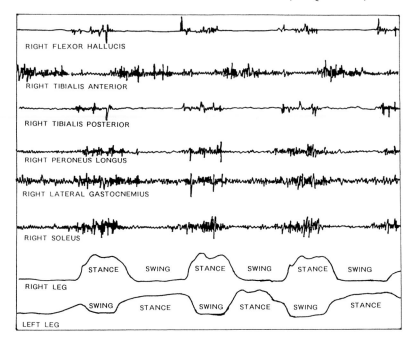

FIGURE 9.   A dynamic electromyogram from a patient with a spastic equinovarus foot deformity. Premature firing is seen in the flexor hallucis muscle, which causes excessive toe flexion. The tibialis anterior muscles show severe spasticity with premature and prolonged firing, which results in forefoot varus. The tibialis posterior and peroneus longus muscles have normal activity. The gastrocnemius and soleus muscle exhibit premature and prolonged firing, resulting in the equinus posture of the ankle.

clearance difficult and preventing initial heel contact. Surgical lengthening of the Achilles tendon is indicated when the patient's foot and ankle position is not adequately controlled by an orthosis or when attempting to free the patient of braces.

Lengthening of the Achilles tendon can be performed percutaneously using the Hoke triple hemisection technique.[8,10,15,20,22] The Achilles tendon rotates approximately 90° on its axis as it inserts on the calcaneus. Because of this rotation, hemisections placed at intermittent levels will sever all the fibers of the tendon (Fig. 10). Subsequently, a dorsiflexion force applied to the foot elongates the tendon without causing discontinuity. If a varus deformity of the foot is present, the proximal and distal cuts are made in the medial half of the tendon and the center cut is placed laterally. If a valgus deformity is present, the proximal and distal cuts are placed laterally and the center cut medially. The foot is then dorsiflexed to the corrected position, allowing the tendon to lengthen.

Varus deformities occur as the result of overactivity of the tibialis anterior muscle. The tibialis anterior muscle frequently will demonstrate continuous electromyographic activity causing the forefoot varus. A spastic varus deformity of the foot interferes with ambulation and makes wearing an orthosis difficult and, if severe, impossible. This deformity is corrected by a split anterior tibial tendon transfer (SPLATT) in which the lateral half of the tibialis anterior tendon is transferred to the lateral side of the foot through a canal in the cuboid bone (Fig. 11). In the case where the bone is severely osteopenic, the lateral portion of the

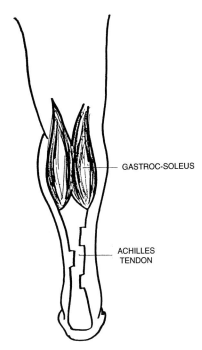

GASTROC-SOLEUS

ACHILLES
TENDON

FIGURE 10.   Lengthening of the Achilles tendon can be done percutaneously by hemisectioning the tendon at three levels. Pressure on the plantar surface of the foot causes the fibers of the tendon to slide and lengthen. The foot is protected in a short leg walking cast for 6 weeks while the tendon heals.

tibialis anterior tendon may be secured to the peroneus brevis or peroneus tertius tendon.

In about 10–20% of stroke and brain-injured patients, the tibialis posterior is also spastic and can contribute to the varus deformity.[10,22] This may be evidenced clinically by the increased heel varus in addition to the forefoot varus caused by the tibialis anterior muscle. This can be corrected by a myotendinous lengthening of the tibialis posterior tendon posterior to the medial malleolus. Because a planovalgus deformity may occur secondarily, a complete release of this tendon is not recommended.

Toe clawing or toe curling is a common accompaniment of the equinovarus foot and can contribute to the ankle equinus. Toe curling is caused by spasticity of the flexor hallucis longus and flexor digitorum muscle as well as the short toe flexor and occasionally the intrinsic muscles of the foot.[11] Spasticity of the extrinsic and intrinsic toe flexors can cause pain, callosities on the dorsum of the toes, and difficulty with wearing shoes. Release of the spastic or contracted extrinsic and intrinsic toe flexors allows for correction of the deformity. Isolated release of the flexor hallucis longus and flexor digitorum longus may result in residual toe curling, especially in patients with traumatic brain injury. The persistent deformity is secondary to spasticity of the flexor digitorum brevis and intrinsic musculature of the foot. Therefore, all intrinsic and extrinsic toe flexor components at the base of each toe are released. This procedure is commonly done

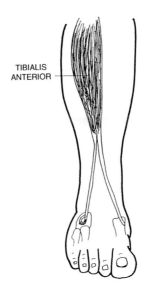

TIBIALIS
ANTERIOR

FIGURE 11. The split anterior tibialis tendon transfer (SPLATT) rebalances the force of this spastic muscle and reliably corrects the varus deformity.

in combination with tendo-Achilles lengthening (TAL) since bringing the foot into a plantigrade position will worsen the toe curling.

Postoperative management for a SPLATT or TAL involves maintaining the patient in a short leg walking cast for 6 weeks. This is followed by use of a molded ankle-foot orthosis in neutral position for an additional 4½ months. Postoperative management or toe flexor release consists of a soft dressing to maintain the toes in the corrected position and immediate ambulation. If associated surgical procedures are performed on the foot, such as SPLATT or TAL, a toe plate is used with the short leg walking cast.

Valgus Foot

Severe valgus or pronation of the foot during stance can occur from over-activity of the peroneus longus muscle.[25] This can occur either alone or in combination with an equinovarus deformity, which is seen during the swing phase and known as the combination foot deformity. In the spastic combination foot deformity, equinovarus is observed during the swing phase from premature firing of the tibialis anterior and gastrocnemius-soleus muscles. The planovalgus deformity occurs during stance from the inappropriate activity of the peroneus longus muscle. The pronation deformity may be accentuated by a premorbid tendency to pes planus or by the presence of an equinus contracture.

Figure 12 shows a dynamic EMG of a patient with a spastic valgus deformity. The spastic valgus deformity is corrected by releasing and then transferring the peroneus longus tendon across the dorsum of the foot and into the navicular bone (Fig. 13). This eliminates the deforming force and actively supports the longitudinal arch. When a combination foot deformity is present, a split anterior tibial tendon transfer is performed along with a tendo-Achilles lengthening and toe flexor release to correct the swing phase abnormalities. Postoperative management involves immobilizing the foot in a short leg walking cast in neutral position for

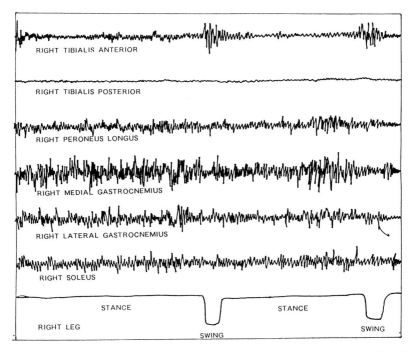

FIGURE 12. A dynamic electromyogram from a patient with a "combination foot deformity" demonstrates severe spasticity with continuous firing of the tibialis anterior, peroneus longus, gastrocnemius, and soleus muscles. The patient has an equinovarus foot deformity during the swing phase and a valgus foot deformity during the stance phase.

6 weeks. Ambulation training can begin on the first postoperative day with weightbearing as tolerated. After the cast is removed, the patient must remain in a rigid ankle-foot orthosis for an additional 4½ months.

CONTRACTURES IN THE LOWER EXTREMITY

This section will address various types of contractures that occur in the hip, knee, and foot.

Hip Flexion Contracture

A severe hip flexion contracture will interfere with nursing care, prevent proper hygiene, and promote the development of pressure sores by limiting patient positioning. An adduction contracture of the hip and a knee flexion contracture are commonly associated with a hip flexion contracture in severely spastic patients. As with any contracture, preoperative radiographs should be obtained prior to performing soft tissue releases in order to rule out the presence of heterotopic ossification joint dislocation or an underlying bony deformity that would prevent correction.

Persistent spasticity of the hip flexors causes a myostatic flexion contracture that can be corrected by release of the sartorius, rectus femoris, tensor fascia lata, iliopsoas, and pectineus muscles at the pelvic brim and gradual hip extension. Approximately 50% of the deformity will be corrected at the time of surgery, as is

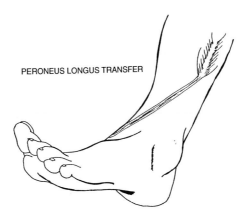

PERONEUS LONGUS TRANSFER

FIGURE 13. The spastic valgus deformity of the foot is corrected by transferring the peroneus longus tendon from the lateral side of the leg across the dorsum of the foot to the navicular bone. If a spastic equinovarus deformity is also present, an Achilles tendon lengthening and SPLATT are carried out at the same time.

true with the release of other contracted joints. A drain is used for 48 hours. Daily wound care and a compressive dressing will help prevent infection in this area where bacterial contamination is likely, and a large dead space remains following surgery. Postoperatively, the patient should be placed in a prone position three times a day for increasing periods, and gentle stretching exercises can be performed to assist in correcting any residual hip flexion deformity. Sitting in a wheelchair is allowed for short periods.

Hip Adduction Contracture

In a nonambulatory patient, excessive hip adduction interferes with nursing care, prevents adequate perineal hygiene, and promotes the development of pressure sores. When a fixed contracture is present, release of the adductor longus, adductor brevis, and gracilis muscles is necessary to eliminate the adduction contracture. Postoperative management involves daily wound care in this potentially contaminated area. The hips are kept in abduction for 4 weeks using casts with an abduction bar or an abduction pillow splint to prevent recurrence of the deformity during wound healing.

Knee Flexion Contracture

A knee flexion contracture causes skin maceration or breakdown in the popliteal fossa and pressure sores on the heels, greater trochanters, and sacrum as a result of limited patient positioning. The knee flexion contracture can be promoted by a hip flexion contracture. A marked increase in hamstring muscle tone in a nonambulatory patient can result in a knee flexion contracture. With severe spasticity of the hamstring muscles or a knee flexion contracture of greater than 60°, attempts to correct the knee position with casting or bracing may result in posterior subluxation of the tibia. If there is an associated hip flexion contracture or spasticity that is not corrected at the same time, the knee flexion contracture is likely to recur after correction and will be resistant to further surgical correction.

Surgical release of the distal hamstring muscles allows gradual correction of the knee flexion contracture.[14,17] As mentioned in the discussion of the crouched gait, distal release of the hamstring tendons does not prevent a patient from becoming ambulatory. Postoperative management involves casting the knee in the position of extension it assumes while being supported under the heel. The long leg cast is changed weekly until full knee extension has been obtained. Forced knee extension during cast changes can result in limb ischemia. Splints are used at night for an additional 4 weeks to maintain the correction.

Hip Extension Contracture

In a nonambulatory patient, a hip extension contracture prohibits sitting and promotes the development of pressure sores. This deformity is seen following severe brainstem injury with a period of decerebrate or decorticate posturing and occurs from severe spasticity of the extensor muscles of the hip. Over time a myostatic hip extension contracture will occur. Release of the contracted hamstring muscles from their origins will allow hip flexion and will improve sitting position.[17] Postoperative management of proximal hamstring release involves gentle hip range of motion. Sitting is also encouraged to increase hip flexion.

Knee Extension Contracture

Severe quadriceps spasticity over time can result in an extension contracture at the knee. This deformity is often seen in combination with a hip extension contracture. Both deformities result in problems with sitting. The knee extension deformity can be corrected by lengthening the quadriceps tendon, which will allow maintenance of quadriceps continuity. The tendon is lengthened using V-Y plasty. Postoperative management involves casting the knee in maximum flexion for 3 weeks. Range of motion exercises, transfer, and ambulation activities are begun after the cast is removed with weightbearing as tolerated.

Foot Contracture Deformities

Severe deformities of the feet are common in patients with spasticity. Even if a patient is nonambulatory these deformities can cause significant problems, including pressure sores, inability to wear shoes or protective footwear, and difficulty positioning the feet on wheelchair leg rests for improved seating position. These deformities should be surgically corrected to maintain a plantigrade foot.

The most common deformity is equinovarus with claw toes. As detailed earlier in this chapter, the procedures to improve muscle balance in this deformity are the split anterior tibial tendon transfer, tendo-Achilles lengthening, and toe flexor release. When the spasticity is severe and of long duration, it is commonly necessary to perform a release of the plantar fascia to correct a cavus deformity as well as a triple arthrodesis in conjunction with the other procedures.

SUMMARY

In patients with spasticity, surgery can be used to improve function and prevent some of the complications associated with increased tone. Adequate preoperative evaluation is mandatory to determine where the deforming forces are acting and who will benefit from surgical intervention. Careful physical examination combined with data obtained from gait analysis, diagnostic nerve blocks, and reports from members of the rehabilitation team are used to help select the appropriate surgical procedures. A managed postoperative rehabilitation program is important to maximize the goals after the surgery is performed.

REFERENCES

1. Baumann JU, Sutherland DH, Hanggi A: Intramuscular pressure during walking: An experimental study using the wick catheter technique. Clin Orthop 145:292–299, 1979.
2. Botte MJ, Waters RL, Keenan MAE, et al: Orthopaedic management of the stroke patient: Part I: Pathophysiology, limb deformity, and patient evaluation. Orthop Rev 27:637–647, 1988.
3. Botte MJ, Waters RL, Keenan MAE, et al: Orthopaedic management of the stroke patient: Part II: Treating deformities of the upper and lower extremities. Orthop Rev 27:891–910, 1988.
4. Close JR, Todd FN: The phasic activity of the muscles of the lower extremity and the effect of tendon transfer. J Bone Joint Surg 41A:189–208, 1959.
5. Esquenazi A, Hirai B: Assessment of gait and orthotic prescription. Phys Med Rehab Clin North Am 2:473–485, 1991.
6. Garland DE, Bailey S: Undetected injuries in head-injured adults. Clin Orthop 155:162–164, 1984.
7. Guanche C, Keenan MAE: Principles of orthopaedic rehabilitation. Phys Med Rehab Clin North Am 3:417–425, 1992.
8. Jordan C: Current status of functional lower extremity surgery in adult spastic patients. Clin Orthop 233:102–109, 1988.
9. Keenan MAE: Surgical decision making for residual limb deformities following traumatic brain injury. Orthop Rev 27:1185–1192, 1988.
10. Keenan MAE, Creighton J, Garland DE, Moore T: Surgical correction of spastic equinovarus deformity in the adult head trauma patient. Foot Ankle 5:35–41, 1984.
11. Keenan MAE, Gorai AP, Smith CW, Garland DE: Intrinsic toe flexion deformity following correction of spastic equinovarus deformity in adults Foot Ankle 7:333–337, 1987.
12. Keenan MAE, Haider T, Stone LR: Dynamic electromyography to assess elbow spasticity. J Hand Surg 15A:607–614, 1990.
13. Keenan MAE, Perry J, Jordan C: Factors affecting balance and ambulation following stroke. Clin Orthop 182:165–171, 1984.
14. Keenan MAE, Ure K, Smith CW, Jordan C: Hamstring release for knee flexion contractures in spastic adults. Clin Orthop 236:221–226. 1988.
15. Kozin SH, Keenan MAE: Principles of surgery for adult brain injury. Curr Orthop 5:75–83, 1991.
16. Murray HH: The stiff knee gait in hemiplegia. Orthop Semin 5:329–332, 1972.
17. Ough JL, Garland DE, Jordan C, Waters RL: Treatment of spastic joint contractures in mentally disabled adults. Orthop Clin North Am 12:143–151, 1981.
18. Perry J, Giovan P, Harris LJ, et al: The determinants of muscle action in the hemiparetic lower extremity. Clin Orthop 131:71–89, 1978.
19. Perry J, Waters RL, Perrin T: Electromyographic analysis of equinovarus following stroke. Clin Orthop 131:47–53, 1978.
20. Piccioni L, Keenan MAE: Surgical management of the spastic equinovarus foot deformity. Operat Tech Orthop 2:146–150, 1992.
21. Stone L, Keenan MAE: Peripheral nerve injuries in the adult with traumatic brain injury. Clin Orthop 233:136–144, 1988.
22. Waters RL, Frazier J, Garland D, et al: Electromyographic gait analysis before and after treatment for hemiplegic equinus and equinovarus deformity. J Bone Joint Surg 64A:284–288,1982.
23. Waters RL, Garland DE, Perry J, et al: Stifflegged gait in hemiplegia: Surgical correction. J Bone Joint Surg 61A:927–933, 1979.
24. Waters RL, Perry J, Garland D: Surgical correction of gait abnormalities following stroke. Clin Orthop 131:54–63, 1978.
25. Young S, Keenan MAE, Stone LR: The treatment of spastic planovalgus deformity in the neurologically impaired adult. Foot Ankle 10:317–324, 1990.

RICHARD D. BUCHOLZ, MD, FACS

MANAGEMENT OF INTRACTABLE SPASTICITY WITH INTRATHECAL BACLOFEN

Division of Neurological Surgery
Department of Surgery
St. Louis University School
   of Medicine
St. Louis, Missouri

Reprint requests to:
Richard D. Bucholz, MD, FACS
Associate Professor
Division of Neurological Surgery
Department of Surgery
Third Floor
St. Louis University School
   of Medicine
3635 Vista at Grand Blvd.
St. Louis, MO 63110

Spasticity is a major problem in the rehabilitation of neurologically impaired patients. Significant disability results from spasms in patients with spinal cord injury, head injury, multiple sclerosis, cerebrovascular accident, and cerebral palsy. These spasms disrupt sleep,[5] render volitional activity difficult, and, in seriously impaired patients, makes nursing care difficult, if not impossible. Although oral pharmacologic management has been the subject of significant research, many patients have restricted lifestyles and disability due to this condition. Many patients cannot derive the full benefits from the available agents because side effects prevent the use of therapeutic dosages.

Many compounds have been used orally to treat spasticity, each with specific advantages and complications. Baclofen, the molecular structure of which is identical to that of gamma-aminobutyric acid (GABA) with the exception of a substitution in the aliphatic chain, stimulates GABA beta receptors and has been proposed for a variety of conditions resulting in spasticity; its effectiveness seems higher in spinal than central conditions. Baclofen was designed to cross the blood-brain barrier, but GABA does not. However, in clinical studies, it became apparent that only limited amounts of drug actually appear within the nervous system after systemic dosage,[3,11] and oral dosages necessary to produce the desired effect may produce significant side effects.[2] Combinations of agents do not appear to be effective.[12]

In response to this problem, many neurosurgical and orthopedic procedures have been developed to relieve the pain and deformity of spasticity, including rhizotomy, myelotomy, and muscle and tendon sections. These procedures are destructive and carry significant risks while not addressing the true problem seen in spasticity: loss of GABA-mediated inhibitory feedback pathways.

The limitations of oral baclofen and the failure of surgical methods led Penn and Kroin to their pioneering work with the intrathecal administration of baclofen.[15] By placing the medication directly on the affected tissue, high levels could be achieved without the side effects associated with oral administration. The development of implantable infusion pumps further refined the technique so that constant perfusion of the spinal cord could be achieved. To individualize treatment for the patient, variable rate electronic pumps have been approved to administer baclofen, or a constant rate infusion pump can be used under investigational protocol. In this chapter, the indications for intrathecal administration of baclofen, surgical considerations, and outcome will be discussed.

PREOPERATIVE EVALUATION

Patient Selection

A baclofen pump should not be considered for initial treatment of a patient suffering from spasticity. Oral medications, as described elsewhere in this volume, should be used extensively and dosage carefully titrated to achieve maximal benefit with minimal side effects. Many patients will experience long-term relief from their symptoms and will not require the discomfort of surgery and expense of a pump insertion.

Patients who have failed pharmacologic therapy should be considered for surgery, including baclofen infusion. Bedridden spinal cord-injured patients devoid of any neurologic function below the level of their lesion with severe spasms in the lower limbs may be treated with total lumbar rhizotomy or subarachnoid phenol injections. Although intrathecal baclofen can be effective, if the patient has no function whatsoever, simply destroying the nerve roots may provide expedient relief without the need for multiple pump refills and pump maintenance. Patients with localized spasticity in specific muscle groups can be considered for orthopedic procedures.

The ideal patient for baclofen infusion has either spinal cord injury or multiple sclerosis with some preserved function below the level of the lesion, allowing the patient to be ambulatory.[7] In this context, the dosage of baclofen can be adjusted to provide maximal relief of spasms while minimizing the weakness usually unveiled by reducing spasticity. Although bedridden patients may be candidates for baclofen, the improvement is usually limited to improved ease of nursing care.[7]

There are significant contraindications to baclofen infusion. Patients should be free of all active infections, and skin over the back should be intact. Any decubiti should be vigorously treated and healed before surgery. Although some patients with complex decubiti refractory to treatment due to spasticity can benefit from placement of a pump, these are special indications for treatment, and options with less risk of infection should be considered. Further, there must be an appropriate area for pump placement on the anterior abdominal wall. Many patients will have had multiple abdominal procedures and/or openings such as colostomies, ileal conduits, or feeding tubes that must be physically separated from the pump pocket. Finally, in patients with spinal cord injuries or those who can be expected to have impairment of cerebrospinal fluid (CSF) circulation, careful evaluation should be performed to ensure that the neuroanatomical source of spasticity is below the level of CSF obstruction.[12] This may require a pretrial evaluation with myelography to ensure communication between the proposed site of infusion and the source of spasticity. If a complete block is present, the patient may be treated more effectively with an ablative procedure such as a phenol injection.

The presence of severe pain alone is not an indication for pump placement. Although pain with spasms can be effectively palliated with intrathecal baclofen, many patients have pain not related to muscle activity. When evaluating a patient, it is important to elicit a history of pain coming on only with spasms. After close questioning, many potential candidates will provide a history of pain unrelated to spontaneous motor activity, and using a pump in these patients may result in a suboptimal outcome, with the patient becoming more fixated on the pain component of his or her symptoms after resolution of spasticity.[10] Complaints of spasticity may have a functional component or provide secondary gain to the patient, which should be eliminated before placement of a pump.

Device Selection

Currently two devices exist—one approved by the Food and Drug Administration and the other undergoing investigation—that have been used for implantation and are capable of delivering constant amounts of subarachnoid baclofen. Each device has its own benefits and drawbacks, and selection of the device should be based on the patient's needs.

The investigational device, manufactured by Infusaid Corp. (Norwood, MA), contains a gas-powered bellows (Fig. 1A). In the act of filling the pump, the gas is compressed into a liquid that slowly expands and turns back into a gas, pushing the drug into the subarachnoid space (Fig. 1B). The rate of infusion is constant with this device, and the duration of infusion, a function of the individual pump's physical characteristics, varies from 2–4 weeks. The daily dosage of medication is determined by the concentration of the drug placed in the reservoir. The device, being purely mechanical and without electronic components, has no battery to wear out and does not require routine replacement. The disadvantages

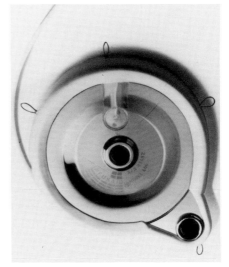

FIGURE 1A. Gas-powered implantable infusion pump manufactured by Infusaid, Inc. This device is available for investigational use only.

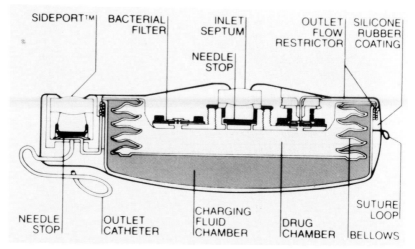

FIGURE 1B. Cross-sectional schematic drawing of Infusaid's pump. The pump is powered by the conversion of liquid within the charging fluid chamber into a gas; the act of filling the pump converts the gas to liquid. As the liquid converts slowly into a gas, the pump is emptied over a 2- to 3-week period. The mechanical bellows separating the drug and gas is designed to last the lifetime of the individual and is the only moving part in this design.

of this unit result from the constant nature of infusion; the rate of delivery cannot be changed on a daily basis, and a permanent change of dosage is accomplished easily only at the time of refill. The device is also susceptible to changes in altitude and temperature.

The other infusion pump, an FDA-approved device produced by Medtronic Corp. (Minneapolis, MN), is a fully electronic pump that can be programmed (Fig. 2). The device monitors the volume of drug remaining and sounds an alarm when near empty. The on-board computer can alter drug delivery several times daily, allowing the physician to titrate the medication against daily activities. For example, spasms at night often interrupt sleep, and a higher level of medication

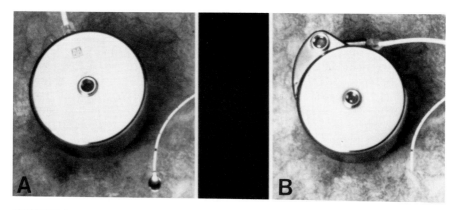

FIGURE 2. *A,* an electronic implantable infusion pump manufactured by Medtronic, Inc. This model does not have a sideport for infusion. The center refilling septum is clearly seen. *B,* a similar pump equipped with a sideport for testing.

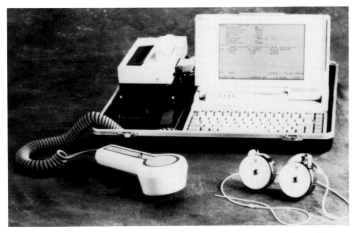

FIGURE 3.   An electronic infusion pump programming unit.

can be given to cover these complaints. Conversely, many patients use their spasticity during the day to assist in ambulation; dosage can therefore be decreased during the day. The delivery of medication can be programmed using an external lap-top computer equipped with a programming wand (Fig. 3) that communicates with the implanted unit using radio waves. The disadvantage of this unit is the need to change the unit when the battery runs out—every 3–4 years with the current technology. Therefore, for an extremely debilitated, chronic, and nonambulatory patient, who will not benefit from the programmable qualities of the electronic pump, it is generally better to enroll the patient into the investigational study involving the gas-powered pump and forego the expense of pump revisions due to battery failure.

PERIOPERATIVE MANAGEMENT

Trial

Most clinicians strongly recommend that once a patient has been chosen to undergo placement of a pump that a trial of subarachnoid infusion of the medication is in order prior to the placement of the pump itself. Although most subarachnoid trials are successful and lead to pump implantation, there are benefits to the trial process. First, electronic pumps are expensive and are supplied to hospitals at a cost greater than $5,000. In contrast, a short trial is relatively inexpensive and, if unsuccessful, avoids the cost and deformity of the patient incurred by placing a valueless pump. Second, by performing a trial with a graded dosage level, the appropriate dosage can be arrived at prior to pump insertion, which greatly simplifies the postoperative course, especially for the gas-powered unit. Third, most clinicians suggest a placebo dose during the trial period to reduce the risk of psychological factors affecting the benefit of the medication. If the patient's response to the placebo is identical to that incurred with the drug, pump placement is not advisable. Finally, if the trial is carried out via a reservoir and catheter rather than with intermittent lumbar punctures, the same catheter can be used for the pump, again greatly simplifying the postoperative course, because changes in the location of drug delivery can alter drug effectiveness.

The trial can be administered either through daily lumbar punctures, a percutaneous lumbar catheter, or by the placement of a combination subcutaneous lumbar catheter/reservoir. Trials given by either catheter method are preferable to intermittent injections for a variety of reasons. First, because daily injections and continuous infusion do not share similar pharmokinetics, injections provide little assistance in determining a postoperative dosage schedule. Second, leakage about the lumbar puncture site, aggravated by multiple punctures, may result in loss of the drug into the epidural space, where it is ineffective, and may lead to inappropriate termination of the trial due to failure of the patient to respond. Finally, multiple punctures are painful in sensate patients, and the chance that the drug will not be delivered to the subarachnoid space is increased.

For these reasons, we choose to perform the trial through a percutaneous catheter with an external continuous infusion pump. This combination has pharmokinetics identical to the subcutaneous pump and allows the patient to ambulate during infusion, an important consideration in partially functional patients who may rely upon their spasticity to assist in walking. Although subcutaneous reservoirs may reduce the risk of infection, intermittent injection does not mimic the pump, and attempts to perform a continuous infusion through a needle into the reservoir usually limits the patient's mobility.

Insertion of the Spinal Catheter

The catheter is placed with the patient in the operating room under general anesthesia regardless of whether a subcutaneous reservoir is placed. The patient is placed in lateral decubitus position such that the side of the abdomen that will receive the pump is superior. A 3-cm incision is made directly over the spinous processes of L3–4 and carried down to the lumbar fascia by sharp dissection. A Touhy needle is inserted between the spinous processes into the subarachnoid space. When the trocar is withdrawn, a steady flow of CSF should be obtained. It is imperative for the surgeon to be confident that the catheter is truly subarachnoid, which can be difficult in patients with complete spinal blocks who have limited amounts of CSF in the lumbar area. If minimal CSF is obtained after multiple attempts, one may conclude that the patient has impaired CSF circulation, which may indicate that the patient is not a candidate for intrathecal therapy.[12] The spinal catheter is inserted to a depth correlating to the highest spinal level responsible for the patient's symptoms. For patients with spasms in the upper extremities, the catheter should be advanced to the high thoracic level. Once the required length of catheter is inserted, a small amount of water-soluble myelographic dye should be injected, and an anteroposterior radiograph of the thoracolumbar junction should be obtained. Although they are radiopaque, the small size of most spinal catheters makes them difficult to visualize on intraoperative radiographs without contrast. Alternatively, the entire procedure can be guided fluoroscopically, but contrast dye is still usually needed. Once the catheter has been shown to be in the correct location, the Touhy needle is removed, the distal end of the catheter is checked for the presence of a steady flow of CSF and then placed into a subcutaneous tunnel. If a percutaneous trial is planned, the end is pulled through the skin approximately 4 cm superior to and 4 cm lateral to midline on the side of the planned pump placement. The path that the tubing takes under the skin should be marked on the skin with indelible ink to help find the catheter when the pump is placed. If a subcutaneous reservoir is planned, the tubing should be taken around the flank to a separate incision below the costal margin on the side planned for the

TABLE 1. Ashworth Scale

Grade	Degree of Muscle Tone
1	No increase in tone
2	Slight increase in tone, giving a "catch" when affected part is moved in flexion or extension
3	More marked increase in tone, but affected part is easily flexed
4	Considerable increase in tone; passive movement difficult
5	Affected part rigid in flexion or extension

Calculated by adding the tone detected with hip flexion, hip abduction, knee flexion, and ankle dorsiflexion on each side and dividing by eight.

pump. A pocket should be made sufficiently large to hold the reservoir. Many reservoirs have tubing to connect them to the catheter; the tubing should be cut so that the connection to the catheter is within the area around the reservoir. All incisions are closed and dressed in a standard fashion.

Determination of Dosage

The trial to determine dosage begins on the first postoperative day with the patient admitted to the neurosurgical floor. Oral baclofen should be tapered off prior to admission; hospitalization may be required in severe cases due to the increased potential for skin breakdown and withdrawal effects, which may include hallucinations.[8] Vital signs should be observed frequently, with special attention to the respiratory rate and pattern. In patients with compromised respiratory function, a pulse oximeter and close nursing observation are required. A very safe and conservative initial dose is 25 μg. The most common side effects include drowsiness, dizziness, nausea, hypotension, headache, and weakness. The progress of the patient is monitored by determining scores on the Ashworth (Table 1) and reflex scales (Table 2) every 4 hours. The goal is to achieve reduced scores on these scales without inducing appreciable side effects. The second dose, 50 μg, is increased daily until reduced scores are achieved or a daily dose of 200 μg is reached. Should the patient experience symptoms of overdosage, the patient can be effectively treated with physostigmine.[9] The appropriate dose of this medication can be given by diluting 4 mg of physostigmine salicylate in 100 mL of injectable normal saline (a final concentration of 0.04 mg/mL) and infused at 5 mL/min (0.2 mg/min) for 10 minutes using a constant infusion pump. The resulting dose of 1–2 mg should reverse any respiratory depression immediately. If respiratory depression persists, the patient should be intubated immediately. Patients who do not respond appreciably during the initial treatment to a daily dose of 200 μg should not undergo placement of an infusion pump.[1]

TABLE 2. Reflex Scale

Score	Description of Reflex
0	No response
1	Hyporeflexia
2	Normal response
3	Mild hyperreflexia
4	Four beats clonus
5	Unsustained clonus, more than four beats
6	Sustained clonus

Calculated by adding the knee and ankle reflex score on each side and dividing by four.

The trial is continued until the patient is free of all spasms but does not manifest any symptoms of respiratory insufficiency. On one day during the trial, the baclofen should be replaced by a placebo injection of saline without the patient's knowledge. The patient should be informed prior to starting the trial that a placebo will be used at some time during the trial; many patients experience dramatic response to the medication only to experience sudden return of symptoms when the placebo is given. Most patients tolerate this experience well if they are informed of this possibility prior to the trial, because it is a reminder to them of how well the medication is working. A response to placebo should indicate the need for additional psychiatric evaluation prior to any surgical intervention.

Insertion of the Pump

The placement of the pump is generally performed with the patient under general anesthesia, and it is technically simple with the exception of filling and programming. The medication is continued as the patient is moved into the operating room for the placement of the pump. The patient is placed in the decubitus position with the side for the pump uppermost (Fig. 4). The back, flank, and abdomen is prepped and draped. For patients with percutaneous catheter, an incision is made in skin over the catheter between the site where the catheter leaves the skin and the midline wound, as indicated by the mark made during the initial operation. The catheter is dissected into this new wound and cut, with the end going through the skin and pulled out under the drapes by an assistant under nonsterile conditions. A tunnel is then made between the incision and the pump pocket. The preferred position for the pump is in either one of the upper abdominal quadrants, but the lower abdominal quadrants can be selected if scarring, previous surgeries, or ostomies prevent the preferred placement. Placement in the lower quadrants frequently results in problems with dressing and belt placement due to the size of these devices. The pump pocket should be made between the abdominal fascia and subcutaneous fat, with the pump sutured directly to the abdominal wall. Some of the subcutaneous fat in obese patients can be removed to accommodate the pump, but the fat should be preserved in thin patients to prevent breakdown of the skin over the pump.

Preparation of the pump for implantation varies with the type of pump. The gas-powered device requires heating and evacuation of air, and detailed instructions

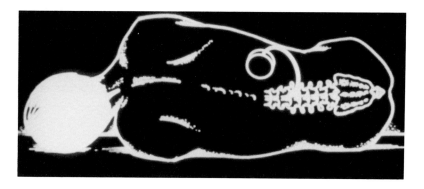

FIGURE 4. Positioning of patient for preferred placement of infusion pump and spinal catheter.

are provided by the manufacturer. The electronic pump requires programming to flush the saline from the subarachnoid catheter quickly, to prime it with baclofen, and then to slowly deliver the daily dose. It is important to use the suture tie points provided on both pumps to anchor the pump to the abdominal muscle fascia with nonreabsorbable suture material to prevent migration or "flipping" of the pump. The patient can usually be discharged the day following placement of the pump.

POSTOPERATIVE CARE

Most patients are seen on a monthly basis, as dictated by the capacity of the implanted pump, the daily dosage, and the concentration of the medication. All patients should keep daily records of their activities, the amount of spasms experienced, and any difficulties encountered with weakness, respiratory problems, or temperature elevations.

The pump is easily refilled through the central septum of the device. Puncture should always be performed with needles designed for this purpose, because the use of standard needles can result in leakage of the septum. Time should be taken while emptying the pump to ensure that the previous dosage of medication is completely removed before refilling.

Many patients will experience partial return of symptoms in the immediate postoperative period and should be warned of this possibility. There are many reasons for this phenomenon, mostly having to do with the daily volume of fluid administered, increased activity of the patient, and the position of the patient during most of the day (upright as opposed to supine during hospitalization). Dosage should not be changed immediately, because many patients accommodate to their new symptom level. Generally, changes of dosages between scheduled refills should be avoided because this requires additional punctures of the septum and complete emptying of the pump reservoir.

Altering dosage is relatively simple with an electronic device and only requires reprogramming the unit using the telemetry wand. Both pumps have to be emptied completely before the dose is changed. Changes in dosage with the gas-powered unit are accomplished by refilling the pump with a higher concentration of medication diluted specifically for the patient. Therefore, for patients with the gas-powered unit, a phone call should be made to the patient the day before the clinic visit and the symptom level ascertained so that changes in dosages can be planned and the new drug concentration made up by the pharmacist.

OUTCOME

Studies involving patients treated for more than 4 years comment on the long-term outcome of patients treated with intrathecal baclofen.[15] Any report describing the outcome from treatment for an intermittent disease such as spasticity must be somewhat subjective, given the nature of the process. Some studies have used objective criteria such as the Ashworth scale or electromyographic recordings to evaluate reduction in phasic muscle activity[5]; these studies have indicated persistent reduction of rigidity and spasms in the vast majority of patients over the long term (Fig. 5).

Dosage

Most patients need an increase in dosage early in the course (Fig. 6), which usually reaches a plateau 6 months following implantation.[1] Patients with continuing

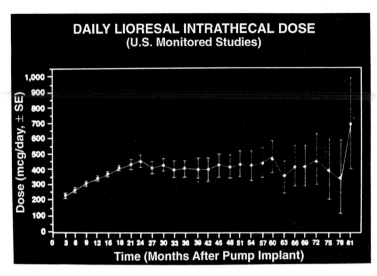

FIGURE 5. Average daily dose of baclofen given to patients for control of intrathecal spasticity. (From Coffey R, Cahill D, Steers W, et al: Intrathecal baclofen for intractable spasticity of spinal origin: Results of a long-term multicenter study. J Neurosurg 78:226–232, 1993; with permission.)

need for ever-escalating dosages probably represent treatment failures. Daily dosages rarely exceed 650 µg daily.

Functional Outcome

Studies looking at the functional outcome from long-term baclofen infusion have found significant improvements in bladder control, dressing ability, and skin

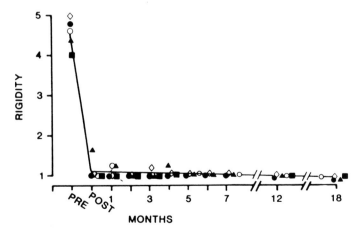

FIGURE 6. Reduction in rigidity in patients undergoing long-term administration of baclofen as determined by the Ashworth scale. (From Penn RD, Kroin JS: Long-term intrathecal baclofen infusion for treatment of spasticity. J Neurosurg 66:181–185, 1987; with permission.)

integrity.[1,14-16] Objective assessment of these capabilities demonstrated persistent improvement.[13] Intrathecal baclofen also helped patients in the use of preserved voluntary function. Many patients experience their most intense spasms when they attempt to volitionally contract muscles; following intrathecal baclofen administration, patients report a greater ability in initiating and controlling movement.[6] In a study involving patients with spasticity from spinal cord injury, Loubser et al. found that all of their patients felt that the control of their spasticity was enhanced with the pump, and none required supplemental antispasmodics.[8] Many patients were able to achieve independence in daily living because of this increased control, and several were able to enter vocational training to allow themselves to become economically self sufficient. In addition, many clinicians have found that baclofen can facilitate bladder management programs in many patients with uncontrolled bowel and bladder emptying reflexes, greatly improving their ability to enter the workplace.[4]

Complications

Complications from treatment with intrathecal baclofen can be considered minor or major depending on whether therapy must be terminated. The incidence of serious complications is rather low, and most minor complications are related to mechanical problems with the subarachnoid catheter or the pump itself. Removal of the system when a serious complication occurs can be quite devastating, because patients quickly become habituated to the relief provided by the pump, and return of the same symptoms experienced prior to pump placement will be perceived by the patient as being far more intense.

In a series of 46 patients treated with baclofen pumps, Teddy et al. found that the most common minor complications were tube dislodgment from the subarachnoid space, disconnection, kinkage, and blockage, which together represented 33% of all complications.[17] All of these problems present in a similar fashion with the prompt recurrence of symptoms, and preoperative diagnosis may be possible with appropriate radiographs in the presence of disconnection, kinkage of the tubing, or dislodgment. Blockage can be detected by injection of diluted myelographic dye under fluoroscopic guidance through the sideport of the device if the pump is so equipped. Injection through the sideport of these pumps, however, can be associated with complications, and the manufacturers of the pumps provide specific limitations to ensure that overpressurization of the sideport does not occur. In spite of these diagnostic measures, most failures will not be diagnosed with any degree of certainty until the pump is explanted and fully tested. Relatively few malfunctions were due to failure of the pump itself (7%) in this series, which used a variety of gas-powered and electronic pumps.

Serious complications involve either infection of the system with the usual concomitant meningitis, breakdown of the wound over the system, or spinal headaches due to continued CSF loss around the lumbar catheter. Infection is usually easily detectable clinically, with obvious erythema or discharge around the pump system, and usually involves skin contaminants such as staphylococcus as opposed to opportunistic or indolent infections. Removal of the complete system is mandatory in all situations, and antibiotic therapy should eradicate meningitis even if subarachnoid infection is not clinically apparent.

Overdosage due to failure of the pump septum, resulting in leakage of concentrated baclofen into the adipose tissue around the pump, has been reported once using one model of the pumps under investigation. The situation apparently has been rectified. The occurrence of this complication underscores the need to use only approved needles for pump refills and testing. Most cases of overdosage are related to improper testing[17] or injection techniques rather than failure of the pump mechanism, and all cases should be managed by removing the medication from the pump and, in severe cases, draining cerebrospinal fluid. Intravenous physostigmine may be helpful in some cases but is contraindicated when cardiovascular depression is present. The presence of a sideport on the pump increases the risk that testing will be performed through this port without removing the medication first; many cases of overdose have occurred by flushing the contents of the spinal catheter into the spine by injecting into the sideport.

There have been sporadic cases of baclofen overdose in patients receiving high levels of medication, above 1000 μg daily.[2] The use of such high dosages is ill advised unless the patient has no other therapeutic options and recognizes the inherent risks associated with these massive dosages.

CONCLUSIONS

Intrathecal baclofen is a highly effective alternative in the treatment of spasticity due to a variety of conditions. Although most effective in conditions involving spasticity primarily in the lower extremities, it also may be useful in cervical or diaphragmatic spasticity. Although certainly not the treatment of first resort, intrathecal baclofen has a lower incidence of side effects that other techniques for treating spasticity refractory to oral agents. The intrathecal method of administration should be considered for other medications and conditions for the treatment of central nervous system conditions that do not respond to oral medication due to the presence of the blood-brain barrier.[14]

ACKNOWLEDGMENTS

I would like to acknowledge Carol Baumann, RN, MSN(R), CNOR, for her review of the manuscript. Figure 1 was supplied by Frances Foote of Infusaid Inc., and Figures 2–4 were supplied by Karl Lindner of Medtronics Inc.

REFERENCES

1. Coffey R, Cahill D, Steers W, et al: Intrathecal baclofen for intractable spasticity of spinal origin: Results of a long-term multicenter study. J Neurosurg 78:226–232, 1993.
2. Delhaas EM, Brouwers JRB: Intrathecal baclofen overdose: Report of 7 events in 5 patients and review of the literature. Int J Clin Pharmacol Ther Toxicol 29(7):274–280, 1991.
3. Faigle JW, Keberle H: The chemistry and kinetics of Lioresal. Postgrad Med J 48(suppl):9–13, 1972.
4. Frost F, Nanninga J, Penn R, et al: Intrathecal baclofen infusion: Effect on bladder management programs in patients with myelopathy. Am J Phys Med Rehabil 68:112–115, 1989.
5. Kravitz HM, Corcos DM, Hansen G, et al: Intrathecal baclofen: Effects on nocturnal leg muscle spasticity. Am J Phys Med Rehabil 71:48–52, 1992.
6. Latash ML, Penn RD, Corcos DM, Gottlieb GL: Effects of intrathecal baclofen on voluntary motor control in spastic paresis. J Neurosurg 72:388–392, 1990.
7. Lazorthes Y, Sallerin-Caute B, Verdie J, et al: Chronic intrathecal baclofen administration for control of severe spasticity. J Neurosurg 72:393–402, 1990.
8. Loubser PG, Narayan R, Sandin KJ, et al: Continuous infusion of intrathecal baclofen: Long term effects on spasticity in spinal cord injury. Paraplegia 29:48–64, 1991.
9. Muller-Schwefe G, Penn RD: Physostigmine in the treatment of intrathecal baclofen overdose: Report of three cases. J Neurosurg 71:273–275, 1989.
10. Muller H, Zierski J: Long term intrathecal baclofen infusion. In Marsden CD (ed): Treating Spasticity: Pharmacological Advances. Toronto, Hans Huber, 1989, pp 55–72.
11. Muller H, Zierski J, Dralle D, et al: Pharmacokinetics of intrathecal baclofen. In Muller H, Zierski J, Penn RD (eds): Local Spinal Therapy of Spasticity. Berlin, Springer Verlag, 1988, p 253.

12. Ochs G, Struppler A, Meyerson BA, et al: Intrathecal baclofen for long term treatment of spasticity: A multicenter study. J Neurol Neurosurg Psychiatry 52:933–939, 1989.
13. Parke B, Penn RD, Savoy SM, Corcos D: Functional outcome after delivery of intrathecal baclofen. Arch Phys Med Rehabil 70:30–32, 1989.
14. Penn RD: Intrathecal baclofen for severe spasticity. Ann NY Acad Sci 531:157–166, 1988.
15. Penn RD, Kroin JS: Long-term intrathecal baclofen infusion for treatment of spasticity. J Neurosurg 66:181–185, 1987.
16. Penn RD, Savoy SM, Corcos D, et al: Intrathecal baclofen for severe spinal spasticity. N Engl J Med 320:1517–1521, 1989.
17. Teddy P, Jamous A, Gardner, et al: Complications of intrathecal baclofen delivery. Br J Neurosurg 6:115–118, 1992.

CRAIG M. McDONALD, MD
ROSS M. HAYS, MD

SELECTIVE DORSAL RHIZOTOMY: PATIENT SELECTION, INTRAOPERATIVE ELECTROPHYSIOLOGIC MONITORING, AND CLINICAL OUTCOME

From the Department of Physical
Medicine and Rehabilitation
and Department of Pediatrics
University of California, Davis
Sacramento, California (CMM)
and
Department of Rehabilitation
Medicine and Department
of Pediatrics
University of Washington
Seattle, Washington (RMH)

Reprint requests to:
Craig M. McDonald, MD
Assistant Professor
Department of Physical Medicine
and Rehabilitation
University of California, Davis,
Medical Center
4301 X Street, Room 2030
Sacramento, CA 95817

Selective dorsal rhizotomy (SDR), the neurosurgical ablation of a select proportion of dorsal rootlets, is specifically designed to reduce spasticity. It has been applied in most instances to children with cerebral palsy and occasionally to patients with spasticity secondary to other upper motor neuron disorders.[5,13,41,47,52,100] Clinical follow-up 8 years[6] and 15 years[32] postoperatively using largely subjective measures of outcome have been encouraging with regard to maintenance of diminished tone, improved function, low incidence of side effects, and patient/parent satisfaction. While various forms of dorsal rhizotomy have been used for almost a century, increasing enthusiasm regarding this procedure and its expanded use in many centers throughout North America has occurred largely within the past decade.

The neurophysiologic basis for SDR, its proper application, long-term side effects, and objectively measured outcomes still remain largely unknown. The electrophysiologic criteria by which a subset of afferents are selected for sectioning has become a matter of increasing controversy. The purpose of this chapter is to summarize the literature concerning the use of SDR in patients with cerebral palsy with emphasis on patient selection, the basis for intraoperative monitoring and rootlet sectioning, and clinical outcome.

NEUROPHYSIOLOGIC ASPECTS OF SPASTICITY IN CEREBRAL PALSY

Cerebral palsy is a nonprogressive disorder of movement and posture due to central nervous system insults acquired any time from the prenatal period through the first 3 years of development. Patients may exhibit variable patterns of spasticity, rigidity, dystonia, tremor, ataxia, weakness, and primitive movement patterns with poor motor control and postural responses. Secondary musculoskeletal complications such as fixed contractures, hip instability, and spinal deformity produce further loss of function. Spasticity is frequently exhibited by these patients and is characterized as a velocity-dependent increase in tonic stretch reflexes and exaggerated tendon jerks.

When a spastic muscle is stretched, afferent signals from the muscle spindle travel up Group 1a phasic/tonic stretch afferents through the posterior roots of the spinal cord. At the segmental level, 1a afferents make direct connections with alpha motoneurons and interneurons.[9] The interneuronal pool also derives afferent input from flexor reflex afferents, secondary muscle afferents, joint receptor afferents, cutaneous afferents, and descending fibers. The interneurons modulate spinal cord reflexes and this interneuronal pool is, in turn, modulated by spinal segmental afferents—collateral propriospinal fibers that travel to distant segments— and the brain via descending fiber tracts.

The neurophysiologic basis for spasticity in cerebral palsy has not been fully elucidated. Increased tone is believed to result from a defect in the descending central-interneuronal control of Group 1a afferents. Unopposed (disinhibited) Group 1a afferent activity results in relative alpha motoneuron over activity segmentally and suprasegmentally via monosynaptic and collateral propriospinal pathways.[7] Decreased descending inhibitory control of gamma efferents may play a further role in cerebral palsy spasticity. The theoretical basis of SDR is a neurolytic reduction in afferent facilitatory influences on the anterior horn cell in the spastic patient who has diminished inhibitory influences from descending tracts.

SELECTIVE DORSAL RHIZOTOMY: SURGICAL PROCEDURE

The historical development of SDR is well described elsewhere.[2,78–80] The term *selective* refers to the selective sectioning of segmental rootlets or fascicles with abnormal neurophysiologic characteristics and sparring of a variable proportion of rootlets with normal responses. This approach, which produced less sensory side effects than previous complete posterior rhizotomies, was introduced by Fasano[28,33] and later modified and further popularized by Peacock.[73–75]

Patient Selection

The procedure needs to be further "selective" with regard to patient selection. The following are favorable selection criteria for selective dorsal rhizotomy as proposed by several authors:[13,40,69,74,77,96]

1. **Pure spasticity (absent athetosis, ataxia, dystonia, rigidity).** SDR is very specific for spasticity and has had limited success in patients with dystonia and athetosis.[6,33,35,73,74]

2. **Function limited primarily by spasticity (spasticity not used for functional benefit).**

3. **Not significantly affected by primitive reflexes/abnormal movement patterns.** Abnormal movement patterns and primitive reflexes are likely to

continue after relief of spasticity[42] and, if significant, can cause persistent motor impairment.

4. **Absence of profound underlying weakness.** Evaluation of strength underlying spasticity is very difficult, particularly in children age 5 and younger.[63] A defect of the pyramidal tract causing decreased muscular strength is often present in patients with cerebral palsy.[32,71] The tone reduction in SDR is felt by many to unmask underlying weakness.

5. **Selective motor control.** Staudt and Peacock[96] use the Rancho Los Amigos evaluation of upright control for hemiplegic patients as a measure of selective motor control out of synergy. Cahan et al.[21] believe the ability to cooperate well with standard manual muscle testing provides evidence for good selective motor control and hence predicts better outcome following SDR.

6. **Some degree of spontaneous forward locomotion.** In one series,[79] six severely spastic children unable to crawl before surgery remained unable to do so afterward, but more than 90% of patients who crawled with difficulty preoperatively showed functional gains after SDR. In another series,[98] all four-point crawlers improved to ambulation with walkers while only 50% of combat style crawlers improved to ambulation with a walker.

7. **Adequate truncal balance/righting responses.** Good trunk strength and control is evidenced by the ability to side sit. Balance, presence of protective responses, and sensory-motor integrative ability are also described as factors associated with successful outcome.[80,96]

8. **Spastic diplegia (absence of total body involvement).** Maximal functional benefit has been shown to occur in children with spastic diplegia.[6] Peacock considers the severely impaired spastic quadriplegic a candidate if spasticity prevents adequate handling and positioning, but the hemiplegic patient generally achieves good functional status without surgical intervention.[80,96]

9. **History of prematurity.** Full-term children with cerebral palsy are more likely to have cortical damage accompanying periventricular leukomalacia[71] and, hence, are less likely to be purely spastic.

10. **Younger patient (age 3–8 preferable).** Steinbok et al.[98] found that no child older than 8 years of age had an improved level of locomotion as a result of SDR. Younger patients may have developed fewer abnormal movement patterns, and they tend to have fewer musculoskeletal deformities. However, the younger diplegics also show the most functional gains without treatment. Children age 2 and younger are felt to have a limited ability to cooperate with the intensive postoperative therapy program.

11. **Minimal or no joint contractures, spinal deformity.** The presence of severe fixed contractures is likely to impede functional progress postoperatively. Berman[13] notes that apparent fixed contractures seen preoperatively often turn out to be functional limitations in range of motion caused by spasticity. This has provided rationale for the recommendation to delay orthopedic procedures such as tendon lengthening until 6–12 months after SDR. It was previously argued that history of prior orthopedic procedures was a contraindication to SDR. However, in one recent study, children with prior orthopedic procedures did as well as those who had never had an orthopedic operation.[98] Some deformities will not be corrected by SDR, and approximately 50–60% of patients require subsequent orthopedic procedures 3–7 years postoperatively.[6] Thus, the neurosurgical and orthopedic procedures are largely complementary, and one approach need not necessarily precede the other.

12. **Adequate cognitive ability to follow directions and participate in therapy.**
The majority (75%) of Peacock's patients have had an IQ greater than 70.[74] The
more intelligent children tended to make the greatest functional gains.
13. **No significant motivational/behavior problems that interfere with therapy.**
14. **Supportive and interactive family committed to postoperative therapy.**

Anesthesia

Anesthesia is induced with either inhalation agents or by intravenous sodium
thiopental. Intubation is done without muscle relaxants or with short-acting
depolarizing (succinylcholine) or nondepolarizing drugs (atracurium or vecuron-
ium).[19] Muscle relaxants cannot be used during nerve root stimulation because
they suppress motor evoked responses. A constant level of maintenance inhalation
agents, such as nitrous oxide, and narcotic analgesics, such as fentanyl, are
used;[19,69] however, patients may still exhibit labile physiologic responses during
root stimulation. The anesthetic effects on the specific neurophysiologic parameters
measured remain largely unknown.

Surgical Exposure

Peacock modified the dorsal rhizotomy as described by Fasano by extending
the laminectomy to L2–L5 and leaving the facet joints intact.[73] This moved the
operative field away from the conus medullaris to the cauda equina, allowing
easier segmental identification of roots and diminished risk of bowel and bladder
deafferentation. Others have performed a laminotomy similar to that described by
Raimondi[88] in hopes of maintaining better spine stability.[2,41,98] Several authors still
prefer a limited laminectomy at the level of the conus.[10,55]

Selective Rootlet Sectioning: Role of Intraoperative Monitoring

STIMULATION TECHNIQUE AND ROOT IDENTIFICATION

Roots are stimulated with an insulated bipolar stimulator (microsurgical
nerve hooks). The conventional technique simulates orthodromic nerve stimulation
with placement of the cathode proximal and anode distal. This convention does
not appear to be essential; recent reports have described no alteration in the
evoked response if the polarity is reversed.[97] Surface or needle recording electrodes are placed over a variable number of target muscles with L2–S2 innervation
(Table 1).[1,49,82–84] Reflex responses in the segmentally appropriate myotomes on

TABLE 1. Segmental Innervation Levels Used in Selective Dorsal Rhizotomy

Target Muscle	Major Root Supplying Muscle[83]	Secondary Level of Innervation[83]	Average Number Roots Innervating Muscle[82]	Compilation of Previous Description for Segmental Innervation[49]
Adductor longus	L3	L4	3.8	L2, L3, (L4)
Vastus medialis	L3	L2	—	L2, L3, L4
Vastus lateralis	L3	L4	3.5	L2, L3, L4
Anterior tibialis	L4	L5	4.2	L4, L5 (S1)
Peroneus longus	L5	S1	4.2	(L4), L5, S1
Gluteus maximus	S1	L5, S2	—	L5, S1, S2
Medial gastrocnemius	S1	S2	4.1	S1, S2
Lateral gastrocnemius	S1	L5	—	S1, S2

the ipsilateral and contralateral side are usually monitored. As many as four to ten additional muscles may be monitored in both lower extremities as well as more distant musculature in the upper extremities, head, and neck.[67,83,97] Roots and divided rootlets are stimulated with a square wave pulse 0.1–0.5 ms in duration, intensity usually 0.2–10 mA, at frequencies of 1–50 Hz. Newberg et al.[68] prefer a stimulation rate of 30 Hz because of potential instability of the compound muscle action potential amplitudes at 50 Hz. Others have not demonstrated significant differences in responses obtained at 35 Hz and 50 Hz. Roots are typically stimulated with a 0.5- to 1.0-second train of stimuli.

Recording of the evoked responses will depend on the choice of electrodiagnostic equipment. Parameters that are commonly used include setting the monitoring equipment to record real-time electromyogram (EMG) responses with the capability of storage at a sweep speed of 50 ms/division, a gain of 200–500 uv/division, high-frequency filter settings of 100 Hz, and low-frequency filter of 10 Hz with an additional 60-Hz filter added. Clinicians using digitized equipment should be aware that significant variability of response, often cited as the hallmark of "abnormal" rootlets, will be artificially created by sampling rate error if the high-frequency filter is set higher than 150 Hz.[95] Digitized distortion of an analog signal's shape, amplitude, and frequency occurs if the sampling rate is not at least twice as high as the high-frequency filter. An alternative approach to avoid distortion is to reduce the sampling time.

Rootlets are initially identified by anatomic characteristics. Dorsal roots are broader and flatter, lighter in color, and are positioned posteriorly so that they can often be differentiated from ventral roots by visual inspection.[80] With a constant current stimulation sensory roots generally have a threshold of 5–20 mA. Ventral roots have a stimulation threshold that is an order of magnitude lower than dorsal roots (usually less than 0.1–0.5 mA). The S1 rootlet is usually the largest; the next largest is L5. The S2 root is usually the first root smaller than its adjacent, superior root. There is no optimum target muscle for S2 because the intrinsic toe flexors may also have some S1 innervation. The S2 root has been both sectioned and spared by various surgeons, but the S3 and S4 roots are avoided at all costs to prevent interruption of bladder innervation.

CRITERIA FOR "NORMAL" AND "ABNORMAL" RESPONSES

In theory, the goal of SDR is to identify a population of rootlets at each spinal level that contain afferents involved in the abnormal or disinhibited pathways (assumed to be contributing to spasticity) and then to permanently disrupt those afferent rootlets in order to decrease spasticity and improve function. The criteria by which those afferents can be distinguished from other sensory fibers is a matter of considerable controversy. The limited understanding of the neurophysiology underlying the selection criteria and the practical application of that knowledge to the intraoperative selection technique continues to evolve as the selective dorsal rhizotomy procedure gains greater popularity and more centers share their clinical experience.

The concept that reflex-mediated, lower motor neuron responsiveness to sensory stimulation could be abnormal in subjects with upper motor neuron impairment was first suggested in 1952 by Magdelary when he demonstrated that inhibition of motor responses to repetitive sensory stimulation (the H reflex recovery curve) was reduced in those with brain injury.[60] In 1967 DeCandia demonstrated similar results in cats.[27] Repetitive orthodromic stimulation of sensory and mixed peripheral nerves reliably induced a reflex discharge depression in spinal motoneurons that was a function of the rate of stimulation.[27] When the rate was increased to about 10 Hz the discharge frequency decreased, and at 30–50 Hz the motoneurons became silent.

Futagi et al. demonstrated that there was less reflex discharge depression and more rapid recovery and facilitation of the H reflex in infants younger than 6 months of age and in children with cerebral palsy.[38,39] A marked effect on the recovery of the H reflex was observed when there was a reduction of the inhibition of central descending pathways to alpha and gamma motoneurons due to damage or immaturity of the brain.[39] A significant correlation also was observed between the degree of abnormality in the recovery curve and the severity of motor handicap in children with spasticity. In their study, analysis of the H reflex recovery curve could separate children with cerebral palsy from normal controls and patients with ataxia, but it did not differentiate between patients with spasticity and those with athetosis.[39]

The experimental findings reported in cats by Decandia[27] and in adult humans by Mayer and Mosser[61] were extrapolated to a substantially different clinical milieu and population by Fasano and became the basis for the intraoperative monitoring technique and selection criteria he popularized for selective dorsal rhizotomy in children with cerebral palsy.[31,33,34] He described specific characteristics of "normal" and "abnormal" dorsal rootlets based on the evoked motor responses to stimulation of bare dorsal roots and rootlets that were consistent with the expectations derived from other investigations of mixed nerve H reflex recovery curve activity (Table 2). Examples of "normal" and "abnormal" responses are shown in Figures 1 and 2. Phillips and Park[84] have also outlined SDR reflex grading criteria in an attempt to standardize the rhizotomy procedure (Table 3). Rootlets that produce 3+ and 4+ responses with ipsilateral and contralateral spread of the evoked response are sectioned (Fig. 3) and others usually spared. If only 1+ and 2+ responses are seen, Phillips and Park advocate sectioning a few of the most actively responding rootlets. Abbot et al.[5] have suggested that a clear correlation exists between the degree of preoperative muscle spasticity and presence of these abnormal EMG response patterns. However, Cohen and Webster[26] found no such correlation.

TABLE 2. Original Characteristics of "Normal" and "Abnormal" Rootlets Described by Fasano[31,33,34]

Normal	Abnormal
1. Threshold between 0.1–0.5 V regardless of frequency of stimulation	1. Lower threshold at 50 Hz, more variable threshold at 1 Hz
2. A single contraction occurs after each stimulus at 1 Hz, but from 5–20 Hz there is a progressive reduction in amplitude of reflex contractions following the first; at 30–50 Hz only the first stimulus is followed by a contraction, with subsequent relaxation occurring during the remaining period of stimulation ("decremental")	2. Loss of temporal inhibition at 50 Hz whereby a sustained tetanic contraction lasts throughout the stimulation period or even longer ("incremental")
3. Limitation in the spatial reflex distribution of the stimulus to one or two muscles in the ipsilateral limb (lack of diffusion)	3. Loss of spatial inhibition characterized by an abnormal diffusion and activation of more proximal or distal innervated ipsilateral muscles and contralateral lower limb muscles

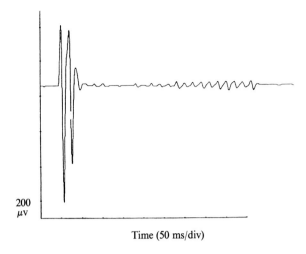

Time (50 ms/div)

FIGURE 1. Example of a normal decremental response to L3 root stimulation at 50 Hz frequency. The evoked response is a surface recording from the adductor longus. Sensitivity is 200 μv/division, and sweep speed is 50 ms/division. (From McDonald C: Selective dorsal rhizotomy: A critical review. Phys Med Rehabil Clin North Am 2:897–915, 1991; with permission.)

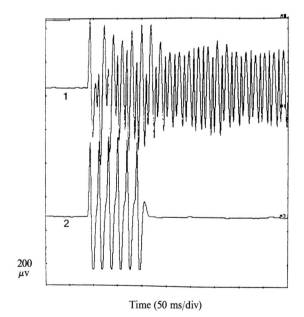

Time (50 ms/div)

FIGURE 2. Example of an abnormal incremental response to S1 root stimulation at 50 Hz frequency. Channel 1 shows the surface recorded evoked response from ipsilateral gastrocnemius, and Channel 2 shows the recorded response from contralateral gastrocnemius. Sensitivity is 200 μv/division and sweep speed is 50 ms/division. Note the abnormal diffusion of the response to the contralateral agonist. (From McDonald C: Selective dorsal rhizotomy: A critical review. Phys Med Rehabil Clin North Am 2:897–915, 1991; with permission.)

TABLE 3.   SDR Reflex Grading Criteria[83]

Grade	Response
0	Unsustained discharge, or single discharge to train of stimuli (normal response)
1+	Sustained response in muscles innervated through the stimulated segment
2+	Sustained response in muscles innervated through the stimulated segment and immediately adjacent segments (e.g., response spreads to L4 and/or S1 innervated muscles when an L5 rootlet is stimulated)
3+	Sustained response in segmentally innervated muscles as well as muscles innervated through segments distant to the stimulated segment
4+	Sustained response in multiple segments of the ipsilateral leg and spread of response to the contralateral leg

The assumption has been that the "abnormal" EMG responses allow identification of the afferent fibers that contribute more to spasticity. It is not known whether use of these criteria identify truly "abnormal" afferent circuits with presumed lack of presynaptic inhibition and sparing of normal afferents. Rootlets

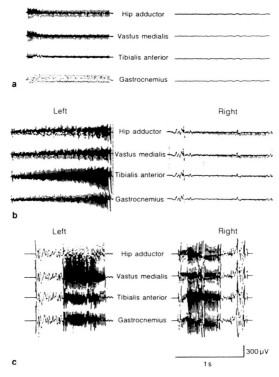

FIGURE 3.   Patterns of response spread within lower limbs to 50 Hz stimulation of posterior nerve roots in a child with spasticity. *A,* stimulation of a left L5 root showing a sustained response with ipsilateral spread only. *B,* stimulation of left L4 root showing mild contralateral spread. *C,* stimulation of left L4 root showing marked contralateral spread. (From Steinbok P, Langill L, Cochrane DD, Keyes R: Observation on electrical stimulation of lumbosacral nerve roots in children with and without lower limb spasticity. Childs Nerv Syst 8:376–382, 1992; with permission.)

that respond incrementally could conceivably either contain different afferent fibers or populations of fibers that synapse on different populations of cells within the cord. In children with cerebral palsy, the dorsal roots themselves are not felt to be abnormal. There is no known anatomic basis for the segregation of sensory axons at the level of the cauda equina. The segregation of large myelinated fibers into more homogenous fascicles occurs proximally, 1–2 mm outside the entry of the rootlet into the dorsolateral sulci of the spinal cord.[55,93]

Storrs and Nashida[102] have further defined the intraoperative stimulation of dorsal rootlets with recording of evoked responses from corresponding myotomes as an extension of the H reflex. They use the ratio of subsequent H_n over H_1 amplitudes (H_n/H_1) that result from 5–50 Hz stimulation to make the criteria for selection of posterior rootlets more objective. Rootlets considered normal show a H_n/H_1 ratio of less than 50% (i.e., a decrement of greater than 50%). Rootlets considered abnormal show a H_n/H_1 ratio of greater than 50%, and at times more than 100% (i.e., a decrement of less than 50%, a stable or even incremental response). The decrement of 50% was arbitrarily chosen and based on previous work on the classic H reflex recovery curve by Mayer and Mosser,[61] who showed that the decrement in amplitudes from H_1 to H_2 (with peripheral tibial nerve stimulation) in normal awake children ages 3–7 averaged 82.3% at 10 Hz (range 70–91%), while the decrement in adults 20–50 years old averaged 56.2% (range 30–70%). Storrs and Nashida do not vary their sectioning criterion with age of the patient despite the age dependency of the response.[38,61] The reliability and reproducibility of the H_n/H_1 ratios obtained by bare rootlet stimulation has not been documented to date. No data exist on H_n/H_1 ratios with rootlet stimulation in normal subjects at various ages, and there have been no trials comparing different decremental ratio criteria.

In practice, objective sectioning criteria are difficult to apply intraoperatively. Fasano et al.[34] and Storrs and Nashida[102] have described rootlets with responses that were mixed showing cyclic fluctuation of amplitude (Fig. 4) and others that showed increased inhibition with resultant lengthening of the refractory period. These responses have been hypothesized to be indicative of either modulation by adjacent abnormal circuits or contiguous mixed rootlets requiring further subdivision. However, these variant responses pose problems when they are not normalized by further subdivision or local sectioning of adjacent rootlets.

More recently, investigators have reported wide variability in the motor responses to dorsal root stimulation. Some surgeons have demonstrated "abnormal" responses (in the form of sustained responses and ipsilateral spread [Fig. 5]) to stimulation in patients who have no spasticity or motor abnormality of any kind and who have undergone laminectomy for extradural lesions or tethered cord release.[26,97] A large series of rhizotomies have been reported with monitoring results in spastic patients that bear no relationship at all to the Fasano criteria.[97] Some clinicians have altogether abandoned the pattern of motor response to dorsal root stimulation observed in a target muscle as a selection criterion.[26,97,98] These more recent difficulties in reproducing the "normal" and "abnormal" responses as they were originally described may be related to variability in the surgical technique or the monitoring process, neither of which has been rigorously studied or standardized. Alternatively, there may be inherent neurophysiologic differences in the motor responses obtained by repetitive stimulation of mixed nerves (reported in the early studies) versus those obtained by stimulation of bare dorsal roots in the rhizotomy intraoperative technique. These theoretical inconsistencies

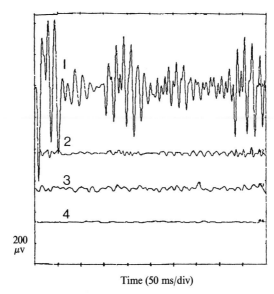

Time (50 ms/div)

FIGURE 4. Example of a response to left L3 posterior root stimulation at 50 Hz frequency. Channels 1–4 show the surface recorded evoked response from the left hip adductor (1), left medial hamstring (2), right hip adductor (3), and left gastrocnemius (4). Sensitivity is 200 µv/division and sweep speed is 50 ms/division. Note the cyclic fluctuation of amplitude in the recording from the left hip adductor.

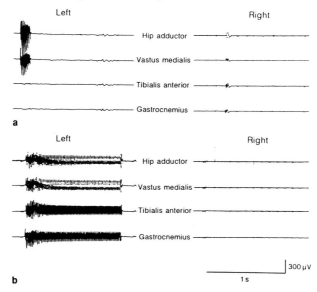

FIGURE 5. Patterns of response spread to 50 Hz stimulation of posterior nerve roots in nonspastic child. *A,* stimulation of left L2 root showing a nonsustained contraction of ipsilateral hip adductor and quadriceps with no spread. *B,* stimulation of left L5 root showing a sustained response with ipsilateral spread. (From Steinbok P, Langill L, Cochrane DD, Keyes R: Observation on electrical stimulation of lumbosacral nerve roots in children with and without lower limb spasticity. Childs Nerv Syst 8:376–382, 1992; with permission.)

TABLE 4. Significance of Evoked Responses in Selective Dorsal Rhizotomy for Determination of Afferent "Abnormality"

Criteria	Phillips & Park[83]	Steinbok et al.[97,98]	Barlot[10]	Spielholz[95]	Cohen & Webster[26]
Lower threshold at 50 Hz	—	Not useful	—	—	Not useful
Unsustained discharge, or single discharge to train of stimuli	0	Rarely seen	0	Rarely seen	Rarely seen
Sustained response in muscles innervated through the stimulated segment	1	0	1	0	0
Sustained response in ipsilateral muscles innervated through the stimulated and immediately adjacent segments	2	Not useful	—	0	Not useful
Spread to ipsilateral leg muscles innervated through distant segments	3	Not useful	—	4	—
Spread to contralateral lower limb muscles at 50 Hz	4	4	3	4	—
Spread to contralateral lower limb muscles at 1 Hz	—	—	4	—	—
Suprasegmental spread to trunk, upper limbs, neck, face	—	4	2	—	—

Scale: 0 = "Normal," 4 = Definitely "Abnormal"

may not have been previously appreciated, and inaccurate assumptions may have been made in the definition of the early selection criteria. The validity of the original criteria has become a matter of increasing controversy as it has become apparent that investigators do not know what truly constitutes a normal response. Table 4 summarizes the impressions of various authors regarding the significance of various evoked responses in SDR for determination of afferent abnormality.

Fasano originally stated that priority should be given to the sectioning of rootlets causing diffusion to the trunk, neck, and upper limb muscles, as well as those associated with triple flexion responses.[33] This diffusion of response to distant myotomes or contralateral side (Fig. 6) is presently being emphasized by some investigators as a more robust indicator of aberrant dorsal roots.[97,98] However, Steinbok, et al.[98] found no difference in tone reduction between patients whose rootlets were sectioned on the basis of sustained responsiveness versus those whose rootlets were sectioned based on extent of abnormal spread. Criterion using extent of spread must be carefully evaluated in the context of recent reports that suggest that the assumptions made about the consistency of segmental innervation of lower extremity musculature are likely to be inaccurate. McDonald et al.[64] have documented this digression from the standard dogma about segmental innervation in their study of children with myelomeningocele. In a series of 123 patients undergoing SDR, Phillips and Park[82,84] demonstrated that approximately 30% of the patients had prefixed, postfixed, and/or asymmetric patterns of lower extremity innervation. Each muscle was found to generally be supplied by three to

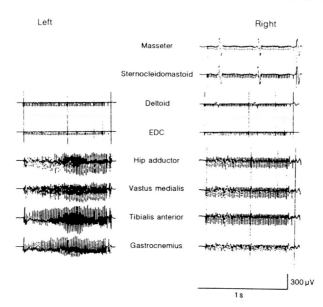

FIGURE 6. Example of a response to left L5 posterior root stimulation at 50 Hz in a child with spasticity. There is contralateral lower limb spread and spread into both upper limbs, sternocleidomastoid, and masseter muscles. (From Steinbok P, Langill L, Cochrane DD, Keyes R: Observation on electrical stimulation of lumbosacral nerve roots in children with and without lower limb spasticity. Childs Nerv Syst 8:376–382, 1992; with permission.)

four different roots.[84] Most surgeons start at S1 and move proximally,[89,100] but anatomic variation is not uncommon. Sacralized lumbar vertebrae and conjoint L5–S1 nerve roots have been observed and can make segmental identification difficult.[100] Without a standardized technique, the influence of these factors is difficult to evaluate or control. The decision regarding sectioning, sparing, or further dissection of roots, fascicles, and rootlets in present practice remains largely a subjective one based on a summation of findings.[68]

A number of other issues influence the reproducibility of responses obtained in SDR intraoperative monitoring. It is possible to vary the distribution of motor response to dorsal root stimulation by intraoperative technique and handling of the nerve roots; contiguous myotomes may be inadvertently stimulated by volume conduction between adjacent spinal segments or through the CSF. The effect of the order of sectioning rootlets has not been systematically evaluated. Fasano et al.[34] noted that sectioning of particular rootlets often resulted in the normalization of reflex properties of adjacent rootlets. Rechecking remaining rootlets frequently was reported to enable some to be preserved due to reduction in disinhibition. The possibility exists that this reduction is in fact refractoriness resulting from repeated mechanical manipulation and/or previous stimulation of the bare nerve tissue. It has not been demonstrated that repetitive stimulation of dorsal rootlets at one segment cannot either sensitize or desensitize the stimulation threshold at adjacent levels that are stimulated subsequently. The order of sectioning might well affect the responses of specific rootlets and alter the decision to section them.

The subjectively observed patterns of muscular contraction may be affected by stimulus strength or distortions of anatomy from contractures or previous orthopedic surgery. Abbott et al.[2] report that they rely principally on clinical palpation and use the EMG response only as a "safety net." They express concern that volume conduction from adjacent contracting muscles may give false positive EMG activity. The characteristics of the EMG response may also be dependent on the type of recording electrodes used. Storrs and Nashida[102] prefer properly placed surface electrodes to needle electrodes, but Newberg et al.[68] and Cohen and Webster[26] use monopolar needles as the active electrode. Gradual decremental responses also can be seen if muscle relaxation is not adequately reversed. Finally, electrical interference is a common problem in the operating room.

Random partial rhizotomies performed in the past resulted in significant clinical reduction of tone but unacceptable loss of cutaneous sensation and proprioception, possibly secondary to the high proportions of rootlets sectioned. There have been no randomized trials comparing SDR as it is currently being performed with alternative techniques such as (1) cutting every other rootlet, which might give equal results in shorter operative time (a 50% random rhizotomy similar in concept to a 4 out of 5 rootlet partial rhizotomy previously performed[43]), or (2) predetermined rhizotomy of a proportion of rootlets with segmental correspondence to specific muscles in which spasticity is observed on clinical examination and determined to be functionally deleterious or most severe.[86] Rhizotomies on hemiplegic patients with unilateral spasticity would help to define the true incidence of abnormal evoked responses, because both sides could be studied. However, these patients are generally quite functional, and such invasive treatment is rarely warranted.

PROPORTION OF ROOTLETS SECTIONED

Normal responses may be uncommon and found in from none to 75% of all dorsal roots tested depending on the patient and author.[19,26,31,67,68,83,97] It is unknown how extensive SDR can be without problematic sensory side effects. Nationwide, there has been a gradual reduction in the number of rootlets being sectioned with presumed decline in the incidence of sensory deficits.[89,98] No study has scientifically documented any critical proportion of afferent sparing necessary for maintenance of sufficient sensory function. Cochrane[25] did not find a correlation between number of abnormal rootlets sectioned and change in tone at 6 months of follow-up. The average proportion of rootlets sectioned has varied from center to center from 25–80% (Table 5). Storrs[100] reports transecting all rootlets at a given segmental level if all respond abnormally. Nelson and Phillips[67] leave at least one rootlet intact at each level. Overlap in the innervation of dermatomes is assumed to be sufficient to spare sensation as long as two adjacent roots are not sacrificed. Cortical somatosensory evoked potentials (SEPs) are not sensitive enough to show abnormality after about 50% of afferent input is lost.[51] Laitenen and coworkers[52] reported a 22% incidence of a diffuse slight deterioration of pin prick sensation after sectioning 60–80% of rootlets. Fasano et al.[31] sectioned less than half of the rootlets in the majority of their patients with favorable results. They believe that more spared afferent input is useful for motor re-education.[33]

The L5 and S1 roots have been reported to be the most frequently abnormal.[46] Lazareff and coworkers[54] report encouraging results with tone reduction throughout the lower extremities and suprasegmentally in patients undergoing a limited SDR involving only the L4, L5 and S1 roots. In this series 40–50% of rootlets were sectioned. The laminectomy was limited to L5 and S1 and operative time was reduced 30 minutes compared with standard SDR. A randomized clinical trial of limited sectioning compared to standard SDR remains to be done.

TABLE 5. Proportion of Rootlets and Levels Sectioned

Authors	Proportion of Studied Rootlets Sectioned	Levels	No. of Rootlets per Level
Peacock & Staudt (1991)	25–50%	L2–S2	—
Fasano et al. (1979, 1988)	<25% (22.5% of patients) 25–50% (75% of patients) >50% (2.5% of patients)	L1–S1	—
Roberts (1990)	38–43%	L2–S1	—
Hurvitz et al. (1989)	25–80%	L2–S1	2–8
Lazareff et al. (1990)	40% (L4) 50% (L5, S1)	L4–S1	7–8 (L4) 10–12 (L5–S1)
Steinbok et al. (1992)	45% (L3–L4) 55% (L2, L5–S2)	L2–S2	3–6
Cahan et al. (1989)	30–80%	L2–S1	—
Kundi et al. (1989)	Approx. 50%	L2–S1	4–10
Oppenheim et al. (1990)	50–75%	L2–S2	5–10
Newberg et al.	64%	L2–S1	2–20
Storrs (1988); Storrs & Nashida (1987)	66.6%	L2–S1 (S1)[†]	3–15
Nelson & Park (1990)	66.6%	L2–S2	—
Phillips & Park (1989)	60–75%	L2–S1	—
Laitinen et al. (1983)	60–80%	T12–S1 C6–C8	—
Barolat (1991)	60–90%	L1–S1	2–3 (L1–L2) 10–15 (S1)
Gros et al. (1967)	*80%	L1–S1 (T11–12)[†]	—
Privat et al. (1976)	*80%	L1–2, S1 (L3)[†]	—

* Neurophysiologic monitoring used only for anatomic localization
† Levels occasionally sectioned

Perioperative Complications

No SDR-associated deaths have been reported in the modern era of SDR. Perioperative complications have included aspiration pneumonia,[1-4,41] intraoperative bronchospasm requiring cessation of the procedure,[1-4] temporary loss of bowel and bladder function,[1,2,35,73] CSF leak,[19,26,109] transient sensory complaints such as anesthesia, dysesthesia, and hyperesthesia,[1,2,35,73,74] transient or permanent hypotonia,[2,25,35,73] spinal subdural hematoma,[98] constipation,[1] ileus,[1,2] urinary tract infection secondary to an indwelling catheter,[80,100] wound infection,[100] and anemia requiring transfusion.[100] Storrs[100] reports two patients with sciatic nerve stretch secondary to hyperextended positioning used for concomitant hamstring releases and one patient with a brachial plexus stretch.

Postoperative Pain Management

Abbott[1] believes a greater density of pain fibers are present in sectioned versus spared rootlets, and he reports a 58% incidence of severe postoperative pain. Analgesics used following SDR include subcutaneous and intravenous morphine sulfate with diazepam for back spasm.[1,98] More recently, several groups have used spinal axis opiates, including epidural morphine via an indwelling catheter for 72 hours,[94] and single low-dose intrathecal morphine given prior to dural closure.[44] These routes of administration have been shown to be effective for early postopertive analgesia and generally free of complications. Abbott[1] has on rare occasions treated the painful dysesthesias with carbamazepine.

Postoperative Care and Therapy

Issues regarding pre- and postoperative nursing care have been discussed elsewhere.[18,92] Most authors stress that intensive and consistent physical therapy that is tailored to the needs of the individual child is essential to ensure maximum physical progress and functional gain during the postoperative period.[1,32,74,94,96] Several therapists have described in detail the typical progression used at their centers for positioning, mobilization, and therapy activities.[30,36,47,57,96,109,111] The goals of postoperative rehabilitation, intensity of therapy, precautions, and the progressive mobilization and activity program for SDR patients have been reviewed elsewhere by McDonald.[62]

Outcome Following Selective Dorsal Rhizotomy

Objective evaluation of treatment outcome in cerebral palsy remains a challenge. The tools for such evaluation are still under investigation and are not widely used. To date, most of the evaluation of progress after SDR has been subjective. The studies are also limited due to lack of adequate controls with similar neurologic involvement and therapy, difficulty eliminating examiner bias, and confounding factors such as previous and subsequent surgery, maturational effects, and variation in type, quality, and frequency of therapy. The following is a summary of studies concerning SDR's effect on (1) neurophysiologic parameters, (2) spasticity, (3) range of motion, and (4) functional outcomes by kinematic gait analysis and gross motor measures. Suprasegmentary benefits and side effects of SDR also are discussed.

Neurophysiologic Parameters

Few studies have examined neurophysiologic correlates of spasticity or electrodiagnostic measures of the integrity of the somatosensory system pre- and post-rhizotomy. The surface recorded EMG response to quick passive stretch in the hamstrings, quadriceps, and calf muscles changed from clonus or a prolonged response (more than 250 ms duration) preoperatively to a more normal duration following SDR.[20,21] Surface EMG analyses of the phasing or temporal characteristics of each muscle (onset and cessation of firing) during ambulation remained abnormal postoperatively in all patients tested.[20,21] The preoperative primitive patterns of mass extensor synergy for stance and flexor synergy for swing was unaffected by SDR. Similarly, another study showed decreased activation burst duration by surface EMG after SDR but persistence of primitive patterns of activation (co-contracture).[84] The motor control deficits that prevent patients from initiating proper sequence of muscle action persist after rhizotomy.

Kundi et al.[51] report that the H_{max}/M_{max} ratio was absent or significantly decreased postoperatively in seven of eight patients tested. This was felt to be consistent with clinically observed reduction in muscle tone secondary to impairment of muscle spindle afferent input.

Two thirds of rhizotomy patients with cerebral palsy had an abnormal pre-operative cortical SEP from stimulating one or more lower extremity nerves (with probability of abnormal SEP being 38% for sural, 29% for posterior tibial, and 27% for peroneal nerve stimulation).[51] Lumbar nerve root potentials were usually present and of normal latency preoperatively. There was a postoperative decrease in the probability of detecting a lumbar root volley from posterior tibial, peroneal, and sural stimulation.[51] However, Kundi and coworkers[22,51] noted a remarkable preservation of cortical SEPs post-SDR following sectioning of 50% of the dorsal roots from L2–S1, with improvement in sural nerve SEPs in some cases. This provided electrophysiologic support for the reports of negligible sensory deficits post-SDR.

EFFECT ON SPASTICITY

To date, most evaluation of the effect of SDR on spasticity has relied on nonstandardized subjective evaluation and standardized but subjective clinical scales such as those proposed by Ashworth and modified by Bohannon and Smith.[17] The decrease in tone that has been reported to occur throughout the lower extremities is clinically pronounced from the immediate postoperative period on, and it has been documented in 60–100% of patients undergoing rhizotomy.[2,5,13,20,24,26,32,34,35,41,52,54,74,77,79,98,102] At 6- to 12-year follow-up, Fasano et al.[34] noted complete or good results for tone reduction in 81% of cases. After 3 years, 5% of patients had recurrence of spasticity, and an additional 2.5% had recurrence when followed 15 years after SDR.[32] Cioffi et al.[24] noted increased spasticity 1 year postoperatively in 1.3–4% of patients depending on muscle tested. Abbott[1] has observed increased spasticity during times of increased stress for months or even years following surgery in 10 spastic quadriplegics. Fasano's colleague Barolat[10] has observed that if fewer than 70% of rootlets are sectioned in the most severely involved patients, the spasticity is likely to recur within 1 or 2 years following the procedure.

It would be useful to document reduction in spasticity post-SDR with reliable and valid quantitative measures. Laitinen et al.[52] used isokinetic dynamometry (Cybex II) in an attempt to quantitate changes in tone post-SDR in several patients with multiple sclerosis. The value of this test for patients with cerebral palsy has not been determined.[16] Others[76,98] have used a myometer to quantitatively measure the force required to overcome the resistance of the muscle tone while moving the joint through the available range of motion. Perhaps the most promising quantitative spasticity measurement system in an electromechanical joint torque device developed by Lehmann and colleagues[56] that objectively differentiates resistance to sinusoidal stretch due to spasticity from that due to passive viscoelastic, inertial, and frictional effects. This system has been successfully applied to 4- to 12-year-old children with cerebral palsy.[85]

The question still remains as to whether an objectively documented reduction in spasticity leads to functional benefits. Landau and Hunt[53] remain unconvinced that spasticity makes a significant contribution to the range of functional motor performance deficits seen with cerebral palsy. Neilson et al.[66] have presented evidence that the major cause of functional disability in cerebral palsy is decreased motor control evidenced by impaired timing and gradation of voluntary movement.

EFFECT ON PASSIVE RANGE OF MOTION

Consistent improvements in passive range of motion have been documented post-rhizotomy in hip extension,[13] hip abduction,[13,24,76,98,108] knee extension/popliteal angle,[13,20,24,76,98,108] and ankle dorsiflexion.[13,20,24,76,78,98,108] Peacock and Staudt[76] observed no change in upper extremity passive range of motion. Several of these studies have graded limitation in the passive range from mild to severe or fixed[13,108] rather than measure actual range with goniometry. Even attempts to establish reliability for goniometric measurements in spastic children have shown variability in interrater and intrarater testing.[8,11,45] No attempt has been made at (1) evaluation of range in SDR patients with blinded examiners or (2) controlled studies comparing range of motion changes in patients undergoing SDR with controls receiving similar intensive therapy.

FUNCTIONAL OUTCOME

Documentation of functional benefits in motor performance post-SDR has not been methodologically rigorous due to the uncontrolled nature of the studies, the use of nonstandardized, subjective scoring of motor skills without elimination of examiner bias, and the presence of confounding variables such as maturation, other surgeries, and variation in quality and intensity of therapy. One approach to objectively assess functional change has been the use of two-dimensional kinematic gait analysis. There have been no published three-dimensional analyses integrating kinematic and force plate data to study joint forces and moments. Studies of gross motor effects have been largely descriptive. A question that remains is whether improved kinematic and gross motor measures translate to an objectively measured improvement in functionally related activities. The Gross Motor Function Measure[91] is a reliable and validated tool that is applicable to cerebral palsy and may prove useful in future efforts to objectively measure change in function.

Kinematic Gait Analysis

Positive Changes. Kinematic gait studies post-SDR have demonstrated increased average velocity[14,20,21,105-107] and stride length.[2,14,20,21,105-107] There has been documented normalization of sagittal plane motion at the hip,[14,21,105-107] knee,[14,20,21,105-107] and ankle.[21] The functional range of movement of the hip was improved with greater terminal stance extension. At the knee there appears to be better stance extension and swing phase flexion allowing for less compensatory hip hiking and circumduction for clearance. Cahan and coworkers[20,21] demonstrated improvement in heel contact on initial floor contact and reduced ankle plantar flexion at initial contact, midstance, terminal stance, and swing.

Stable Variables. There have not been statistically significant changes in cadence (steps per minute),[14,21,105-107] single limb support time or swing/stance time,[19] and thigh mid-range point.[14,106] Hip rotation is unlikely to change because of persistent femoral anteversion in many cases.

Negative Changes. Postoperatively Vaughn et al.[105,106] and Giuliani[42] found patients to exhibit a flexed knee position at heel strike and greater flexion for knee mid-range than normal. This change has been felt to possibly be secondary to knee extensor weakness and returned to a more normal value after 3 years.[105] Cahan et al.,[21] showing decreased but persistent knee flexion at initial heel contact and throughout stance, postulated that the findings were due to weakened plantar flexors. In addition, several patients demonstrated excessive ankle dorsiflexion during midstance and terminal stance secondary to weak plantar flexors or previously overlengthened Achilles tendons.[20,21] Patients may need orthoses following SDR to limit dorsiflexion, control hind foot inversion/eversion, and provide knee stability. Persistent premature heel rise at midstance was seen in 8 of 14 patients, probably secondary to persistent extensor synergy or plantar flexion contractures.[20,21] Subtalar pronation may be substituting for dorsiflexion in the case of limited ankle range.

   Gross Motor Effects.   Functional improvements following rhizotomy are felt to not always translate into an improved level of ambulation.[98] Berman and coworkers[13,14] have shown significant improvement post-SDR in their "mean functional movement" scale in community ambulators, household ambulators, and nonambulators. The nonambulators made the least gains in function. Improvements have been seen in rolling,[13,14] side sitting,[3,13,14,19,20,74,79] tailor sitting,[20] prone kneeling,[13,14] kneel standing,[13,14,111] half-kneeling,[3,13,14,20,111] crawling,[13,14,74,79,111] standing,[13,14,32,74,98,111] and walking.[6,13,14,32,33,35,52,54,74,79,98] The community ambulators and household ambulators improved most in half-kneeling, and nonambulators improved most in long sitting and side sitting.[13] Peacock and coworkers[6,74] report the most functional gains to be experienced by children with spastic diplegia. Progression from nonambulatory status to ambulation tended to occur in younger patients; however, the effects of maturation were not considered. No studies have included controls.

   Energy Expenditure.   Spasticity has been felt to decrease mechanical efficiency of locomotion, increase muscle oxygen requirements, and, hence, increase energy cost. Energy expenditure indices based on oxygen uptake (mL/kg/ meter) and heart rate have been shown to be higher at a given walking speed for children with cerebral palsy compared to normals.[90] Mechanical efficiency (ratio of external work in watts to internal work in oxygen consumption) is a constant (22–24%) in normal individuals regardless of age, sex, or level of conditioning. However, it has been shown to be reduced by increased muscular tone. Mechanical efficiency has been estimated in a proportion of children with spastic diplegia using a bicycle ergometer at steady state workloads.[48] The mean mechanical efficiency for these patients was 14.7% versus 22% for age-matched controls. Improvement in mechanical efficiency post-SDR would be independent of therapy and provide objective and convincing evidence of tone reduction leading to functional benefit in terms of lower energy cost.

   Improvement in growth parameters in patients with weight at or below the fifth percentile pre-SDR has been demonstrated 1 year or more after SDR.[110] The authors who reported this finding believe this to be supportive of the idea that spasticity contributes to increased energy requirements and therefore diminished growth. However, this study had no control group.

Suprasegmental Effects

   Peacock[73,74] has proposed that SDR reduces afferent input to ascending collaterals of the posterior spinal root neurons. These collaterals (which may be present in the fasciculi proprii or propriospinal tracts[29]) synapse with anterior horn cells at many levels and with brainstem nuclei and provide the anatomic rationale for suprasegmental benefits of SDR and for efficacy of a more limited rhizotomy involving the L4–S1 segments as reported by Lazareff et al.[54] Spread of the intraoperative evoked response from stimulation of lumbosacral rootlets into muscles of the upper limbs, face, and neck have been observed in 15% of stimulated rootlets.[97]

   In uncontrolled studies, there have been largely descriptive reports of benefits involving systems outside the segmental distribution of the sectioned L2–S2 rootlets.

These include improved tone and control in the upper extremities, including fine motor skills,[6,13,14,25,26,31,32,34,35,41,43,50,74,79,98] improved speech,[26,31,34,41,43,74,79,87,98] increased voice volume and endurance,[25,98] occasional reduced seizures,[74] reduced nystagmus,[87] less drooling,[13,25,87,98] improved temperament and concentration,[13,25,74] improved swallowing,[31,32,34] improved asthma,[98] less constipation,[15] and improved bowel and bladder control.[74]

SIDE EFFECTS OF SELECTIVE DORSAL RHIZOTOMY

Hypotonia. Marked and diffuse hypotonia has been noted to occur immediately postoperatively in many patients.[6,13,25,31,33,74] This is usually transitory but may last 6 months[34,54] or even years.[74] Fasano and coworkers[31,33] ascribe the initial loss of tone and voluntary power to postoperative spinal shock. They noted more marked and long-lasting hypotonia to occur in only 5% of patients—usually those in which a higher percentage of rootlets were sectioned. Fasano sectioned more than 50% of rootlets in only 2.5% of patients.[31,34] Peacock, on the other hand, often sectioned 50% of rootlets or more[70] and noted 35% of patients to exhibit hypotonia postoperatively.[6] Hypotonia persisted in 62% of these patients at 3–7 years of follow-up but was not felt to be functionally detrimental. Peacock has sectioned a smaller proportion of rootlets in recent years, but the impact on hypotonia has not been published.

Weakness. The tone reduction in SDR is felt by many to unmask underlying muscular weakness. Investigators have noted impaired strength postoperatively in the trunk extensors,[6,47] abdominals,[6,47] hip extensors,[6,20,47,96,111] hip abductors,[6,47,96,111] hip adductors,[47] knee extensors,[47,105,106,111] ankle plantar flexors,[6,20,21,96,111] and ankle dorsiflexors.[2] Strengthening is a priority for postoperative therapy programs.

The motor impairment in cerebral palsy rarely arises from increased tone alone. There is an associated defect of the pyramidal tract that causes a decrease in strength.[13,32,71] Traction on the anterior roots during surgery and the deafferentation of motor neurons may also contribute to postoperative weakness. Berman[13] showed that patients with more severely involved impairments made smaller gains in voluntary movement after their spasticity was alleviated. This may be secondary to an increased degree of pyramidal tract involvement. Unfortunately, muscle strength is extremely difficult to estimate in the presence of spasticity. Steinbok et al.[98] believe that perservation of a greater proportion of L3–L4 posterior rootlets decreases the likelihood of knee extensor weakness after SDR. However, an unexpected finding in patients with relative L4 sparring was in-toeing, possibly secondary to imbalance between medial and lateral hamstrings.[98]

Sensory Changes. Loss of sensation in a dermatomal distribution is generally felt to require complete lesions in several adjacent posterior roots. Loss of pin prick sensation or hypoesthesia in one or more dermatomes appears to be rare after SDR with anywhere from 0–6%[1,2,6,26,34,35,74,98,100] to 22%[52] of patients showing mild permanent deficits. Most patients with hypoesthesia experience resolution of symptoms over several weeks after SDR.[33,73] Impaired position sensation[1,6,19,33] and two-point discrimination[19,100] have been observed but have not had any functional implications. There have been two reported cases of trophic ulcers after SDR[87] and no reports of neuropathic (Charcot) arthropathy.

Transient dysesthesia and hypersensitivity (often involving the soles of the feet) are common and reported in 2.5–40% of patients.[1,2,10,35,47,74,83,98,105,109] These sensations usually resolve within several weeks. Sharp section of rootlets with microscissors rather than electrocoagulation was felt by Storrs[101] to reduce the postoperative dysesthesias.

Using transcutaneous electrical stimulation after SDR, Phillips and Park[83] demonstrated an increase in cognitive sensory threshold stimulating the L5 dermatome at 5 Hz. This was felt to represent a small sensory change not clinically detectable. As previously mentioned, cortical somatosensory evoked potentials remain surprisingly intact after SDR. Park and coworkers[72] have obtained consistent sensory nerve action potentials with ipsilateral sural nerve stimulation and ventral root recordings. They believe this to be electrophysiologic evidence for the presence of afferent fibers in human ventral roots. This may help to explain the preservation of sensation with partial or near-total dorsal rhizotomy.

Bladder Dysfunction.   Permanent bladder complications secondary to SDR have long been felt to be exceedingly rare so long as roots at and distal to S3 are avoided. Many surgeons avoid S2 and distal roots (see Table 5). One might predict a tendency among centers worldwide to under-report the occurrence of permanent neurogenic bladder. Despite this hypothetical reporting bias, evidence is emerging to suggest that this procedure is not free of neurogenic complications to the bladder. Abbott[1] reports that one patient out of 250 was still dependent on a catheterization program 18 months after rhizotomy. Steinbok et al.[98] reports a 2% incidence (1 of 50 patients) of persistent urinary difficulties 1 year after SDR. Transient urinary retention requiring intermittent catheterization for several weeks to months has been reported post-SDR in 1–24% of patients.[1,28,34,52,74,98]

Abbott[1] has postulated that some variability in segmental afferent supply to the bladder may exist and that afferents involved in the bladder's reflex circuits may rarely be isolated to a single root within the target zone of SDR surgery. For example, some children have nearly all pudendal afferent activity carried by only the S2 roots.[28] Alternatively, neuroanatomic circuits that provide the anatomic basis for suprasegmental effects may also apply to "subsegmental" levels (S2 and distal), allowing the possibility of reduction in bladder tone. In one series,[65] cystometrogram documented spastic bladders in 8% of the general population of cerebral palsy patients. These children may be dependent on the generation of higher intravesicular pressures to void, and, hence, they may be the population at greatest risk for post-SDR bladder complications.

Abbott[1] now advocates preoperative cystometrograms for patients whose histories suggest spastic bladder (recurrent UTIs, daytime enuresis, urinary dribbling, or delayed toilet training). Abbott and colleagues[1,28] now record dorsal root action potentials (DRAP) from the S1–S3 roots intraoperatively after electrical stimulation of the pudendal nerve via dorsal penile or clitoral branches. S1 to S2 rootlets carrying significant pudendal activity are spared. Preliminary findings show this monitoring to result in the prevention of persistent micturition dysfunction.[28]

Sexual Dysfunction.   No data exist on incidence of sexual dysfunction following rhizotomy because no series has sufficiently followed patients into adult life. Deletis et al.,[28] showing that in some children nearly all pudendal afferent activity was carried by only the S2 roots, gives legitimate cause for concern, particularly given the willingness of some surgeons to sacrifice S2 level rootlets.

Hip Subluxation and Dislocation.   Muscle imbalance, coxa valga, and femoral anteversion are all factors putting children with cerebral palsy at risk for hip subluxation and frank dislocation. It has been hoped that tone reduction following SDR might prevent progression to hip dislocation. On the other hand, sparing the L1 rootlet could theoretically result in decreased hip extensor and hip abductor tone relative to hip flexor tone and accelerate the progression to dislocation for a hip at risk. The question has not been resolved because the precise natural history of hip deformity in spastic cerebral palsy is largely unknown.

Greene et al.[42a] have recently reported rapid subluxation of the hips in six children who had undergone SDR within 12 months. All children with preexisting hip dysplasia (lateral extrusion index greater than 33%) appeared to be at higher risk for rapid progressive subluxation when compared to children with normal hips. Five of six of these patients had spastic quadriplegia. Abbott[1] reports six ambulatory patients who required femoral varus derotation osteotomies for hip dislocation following SDR. Stempien et al.[99] showed hip placement to remain stable for nearly 90% of hips at 1 year of follow-up. The hips that progressed to dislocation were at risk preoperatively. Those not at risk prior to SDR did not dislocate over the first postoperative year.

Spinal Deformity. Late onset kyphoscoliosis due to the extensive laminectomy/laminotomy is a theoretical risk that will not be proved or disproved until adequate long-term follow-up is available on large numbers of patients. Numerous reports describe the frequent occurrence of spinal deformity in children after laminectomy.[23,37,104] Among several causative factors were early age of surgery, cervical and thoracic site of laminectomy, and muscular paralysis. The destruction of the lateral facet joints also contributes to postlaminectomy scoliosis and kyphosis.[58,59] Arens, Peacock, and Peter[6] cite a previous study[112] as demonstrating that no spinal deformities occur following multiple-level lumbar laminectomy without facetectomy in children. Unfortunately, this study only included six children with lumbar laminectomies. All of these children were younger than 15, and three did not have postoperative spinal roentgenograms. In addition, none of the patients in this series had the trunk weakness associated with cerebral palsy. Bell et al.[12] has reported a significant incidence of spinal deformity (47%) following multiple-level thoracic and lumbar laminectomies; an age of 12 and younger and thoracic level are the strongest risk factors.

Peter et al.[81] found scoliosis (with long mobile primary curves 10–60° in 16% of patients after SDR. This percentage was felt to be below or similar to that generally seen in patients with cerebral palsy; however, the true incidence and natural history of scoliosis in a series of patients with characteristics similar to patients undergoing rhizotomy is not known. In this same series Peter and coworkers found 9% of patients to have spondylolysis and/or grade 1 spondylolisthesis at 1–7 years of follow-up. This was double the expected rate in the normal population. It was hypothesized that increased lordosis and posterior column weakness caused by L2–S1 laminectomy could theoretically add stress on the pars and predispose to spondylolysis.

Suk[103] has shown in young rabbits that a slowly progressive and significant scoliosis occurs with unilateral posterior rhizotomy involving three adjacent roots. The apex of the curvature was toward the side of the rhizotomy. It was felt that sensory and proprioceptive derangement played a major role.

CONCLUSIONS

The experience thus far suggests that SDR can be useful for spasticity in cerebral palsy when patients are carefully selected. Younger children with spastic diplegia who are seriously impaired by spasticity but have retained good selective motor control and some degree of forward locomotion appear to make the most functional gains in uncontrolled studies. A significant percentage of patients require subsequent orthopedic procedures for persisting musculoskeletal deformities.

The significance of "normal" and "abnormal" responses to intraoperative stimulation of posterior rootlets remains largely unknown and has recently become a matter of increasing controversy. The decision regarding sectioning, sparing, or further dissection of rootlets is largely a subjective one based on a summation of findings. Investigators do not know what truly constitutes a "normal" response, or whether the presence of an "abnormal" evoked response actually enables the surgeon to section afferents that contribute more to spasticity. The relation between proportion of rootlets sectioned and clinical outcome including incidence of side effects is also unknown.

Post-SDR spasticity appears decreased on subjective evaluation, passive range of motion improved, and gait dynamics partly improved, but weakness, primitive movement patterns, and impaired motor control persist. Thus, intensive therapy appears necessary to maximize ultimate functional gains. There have been no controlled studies to date documenting the intensity, type, or duration of therapy needed after SDR. A randomized clinical trial may be necessary before the functional benefits of SDR can be adequately elucidated.

Hypotonia and unmasked weakness appear to be the most common and troubling side effects. Sensory deficits and bladder problems are rare; however, it is becoming apparent that persistent difficulty voiding is a real risk, particularly with S2-level rhizotomy. These problems may be further attenuated by a more limited SDR involving the L4–S1 roots. SDR may be causally associated with rapid hip subluxation/dislocation in children with at-risk hips, and this requires further study. The possibility of progressive spinal deformity is a valid concern and may provide further rationale for a more limited SDR requiring L5–S1 laminectomy. It will be many years before the proper application of this surgical intervention (based on sound data) is defined and the risks and long-term complications fully known.

ACKNOWLEDGMENT

The author wishes to thank Judy DeTour for her assistance with manuscript preparation.

REFERENCES

1. Abbott R: Complications with selective posterior rhizotomy. Pediatr Neurosurg 18:43–47, 1992.
2. Abbott R, Forem SL, Johann M: Selective posterior rhizotomy for the treatment of spasticity: A review. Childs Nerve Syst 5:337–346, 1989.
3. Abbott R, Forem S, Johann M, et al: Selective posterior rhizotomy for the treatment of spasticity: Short term outcome. Childs Nerv Syst 4:179, 1988.
4. Abbott R, Johann M, Forem S, et al: Difficulties encountered in treating spasticity. Childs Nerv Syst 5:265, 1989.
5. Abbott R, Johann M, Spielholz N, et al: Selective posterior rhizotomy and spasticity: Relationship between intraoperative abnormal muscle contractions and the tone examination. Neurosurg State Art Rev 4:471–475, 1989.
6. Arens LJ, Peacock WJ, Peter J: Selective posterior rhizotomy: A long term follow-up study. Childs Nerv Syst 5:148–152, 1989.
7. Ashby P, Verrier M, Lightfoot E: Segmental reflex pathways in spinal shock and spasticity in man. J Neurol Neurosurg Psychiatry 37:1352–1360, 1974.
8. Ashton BB, Pickles B, Roll IW: Reliability of goniometric measurements of hip motion in spastic cerebral palsy. Dev Med Child Neurol 20:87–94, 1978.

9. Baldissera PW, Hultborn H, Illert M: Integration in spinal neuronal systems. In Brooks VB (ed): Handbook of Physiology. The Nervous System, Motor Control. Sec 1., Vol 2. Bethesda, MD, American Physiology Society, 1981, pp 509–595.

10. Barolat G: Dorsal selective rhizotomy through a limited exposure of the cauda equina at L-1. J Neurosurg 75:804–807, 1991.

11. Bartlett MD, Wolf LS, Shurtleff DB, et al: Hip flexion contractures: A comparison of measurement methods. Arch Phys Med Rehabil 66:620–625, 1985.

12. Bell D, Walker J, Orrell K: Spinal deformity following multiple-level thoracic and lumbar laminectomy in children. J Pediatr Orthop 10:685, 1990.

13. Berman B: Selective posterior rhizotomy: Does it do any good? Neurosurg State Art Rev 4:431–444, 1989.

14. Berman B, Vaughan CL, Peacock WJ: The effect of rhizotomy on movement in patients with cerebral palsy. Am J Occup Ther 44:511–516, 1990.

15. Binder H, Eng GD: Rehabilitation management of children with spastic diplegic cerebral palsy. Arch Phys Med Rehabil 70:482–489, 1989.

16. Bohannon RW: Variability and reliability of the pendulum test for spasticity using the Cybex II isokinetic dynamometer. Phys Ther 67:659–661, 1987.

17. Bohannon RW, Smith MB: Interrater reliability of a modified Ashworth scale. Phys Ther 67:206–207, 1987.

18. Brucker JM: Selective dorsal rhizotomy: Neurosurgical treatment of cerebral palsy. J Pediatr Nursing 5:105–114, 1990.

19. Cahan LD: Selective dorsal rhizotomy for children with cerebral palsy. Contemp Neurosurg 10:1–6, 1988.

20. Cahan LD, Adams JM, Beeler L, et al: Clinical, electrophysiologic, and kinesiologic observations in selective dorsal rhizotomy in cerebral palsy. Neurosurg State Art Rev 4:474–477, 1989.

21. Cahan LD, Adams JM, Perry J, et al: Instrumented gait analysis after selective dorsal rhizotomy. Develop Med Child Neurol 32:1037–1043, 1990.

22. Cahan LD, Kundi MS, McPherson D, et al: Electrophysiologic studies in selective dorsal rhizotomy for spasticity in children with cerebral palsy. Appl Neurophysiol 50:459–462, 1987.

23. Cattell HS, Clark GL Jr: Cervical kyphosis and instability following multiple laminectomy in children. J Bone Joint Surg 49A:713–720, 1967.

24. Cioffi M, Feathergill B, Beeker B, et al: Clinical outcome of children following selective posterior rhizotomy. Develop Med Child Neurol 32(suppl 62):5, 1990.

25. Cochrane DD: Local and remote effects of selective dorsal rhizotomy for the treatment of spasticity in children with cerebral palsy. Neurosurgery 26:712–713, 1990.

26. Cohen AR, Webster HC: How selective is selective posterior rhizotomy? Surg Neurol 35:267–272, 1991.

27. DeCandia M, Provini L, Taborikova H: Mechanisms of the reflex discharge depression in the spinal motoneuron during repetitive orthodromic stimulation. Brain Res 4:284–291, 1967.

28. Deletis V, Vodusek D, Abbott R, et al: Intraoperative monitoring of dorsal sacral roots. Minimizing the risk of iatrogenic micturition disorders. Neurosurgery 30:72–75, 1992.

29. Dimitrijevic MR, Nathan PW: Studies of spasticity in man. II. Analysis of stretch reflexes in spasticity. Brain 90:333–358, 1967.

30. Elk B: Pre-operative assessment and post-surgical occupational therapy for children who have undergone a selective posterior rhizotomy. S Afr J Occup Ther 14:45–50, 1984.

31. Fasano VA, Barolat-Romana G, Zeme S, et al: Electrophysiological assessment of spinal circuits in spasticity by direct dorsal root stimulation. Neurosurgery 4:146–151, 1979.

32. Fasano VA, Broggi G: Functional posterior rhizotomy. Neurosurg State Art Rev 4:409–412, 1989.

33. Fasano VA, Broggi G, Barolat-Romana G, et al: Surgical treatment of spasticity in cerebral palsy. Childs Brain 4:289–305, 1978.

34. Fasano VA, Broggi G, Zeme S: Intraoperative electrical stimulation for functional posterior rhizotomy. Scand J Rehabil Med Suppl 17:149–154, 1988.

35. Fasano VA, Broggi G, Zeme S, et al: Long-term results of posterior rhizotomy. Acta Neurochir Suppl 30:435–439, 1980.

36. Feathergill B, Cioffi M, Becker B: Selective posterior rhizotomy treatment protocol for physical therapy. Rhizotomy Program, Rehabilitation Institute of Chicago, 1989.

37. Fraser RD, Paterson DC, Simpson DA: Orthopaedic aspects of spinal tumors in children. J Bone Joint Surg 59B:143–151, 1977.

38. Futagi Y, Abe J: H-reflex study in normal children and patients with cerebral palsy. Brain Dev 7:414–420, 1985.

39. Futagi Y, Abe J, Tanaka J: Recovery curve of the h-reflex in normal infants, central coordination disturbance cases and cerebral palsy patients within the first year. Brain Dev 10:8–12, 1988.
40. Gaebler-Spira DJ: Rehabilitation and patient selection for selective posterior rhizotomy. Presented at The Child with Cerebral Palsy and Selective Posterior Rhizotomy, Instructional course. American Academy for Cerebral Palsy and Developmental Medicine, Orlando, October 5, 1990.
41. Gaskill SJ, Wilkens K, Marlin AE: Selective posterior rhizotomy to treat spasticity associated with cerebral palsy: A critical review. Tex Med 88:68–71, 1992.
42. Giuliani CA: Dorsal rhizotomy for children with cerebral palsy: Support for concepts of motor control. Phys Ther 71:248–259, 1991.
42a. Greene WB, Dietz FR, Goldberg MJ, et al: Rapid progression of hip subluxation in cerebral palsy after selective posterior rhizotomy. J Pediatr Orthop 11:494–497, 1991.
43. Gros C, Ouaknine G, Vlahovitch B, et al: Laradicutomie selective posterieure dans le traitement neuro-chirurgical de l'hypertonie pyramidale. Neurochirurgie 13:505–518, 1967.
44. Harris MM, Kahana MD, Park TS: Intrathecal morphine for postoperative analgesia in children after selective dorsal root rhizotomy. Neurosurgery 28:519–522, 1991.
45. Harris SR, Smith LH, Krukowski L: Goniometric reliability for a child with spastic quadriplegia. J Pediatr Orthop 5:348–351, 1985.
46. Hurvitz EA, Leonard JA, Venes JL, et al: Electrodiagnostic findings in selective dorsal rootlet rhizotomy and their correlation to clinical picture. Arch Phys Med Rehabil 70(Oct):A-44, 1989.
47. Irwin-Carruthers SH, Davids LM, Van Rensburg CK, et al: Early physiotherapy in selective posterior rhizotomy. Physiotherapy 41:44–49, 1985.
48. Jones J, McLaughlin JF: Mechanical efficiency of children with spastic cerebral palsy. Dev Med Child Neurol (suppl 59)31:6, 1989.
49. Kendall FP, McCreary EK: Muscles: Testing and Function. 3rd ed. Baltimore, Williams & Wilkins, 1983, pp 47–51.
50. Kinghorn J: Upper extremity functional changes following selective posterior rhizotomy in children with cerebral palsy. Am J Occup Ther 46:502–507.
51. Kundi M, Cahan L, Starr A: Somatosensory evoked potentials in cerebral palsy after partial dorsal root rhizotomy. Arch Neurol 46:524–527, 1989.
52. Laitinen LV, Nilsson S, Fugl-Meyer AR: Selective posterior rhizotomy for treatment of spasticity. J Neurosurg 58:895–899, 1983.
53. Landau WM, Hunt CC: Dorsal rhizotomy, a treatment of unproven efficacy. J Child Neurol 5:174–178, 1990.
54. Lazareff JA, Mata-Acosta AM, Garcia-Mendez MA: Limited selective posterior rhizotomy for the treatment of spasticity secondary to infantile cerebral palsy: A preliminary report. Neurosurgery 27:535–538, 1990.
55. Lazareff JA, Vaencia Mayoral PF: Histological differences between rootlets sectioned during selective posterior rhizotomy by two surgical techniques. Acta Neurochir (Wien) 105:35–38, 1990.
56. Lehmann JR, Price R, de Lateur, BJ, et al: Spasticity: Quantitative measurements as a basis for assessing effectiveness of therapeutic intervention. Arch Phys Med Rehabil 70:6–15, 1989.
57. Lewin JE, Lewis L: Treatment protocol for occupational therapy sample long-term goals. Rhizotomy Program, Rehabilitation Institute of Chicago, 1989.
58. Longstein JE: Post-laminectomy kyphosis. Clin Orthop 128:93–100, 1977.
59. Longstein JE: Postlaminectomy kyphosis. In Chou SN, Seljeskog EL (eds): Spinal Deformities and Neurological Dysfunction. New York, Raven Press, 1978, pp 53–63.
60. Magdelary JW, Teasdall RD, Park AM, Languth HW: Electrophysiological studies of reflex activity with lesions of the nervous system. Bull Johns Hopkins Hosp 91:219–244, 1952.
61. Mayer RF, Mosser RS: Excitability of motoneurons in infants. Neurology 19:932–945, 1969.
62. McDonald CM: Selective dorsal rhizotomy: A critical review. Phys Med Rehabil Clin North Am 2:891–915, 1991.
63. McDonald CM, Jaffe KM, Shurtleff DB: Assessment of muscle strength in children with meningomyelocele: Accuracy and stability of measurements over time. Arch Phys Med Rehabil 67:855–861, 1986.
64. McDonald CM, Jaffe KM, Shurtleff DB, Menelaus MB: Modifications to the traditional description of neurosegmental innervation in myelomeningocele. Dev Med Child Neurol 33:473–481, 1991.
65. McNeal DM, Hawtrey CE, Wolraich ML, Mapel JR: Symptomatic neurogenic bladder in a cerebral palsy population. Dev Med Child Neurol 25:612–616, 1983.

66. Neilsen PD, O'Dwyer NJ, Nash J: Control of isometric muscle activity in cerebral palsy. Dev Med Child Neurol 32:778–788, 1990.
67. Nelson KR, Phillips LH: Neurophysiologic monitoring during surgery of peripheral and cranial nerves, and in selective dorsal rhizotomy. Semin Neurol 19:141–149, 1990.
68. Newberg NL, Gooch JL, Walker ML: Intraoperative monitoring in selective dorsal rhizotomy. Pediatr Neurosurg 17:124–127, 1991-92.
69. Oppenheim WL: Selective posterior rhizotomy for spastic cerebral palsy: A review. Clin Orthop 253:200–229, 1990.
70. Oppenheim WL, Peacock WJ, Staudt LA, et al: Selective posterior rhizotomy for cerebral palsy. Presented at the Symposium on Selective Posterior Rhizotomy—Issues and Answers. San Francisco, October 26, 1989.
71. Park TS, Phillips LH, Torner JC: Magnetic resonance imaging in selective dorsal rhizotomy for spastic cerebral palsy. Neurosurg State Art Rev 4:485–495, 1989.
72. Park TS, Shaffrey ME, Phillips LH, et al: Electrophysiologic evidence for afferent fibers in human ventral roots. Childs Nerv Syst 6:320, 1990.
73. Peacock JW, Arens LJ: Selective posterior rhizotomy for the relief of spasticity in cerebral palsy. S Afr Med J 62:119–124, 1982.
74. Peacock WJ, Arens LJ, Berman B: Cerebral palsy spasticity. Selective posterior rhizotomy. Pediatr Neurosci 13:61–66, 1987.
75. Peacock WJ, Eastman RW: The neurosurgical management of spasticity. S Afr Med J 60:849–850, 1981.
76. Peacock WJ, Staudt LA: Functional outcomes following selective posterior rhizotomy in children with cerebral palsy. J Neurosurg 74:380–385, 1991.
77. Peacock WJ, Staudt LA: Selective posterior rhizotomy. Contemp Neurosurg 12:1–5, 1990.
78. Peacock WJ, Staudt LA: Selective posterior rhizotomy: Evolution of theory and practice. Pediatr Neurosurg 17:128–134, 1991–92.
79. Peacock WJ, Staudt L: Selective posterior rhizotomy: History and results. Neurosurg State Art Rev 4:403–408, 1989.
80. Peacock WJ, Staudt LA: Spasticity in cerebral palsy and the selective posterior rhizotomy procedure. J Child Neurol 5:179–185, 1990.
81. Peter JC, Hoffman EB, Arens LJ, Peacock WJ: Incidence of spinal deformity in children after multiple level laminectomy for selective posterior rhizotomy. Childs Nerv Syst 6:30–32, 1990.
82. Phillips LH, Park TS: Electrophysiologic mapping of the segmental anatomy of the lower extremity. Muscle Nerve 14:1213–1218, 1991.
83. Phillips LH, Park TS: Electrophysiologic studies of selective posterior rhizotomy patients. Neurosurg State Art Rev 4:459–469, 1989.
84. Phillips LH, Park TS: Ventral root mapping: Segmental innervation patterns determined by direct cauda equina stimulation. Muscle Nerve 11:967, 1988.
85. Price R, Bjornson KF, Lehmann JF, et al: Quantitative measurement of spasticity in children with cerebral palsy. Develop Med Child Neurol 33:585–595, 1991.
86. Privat JM, Benezech J, Frerebeau P, et al: Sectorial posterior rhizotomy, a new technique of surgical treatment for spasticity. Acta Neurochir 35:181–195, 1976.
87. Purohit AK, Dinakar I: Selective posterior rhizotomy for spasticity. Childs Nerv Syst 6:320–321, 1990.
88. Raimondi AJ, Gutierrez FA, DiRocco C: Laminotomy and total reconstruction of the posterior arch for spinal canal surgery in childhood. J Neurosurg 45:550–560, 1976.
89. Roberts TS: Selective dorsal rhizotomy. In Spasticity: Measurement and management. The Duncan Seminar, Children's Hospital and Medical Center, Seattle, 1990.
90. Rose J, Gamble JG, Burgos A, et al: Energy expenditure index of walking for normal children and for children with cerebral palsy. Develop Med Child Neurol 32:333–340, 1990.
91. Russell DJ, Rosenbaum PL, Cadman DT: The gross motor function measure: A means to evaluate the effects of physical therapy. Develop Med Child Neurol 31:341–352, 1989.
92. Shiminski-Maher T: Selective posterior rhizotomy in the nursing practice. J Neurosci Nurs 21:308–312, 1989.
93. Sindou M, Quoex C, Baleydier C: Fiber organization at the posterior spinal cord—rootlet junction in man. J Comp Neurol 153:15–26, 1974.
94. Sparkes ML, Klein AS, Duhaime A, Mickle JP: Use of epidural morphine for control of postoperative pain in selective dorsal rhizotomy for spasticity. Pediatr Neurosci 15:229–232, 1989.
95. Spielholz NI: Selective posterior rhizotomy for relief of spasticity. Proceedings of the American Association of Electromyography and Electrodiagnosis, 1989.

96. Staudt LA, Peacock WJ: Selective posterior rhizotomy for treatment of spastic cerebral palsy. Pediatr Phys Ther 1:3–9, 1989.
97. Steinbok P, Langill I, Cochrane DD, Keyes R: Observations on electrical stimulation of lumbosacral nerve roots in children with and without lower limb spasticity. Childs Nerv Syst 8:376–382, 1992.
98. Steinbok P, Reiner A, Beauchamp RD, et al: Selective functional posterior rhizotomy for treatment of spastic cerebral palsy in children. Pediatr Neurosurg 18:34–42, 1992.
99. Stempien L, Gaebler-Spira D, Dias L, et al: The natural history of the hip in cerebral palsy following selective posterior rhizotomy. Develop Med Child Neurol 32:5–6, 1990.
100. Storrs BB: Selective posterior rhizotomy. Presented at The Child with Cerebral Palsy and Selective Posterior Rhizotomy, Instructional course. American Academy of Cerebral Palsy and Developmental Medicine, Orlando, October 5, 1990.
101. Storrs BB: Selective posterior rhizotomy for treatment of progressive spasticity in patients with myelomeningocele. Pediatr Neurosci 13:135–137, 1987.
102. Storrs BB, Nashida T: Use of the "h" reflex recovery curve in selective posterior rhizotomy. Pediatr Neurosci 14:120–123, 1988.
103. Suk SI, Song HS, Lee CK: Scoliosis induced by anterior and posterior rhizotomy. Spine 14:692–697, 1989.
104. Tachdjian MO, Matson DD: Orthopaedic aspects of intra-spinal tumors in infants and children. J Bone Joint Surg 47A:223–248, 1965.
105. Vaughan CL, Berman B, Peacock WJ: Cerebral palsy and rhizotomy. A 3-year follow-up evaluation with gait analysis. J Neurosurg 74:178–184, 1991.
106. Vaughan CL, Berman B, Peacock WJ: Gait analysis and rhizotomy: Past experience and future considerations. Neurosurg State Art Rev 4:445–458, 1989.
107. Vaughan CL, Berman B, Staudt LA, et al: Gait analysis of cerebral palsy before and after rhizotomy. Pediatr Neurosci 14:297–300, 1988.
108. Walker ML, Tippets R, Liddell K: Long-term follow-up on results of selective dorsal rhizotomy for the relief of spasticity in cerebral palsy children. Childs Nerv Syst 5:265, 1989.
109. Wiley MB: Inpatient physical therapy after dorsal rhizotomy. Neurosurg State Art Rev 4:413–416, 1989.
110. Wilner LJ, Gaebler-Spira D: Growth parameters of cerebral palsy children: Status post selective posterior rhizotomy. Arch Phys Med Rehabil 70(Oct):A-45–46, 1989.
111. Wilson JM: Outpatient-based physical therapy program for children with cerebral palsy undergoing selective dorsal rhizotomy. Neurosurg State Art Rev 4:417–429, 1989.
112. Yasukoka S, Peterson HA, MacCarty CS: Incidence of spinal column deformity after multilevel laminectomy in children and adults. J Neurosurg 57:441–445, 1982.

INDEX

Entries in **boldface** type signify complete articles.